Lecture Notes in Artificial Intelligence   37

Edited by J. G. Carbonell and J. Si

Subseries of Lecture Notes in

T0230145

Han La Poutré   Norman M. Sadeh
Sverker Janson (Eds.)

Agent-Mediated Electronic Commerce

Designing Trading Agents and Mechanisms

AAMAS 2005 Workshop, AMEC 2005
Utrecht, Netherlands, July 25, 2005
and IJCAI 2005 Workshop, TADA 2005
Edinburgh, UK, August 1, 2005
Selected and Revised Papers

 Springer

Series Editors

Jaime G. Carbonell, Carnegie Mellon University, Pittsburgh, PA, USA
Jörg Siekmann, University of Saarland, Saarbrücken, Germany

Volume Editors

Han La Poutré
CWI
Centre for Mathematics and Computer Science
Kruislaan 413, 1098 SJ Amsterdam, Netherlands
E-mail: hlp@cwi.nl

Norman M. Sadeh
Carnegie Mellon University
ISRI - School of Computer Science
5000 Frobes Avenue, Pittsburgh, PA 15213-3891, USA
E-mail: sadeh@cs.cmu.edu

Sverker Janson
Swedish Institute of Computer Science
Box 1263, 164 29 Kista, Sweden
E-mail: sverker@sics.se

Library of Congress Control Number: 2006934011

CR Subject Classification (1998): I.2.11, K.4.4, C.2, H.3.4-5, H.5.3, I.2, J.1

LNCS Sublibrary: SL 7 – Artificial Intelligence

ISSN   0302-9743
ISBN-10   3-540-46242-2 Springer Berlin Heidelberg New York
ISBN-13   978-3-540-46242-2 Springer Berlin Heidelberg New York

Springer is a part of Springer Science+Business Media

springer.com

© Springer-Verlag Berlin Heidelberg 2006
Printed in Germany

Typesetting: Camera-ready by author, data conversion by Scientific Publishing Services, Chennai, India
Printed on acid-free paper   SPIN: 11888727   06/3142   5 4 3 2 1 0

Preface

As use of automated agent trading, online auctions and other forms of agent-mediated electronic commerce is gaining prominence in everyday economic activities, interest in further advancing these technologies is also continuing to grow. The present volume presents a snapshot of research on Designing Trading Agents and Mechanisms for Agent-Mediated Electronic Commerce. The book has been built around a collection of articles initially presented at two highly respected international workshops held in the summer of 2005:

– The 2005 workshop on Agent-Mediated Electronic Commerce VII: Designing Mechanisms and Systems (AMEC VII, 2005) collocated with the AAMAS 2005 conference held in Utrecht, The Netherlands, in July 2005. AMEC 2005 was the seventh in a series of international workshops on research at the intersection between computer science, operations research, artificial intelligence, distributed systems, and economics, including game theory. Research presented at this workshop has traditionally addressed a mix of both theoretical and practical issues, looking at behavioral and organizational dimensions of agent-mediated electronic commerce as well as at complex computational, information and system-level challenges. An extended version of an article originally presented at AMEC2004 has also been included.

– The 2005 workshop on Trading Agent Design and Analysis (TADA 2005), collocated one week later with the International Joint Conference on Artificial Intelligence (IJCAI 2005) in Edinburgh, Scotland. The TADA workshop was the third of its kind and focused more specifically on trading agent technologies and mechanism design. This includes discussions of agent architectures and decision-making algorithms along with theoretical analyses and empirical evaluations of agent strategies in different trading contexts. The workshop also serves as the primary discussion forum for the Trading Agent Competition (TAC) research community. TAC is an annual tournament that currently revolves around two different trading scenarios: a scenario that focuses on trading for flight reservations, hotel bookings and tickets at special events ("TAC Travel") and a scenario that models trading for consumer orders and component procurement in a PC assembly supply chain ("TAC Supply Chain Management" or "TAC-SCM"). Participants in the competition develop software agents that compete against one another through several rounds. The rounds, enabled by game servers at SICS (www.sics.se/tac), span several weeks and feature hundreds of games pitting different groups of agents against one another. The competition, which over the years has attracted the participation of several hundred researchers, has grown to become a major catalyst for automated trading and agent-mediated e-commerce research.

We hope that this book will be both a useful resource and a source of inspiration for researchers, students, and practitioners in agent-mediated electronic commerce and trading agents.

Han La Poutré
Norman Sadeh
Sverker Janson

Short Bios

Han La Poutré is research group leader at CWI in Amsterdam (The Netherlands), heading the theme group "Computational Intelligence and Multi-agent Games." He also is a full professor of "e-Business and Computer Science" at the Department of Information Systems at Eindhoven University of Technology. Both in 1999 and 2005, his research group was rated excellent in the six-yearly evaluation of the CWI by NWO (the Netherlands Organization for Scientific Research). Han served as Co-chair of the AMEC-VII workshop.

Norman Sadeh is an Associate Professor in the School of Computer Science at Carnegie Mellon University (CMU), where among other things he founded and directs the e-Supply Chain Management Laboratory. He is also the original proposer of the Supply Chain Trading Agent Competition (TAC- SCM), which over the years has been refined under a collaboration between CMUs e-Supply Chain Management Laboratory, SICS and the University of Minnesota. Norman served as Co-chair of the AMEC-VII workshop.

Sverker Janson is director of the Intelligent Systems Laboratory at SICS, Swedish Institute of Computer Science. He is co-designer of the original 2003 TAC SCM game, with Raghu Arunachalam, Norman Sadeh, Joakim Eriksson, and Niclas Finne. His lab designed and developed the game servers and agentware for TAC, TAC Travel and TAC SCM, and operates the competition since 2002. Sverker served as Chair of the TADA 2005 workshop.

Organization

Committees

Program Committee AMEC VII 2005

Jean-Marie Andreoli, Xerox Research Centre Europe, France
Martin Bichler, Technical University Munich, Germany
Dave Cliff, Hewlett-Packard, UK
Frank Dignum, Utrecht University, The Netherlands
Peyman Faratin, MIT, USA
Shaheen Fatima, University of Liverpool, UK
Mark Fox, University of Toronto, Canada
Amy Greenwald, Brown University, USA
Sverker Janson, SICS, Sweden
Nick Jennings, Southampton University, UK
Jeff Kephart, IBM T.J. Watson Research Center, USA
Han La Poutré, CWI Amsterdam, The Netherlands (Co-chair)
Kate Larson, University of Waterloo, Canada
Rudolf Muller, Maastricht University, The Netherlands
David Parkes, Harvard University, USA
Jeffrey Rosenschein, Hebrew University, Israel
Norman Sadeh, Carnegie Mellon Univerisity, USA (Co-chair)
Carles Sierra, IIIA - CSIC, Spain
William Walsh, IBM T.J. Watson Research Center, USA
Michael Wellman, University of Michigan, USA
Mike Wooldridge, University of Liverpool, UK

Additional Reviewers AMEC VII 2005

Tomas Klos, CWI Amsterdam, The Netherlands
Gopal Ramchurn, Southampton University, UK

Organizing Committee TADA 2005

Sverker Janson, SICS (Chair)
David Parkes, Harvard University
Michael Wellman, University of Michigan

Program Committee TADA 2005

Dave Cliff, Deutsche Bank
John Collins, University of Minnesota
Maria Fasli, Essex University
Amy Greenwald, Brown University
Nick Jennings, Southampton University

Tracy Mullen, Penn State University
Jörg P Müller, Siemens
Sun Park, Yonsei University
Norman Sadeh, Carnegie Mellon University
Peter Stone, University of Texas at Austin
William Walsh, IBM Research
Christof Weinhardt, University of Karlsruhe
Michael Wellman, University of Michigan
Peter Wurman, North Carolina State University
Dongmo Zhang, University of Western Sydney

Additional Reviewers TADA 2005

Esther David
Casey Marks
Victor Naroditskiy
Alex Rogers

Table of Contents

PART 3: AMEC VI 2004

Learning Environmental Parameters for the Design of Optimal English Auctions with Discrete Bid Levels

A. Rogers[1], E. David[1], J. Schiff[2], S. Kraus[3], and N.R. Jennings[1]

[1] Electronics and Computer Science, University of Southampton, Southampton, SO17 1BJ, UK
[2] Department of Mathematics, Bar-Ilan University, Ramat-Gan 52900, Israel
[3] Department of Computer Science, Bar-Ilan University, Ramat-Gan 52900, Israel
{acr, ed, nrj}@ecs.soton.ac.uk, {schiff@math, sarit@cs}.biu.ac.il

Abstract. In this paper we consider the optimal design of English auctions with discrete bid levels. Such auctions are widely used in online internet settings and our aim is to automate their configuration in order that they generate the maximum revenue for the auctioneer. Specifically, we address the problem of estimating the values of the parameters necessary to perform this optimal auction design by observing the bidding in previous auctions. To this end, we derive a general expression that relates the expected revenue of the auction when discrete bid levels are implemented, but the number of participating bidders is unknown. We then use this result to show that the characteristics of these optimal bid levels are highly dependent on the expected number of bidders and on their valuation distribution. Finally, we derive and demonstrate an online algorithm based on Bayesian machine learning, that allows these unknown parameters to be estimated through observations of the closing price of previous auctions. We show experimentally that this algorithm converges rapidly toward the true parameter values and, in comparison with an auction using the more commonly implemented fixed bid increment, results in an increase in auction revenue.

1 Introduction

The popularity of online internet auctions has increased dramatically over recent years, with total online auction sales currently exceeding $30 billion annually. This popularity has prompted much research into agent mediated auctions and specifically the development of autonomous software agents that are capable of fulfilling the role of auctioneer or bidder on behalf of their owner. Now, much of the theoretical work on these agent mediated auctions has focused on direct sealed bid protocols, such as the second-price (Vickrey) auction. These protocols are attractive as they are economically efficient and provide simple dominant bidding strategies for participating agents. However, despite these properties, such sealed bid protocols are rarely used in practice [14]. The vast majority of current online and real world auctions implement variants of a single auction protocol, specifically, the oral ascending price (English) auction with discrete bid levels [8]. Under this protocol, the auctioneer announces the price of the next bid and waits until a bidder indicates their willingness to pay this amount. Upon receiving such an indication, the price moves on to another higher discrete bid price, again proposed by the auctioneer. The auction continues until there are no bidders willing to pay the bid price requested by the auctioneer. At this point, the object is allocated to the current highest bidder and that bidder pays the last accepted discrete bid price.

H. La Poutré, N. Sadeh, and S. Janson (Eds.): AMEC and TADA 2005, LNAI 3937, pp. 1–15, 2006.

Now, despite its apparent popularity, an auctioneer implementing an English auction with discrete bid levels is faced with two complementary challenges. Firstly, it must determine the actual discrete bid levels to be used. The standard academic auction literature provides little guidance here since it commonly assumes a continuous bid interval, where bidders incrementally outbid one another by an infinitesimally small amount. However, discrete bid levels do have an effect, and have been investigated by Rothkopf and Harstad [13]. They showed that the revenue of the auction is dependent on the number and distribution of discrete bid levels implemented and, in general, the use of discrete bid levels reduces the revenue generated by the auction. Conversely, the discrete bid levels also act to greatly reduce the number of bids that must be submitted in order for the price to reach the closing price. This has the effect of increasing the speed of the auction and, hence, reduces the time and communication costs of both the auctioneer and bidders. By analysing the manner in which the discrete bid auction could close and then calculating the expected revenue of the auctioneer in a number of limited cases (which we detail in section 2), they were able to derive the optimal distribution of bid levels that would maximise this revenue. In previous work, we extended this result to the general case, and we can now determine the optimal bid levels for an auction in which the environmental parameters are given [4]. Specifically, these parameters are the number of bidders participating in the auction and the bidders' valuation distribution .

Thus, performing this optimal auction design introduces the second of the two challenges; that of determining, for the particular setting under consideration, the values of these environmental parameters. While, in some settings these may be well known, in most cases they will not. Thus, in this paper, we tackle the problem of determining the optimal discrete bid levels when these values must be estimated through observations of previous auctions. In so doing, we extend the state of the art in three ways:

1. We extend previous work by deriving an expression that describes the expected revenue of a discrete bid auction when the number of bidders participating is unknown but can be described by a probability distribution.
2. We use this expression to calculate the optimal bid levels that maximise the auctioneers' revenue in this case. We demonstrate that the optimal discrete bid levels produced by this method are dependent on the distribution of the number of participating bidders and on the distribution that describes the bidders' valuations.
3. We show that this expression allows us to use machine learning, and specifically Bayesian inference, in an online algorithm that generates sequentially better estimates for the parameters that describe the two unknown distributions (i.e. the distribution of the number of bidders participating in any auction and the distribution of the bidders' valuation) by observing only the closing price of previous auctions.

The results that we provide may be used in the design of online auctions or may be used by automated trading agents that are adopting the role of an auctioneer within a multi-agent system. In such settings these auction protocols are attractive as they provide a relatively simple bidding strategy for the agents, yet, unlike second price sealed bid auctions, do not require the bidders to reveal their full private information to the auctioneer. In this setting, there is a need to fully automate the design of such auction mechanisms, and the work presented here represents a key step in this direction.

The remainder of the paper is organised as follows: in section 2 we present related work and in section 3 we describe our auction model and present the previously derived results for the expected revenue of this auction (in order to make this paper self-contained). In section 4 we extend this result to the case that the number of bidders participating in the auction is described by a distribution and we use this new result to derive optimal discrete bid levels in this case. In section 5 we present our Bayesian inference algorithm and finally we conclude and discuss future work in section 6.

2   Related Work

The problem of optimal auction design has been studied extensively for the case of auctions with continuous bid increments [12,10]. In contrast, auctions with discrete bid levels have received much less attention, and much of the work that does exist is based on the assumption that there is a fixed bid increment and thus the price of the auction ascends in fixed size steps [15,3,16]. In contrast, Rothkopf and Harstad considered the more general question of determining the optimal number and distribution of these bid levels [13]. They provided a full discussion of how discrete bid levels affect the expected revenue of the auction and they considered two different distributions for the bidders' private valuations (uniform and exponential). In the case of the uniform distribution, they considered two specific instances: (i) two bidders with any number of allowable bid levels, and (ii) two allowable bid levels with any number of bidders. In the first instance, evenly spaced bid levels (i.e. a fixed bid increment) was found to be the optimal. In the second instance, the bid increment was shown to decrease as the auction progressed. Conversely, for the exponential distribution (again with just two bidders), the optimal bid increment was shown to increase as the auction progressed.

In previous work, we extended the analysis of Rothkopf and Harstad [13], and, rather than analyse the ascending price English auction in limited cases, we presented a general expression that relates the revenue to the actual bid levels implemented. For a uniform valuation distribution we were able to derive analytical results for the optimal bid levels, and in general, we were able to numerically determine the optimal bid levels for any bidders' valuation distribution, any number of bid levels and any number of bidders. In addition, we showed that in general, increasing the number of discrete bid levels, causes the revenue to approach that of a continuous bid auction.

In this paper, we extend this previous work and address the problem of estimating the number and valuation distribution of the bidders through observing the closing price of previous auctions. This problem is similar to that studied in the econometrics literature, where it has been used to identify the behaviour of bidders in real world auctions [6]. More recently, it has received attention within electronic commerce, with the goal of determining the reserve price in a repeated procurement auction [2]. Typically, this work uses statistical maximum likelihood estimators to determine the parameters that describe the bidders' valuation distribution through observations of their bidding behaviour. In our case, this task is somewhat different as much of this information is lost in the discretisation of the bids. Thus, we use the expression that we have already derived for the revenue of the discrete bid auction, and use Bayesian inference to infer parameter values through observations of the closing price of previous auctions. This

$$l_{i-1} \qquad l_i \qquad l_{i+1}$$

Case 1

Two or more bidders have valuations between $[l_i, l_{i+1})$ and none have valuations $x \geq l_{i+1}$.

Case 2

One bidder has a valuation $x \geq l_{i+1}$, one or more bidders have valuations in the range $[l_i, l_{i+1})$ and the bidder with the highest valuation was the current highest bidder at l_i.

Case 3

One bidder has a valuation $x \geq l_i$, one or more bidders have valuations in the range $[l_{i-1}, l_i)$, and the bidder with the highest valuation was not the current highest bidder at l_{i-1}.

Fig. 1. Diagram showing the three cases whereby the auction closes at the bid level l_i. In each case, the circles indicate a bidder's private valuation and the arrow indicates the bid level at which that bidder was selected as the current highest bidder.

method is attractive, as rather than providing a single parameter estimate at each iteration, it provides a full distribution that describes the auctioneer's belief over the entire range of possible parameter values. Thus indicating the confidence that the auctioneer should have in his current estimate [9]. In addition, Bayesian inference tends to be computationally simpler than maximum likelihood methods, since it does not require us to maximise a function over several dimensions [1].

3   Auction Model and Expected Auction Revenue

In this work we consider a common model of an English auction that was used by Rothkopf and Harstad [13]. In this model, n risk neutral bidders are attempting to buy a single item from a risk neutral auctioneer. Bidders have independent private valuations, x_i, drawn from a common continuous probability density function, $f(x)$, within the range $[\underline{x}, \bar{x}]$, and with a cumulative distribution function, $F(x)$, where with no loss of generality, $F(\underline{x}) = 0$ and $F(\bar{x}) = 1$. The bidders participate in an ascending price auction, whereby the bids are restricted to discrete levels which are determined by the auctioneer. We assume there are $m+1$ discrete bid levels, starting at l_0 and ending at l_m (at this point, we make no constraints on the actual number of these bid levels).

The auction starts with the auctioneer announcing the first discrete bid level (i.e. the reserve price of the auction) and asks the bidders to indicate their willingness to pay this amount. In traditional English auction houses, this indication is normally accomplished by a nod to the auctioneer, while in current online auctions such as www.onsale.com it requires a click of a mouse. If no bidders are willing to pay this amount within a predetermined and publically announced interval, the auction closes and the item remains unsold. However, if a bid is received, the auction proceeds and the auctioneer again requests bidders willing to pay the next discrete bid level. If no bidders are willing to pay this new price, the auction then closes and the item is sold to the current highest bidder.

Now, in order to determine the optimal bid levels that the auctioneer should announce, an expression for the expected revenue of the auction must be found. Rothkopf and Harstad considered this problem and identified three mutually exclusive cases that described the different ways in which the auction could close at any particular bid level [13]. These cases are shown in figure 1. They then calculated the probability of each case occurring in a number of limited cases. In our earlier work we have been able to use the same descriptive cases, but derive a general result for each probability [4]. Thus we are able to describe the probability of the auction closing at any particular bid level:

$$P_n(l_i) = \begin{cases} [1 - F(l_i)] \left[\frac{F(l_{i+1})^n - F(l_i)^n}{F(l_{i+1}) - F(l_i)} \right] & i = 0 \\ \\ [1 - F(l_i)] \left[\frac{F(l_{i+1})^n - F(l_i)^n}{F(l_{i+1}) - F(l_i)} + \frac{F(l_{i-1})^n - F(l_i)^n}{F(l_i) - F(l_{i-1})} \right] & 0 < i \le m \end{cases} \tag{1}$$

Note that the subscript in P_n indicates that the expression is in terms of the actual number of bidders, n, who participate in the individual auction, and that we define $F(l_{m+1}) = 1$. Now, the expected revenue of the auctioneer is simply found by summing over all possible bid levels and weighting each by the revenue that it generates:

$$E_n = \sum_{i=0}^{m} l_i P_n(l_i) \tag{2}$$

Thus, by substituting equation 1 into this expression and performing some simplification, we get the result:

$$E_n = \sum_{i=0}^{m} \frac{F(l_{i+1})^n - F(l_i)^n}{F(l_{i+1}) - F(l_i)} \left[l_i [1 - F(l_i)] - l_{i+1} [1 - F(l_{i+1})] \right] \tag{3}$$

In our previous work we used this result to generate optimal bid levels when the number of bidders and the bidders valuation distribution are known.

4   Optimising over Uncertainty in the Number of Bidders

Now, we wish to deal with the more general case that the number of bidders participating in the auction is not known by the auctioneer. To do so, we have to carefully define what we mean by participation. Thus, a bidder is said to be participating in (or has entered) the auction, if they have generated a valuation for the item being sold, are present and are prepared to bid. It is this number of bidders (plus their valuation distribution and the discrete bid levels implemented) that determines the expected revenue of the auction (as described in equation 3). However, in the English auction considered here, not all of the bidders who are participating will necessarily submit bids to the auctioneer (i.e. many will find that the other bidders have raised the price beyond their own private valuation and thus they have no opportunity to bid). Thus, the auctioneer is not able to determine the number of bidders who are participating by simply observing the bids.

In addition, in any specific setting, the number of bidders participating in an auction is unlikely to be fixed but will most likely be described by a probability distribution.

Levin and Smith showed this by considering an auction model in which the number of bidders participating was endogenously determined [7]. They modeled a pool of potential bidders, and showed that, at equilibrium, each potential bidder has a fixed probability of actually participating in (or entering) the auction. The number of bidders participating in any auction was thus described by a binomial distribution. Bajari and Hortacsu considered a similar model and compared their model to data collected from eBay auctions selling collectable U.S. coins [1]. They note that in such online auctions, the pool of potential bidders is extremely large. However, the fact that, in general, only a small number of bids are observed, suggests that the probability that a potential bidders participates in any individual auction is very low. Thus, they assume that, in such cases, a Poisson distribution is an appropriate approximation for the binomial proposed by Leven and Smith. In light of this work, we describe the number of bidders participating in any auction by a Poisson distribution and thus the probability that n bidders participate is given by:

$$P(n) = \frac{v^n e^{-v}}{n!} \tag{4}$$

Here the parameter v describes the mean of this distribution and thus represents the expected or average number of participants in any individual auction. Given this distribution, we can extend the results described in the previous section and express the probability of the auction closing at any bid level, in terms of the parameter v, rather than n. To do so, we simply sum the probability given in equation 1 multiplied by the probability of that number of bidders actually occurring:

$$P_v(l_i) = \sum_{n=0}^{\infty} P(n) P_n(l_i) \tag{5}$$

Now substituting equations 1 and 4 into this expression and making use of the identity $\sum_{n=0}^{\infty} v^n / n! = e^v$ allows us to derive the result:

$$P_v(l_i) = \begin{cases} [1 - F(l_i)] \left[\frac{e^{v[F(l_{i+1})-1]} - e^{v[F(l_i)-1]}}{F(l_{i+1}) - F(l_i)} \right] & i = 0 \\ [1 - F(l_i)] \left[\frac{e^{v[F(l_{i+1})-1]} - e^{v[F(l_i)-1]}}{F(l_{i+1}) - F(l_i)} + \frac{e^{v[F(l_{i-1})-1]} - e^{v[F(l_i)-1]}}{F(l_i) - F(l_{i-1})} \right] & 0 < i \leq m \end{cases} \tag{6}$$

Now finally, as before, we are able to perform a weighted sum over all of the discrete bid levels to determine the expected revenue of the auctioneer given the uncertainty in the number of bidders that are participating in any specific auction:

$$E_v = \sum_{i=0}^{m} \frac{e^{v[F(l_{i+1})-1]} - e^{v[F(l_i)-1]}}{F(l_{i+1}) - F(l_i)} \left[l_i [1 - F(l_i)] - l_{i+1} [1 - F(l_{i+1})] \right] \tag{7}$$

This is a key result. It expresses the expected revenue of the auction in terms of the actual bid levels implemented, the bidders valuation distribution and, v, the mean number of bidders who participate in each auction. We use this result in the next section to derive optimal bid levels in spite of the inherent uncertainty in the number of bidders who will participate in any individual auction.

$$for\ i=0{:}m$$
$$l_i \leftarrow \begin{cases} a+i*(\bar{x}-a)/m & where \quad a=\max(\underline{x},\bar{x}/2) & \text{// uniform} \\ 1/\alpha + i*(2/\alpha m) & & \text{// exponential} \end{cases}$$
$$d \leftarrow \infty$$
$$while\ d > stopping\ condition,$$
$$l'_0 \leftarrow \arg\max_{l_0} E_v(l_0,\ldots,l_m) \quad where \quad \underline{x} \geq l_0 < l_1$$
$$for\ i=1{:}m\text{-}1$$
$$l'_i \leftarrow \arg\max_{l_i} E_v(l_0,\ldots,l_m) \quad where \quad l_{i-1} < l_i < l_{i+1}$$
$$l'_m \leftarrow \arg\max_{l_m} E_v(l_0,\ldots,l_m) \quad where \quad l_{m-1} < l_m \leq \bar{x}$$
$$d \leftarrow 0$$
$$for\ i=0{:}m,$$
$$d \leftarrow \max(d, \mathrm{abs}(l'_i - l_i))$$
$$l_i \leftarrow l'_i$$

Fig. 2. Pseudo-code algorithm for calculating solutions for the optimal bid levels

4.1 Optimal Discrete Bid Levels

The expression presented in the last section describes the expected revenue of the auction when discrete bid levels $l_0 \ldots l_m$ are used. Thus, in order to find the optimal bid levels in this case, we must find the values $l_0 \ldots l_m$ that maximise this expression. In general, it is not possible to perform this maximisation analytically, so we must use a numerical algorithm. Now, given that there are many numerical multi-dimensional optimisation algorithms available (see Numerical Recipes [11] for examples), two key features of this problem guide our choice. Firstly, since each term in the summation in equation 7 contains only pairs of bid levels (i.e. l_i and l_{i+1}), we note that maximising this expression, and thus solving $\delta E_v / \delta l_i = 0$, is equivalent to solving a tri-diagonal set of $m+1$ simultaneous equations, that, by denoting $\delta E_v / \delta l_i$ as f_i, we can write as:

$$\begin{aligned} f_0(l_0, l_1) &= 0 \\ f_i(l_{i-1}, l_i, l_{i+1}) &= 0 \quad \text{for } i = 1 \text{ to } m-1 \qquad (8) \\ f_m(l_{m-1}, l_m) &= 0 \end{aligned}$$

Secondly, the solutions to these equations are constrained such that their ordering remains constant i.e. $l_{i-1} < l_i < l_{i+1}$. A general purpose optimisation package will fail to exploit the first feature and will be heavily constrained by the second. However, we can produce a simple and efficient numerical algorithm by using Jacobi iteration whereby we iteratively solve the $m+1$ simultaneous equations [5]. That is, we fix all other bid levels, and we find the value of l_i that maximises equation 7 given that $l_{i-1} < l_i < l_{i+1}$. The expression is well behaved in this range and has a single maximum that can be found using hill climbing or a gradient based method. We update all l_i and then iterate the process until the bid levels converge to the necessary accuracy.

We present this algorithm in figure 2, noting that the expression $E_v(l_0, \ldots, l_m)$ represents the revenue expression in equation 7. Whilst we do not prove the convergence properties of this iterative algorithm here, in our experiments it converged reliably given

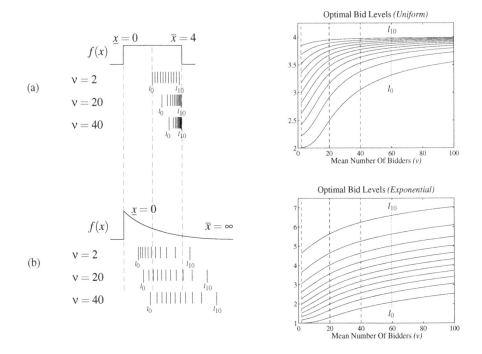

Fig. 3. Optimal bid levels for (a) uniform and (b) exponential valuation distributions

that two starting conditions for l_i were satisfied. Specifically, at the first iteration, no bid level may be outside the upper limit of the bidders' valuation distribution (i.e. $l_i \leq \bar{x}$) and l_0 must be greater or equal to the reserve price predicted for the equivalent continuous bid auction (i.e. for a uniform bidders' valuation distribution $l_0 \geq \max(\underline{x}, \bar{x}/2)$). We provide suitable starting conditions for the two valuation distributions that we consider in the next section in the algorithm.

4.2 Comparison of Valuation Distributions

The numerical solution described in the previous sections allows us to calculate the optimal discrete bid levels for any value of v (i.e. the mean number of bidders present in any auction) and any bidders' valuation distribution. In this section, we compare the optimal bid levels over a range of values of v when two different bidders' valuation distributions are used. Specifically, we compare the exponential distribution, proposed by Rothkopf and Harstad, with the more common uniform distribution, and, to allow us to compare these two directly, we chose their parameters so that the expected closing price of the auctions are similar in both cases. Thus for the uniform distribution, we consider a range of [0,4] meaning $f(x) = \frac{1}{\bar{x}-\underline{x}}$ and $F(x) = \frac{x-\underline{x}}{\bar{x}-\underline{x}}$ where $\underline{x} = 0$ and $\bar{x} = 4$. For the exponential distribution, we have $f(x) = \alpha e^{-\alpha x}$ and $F(x) = 1 - e^{-\alpha x}$ where $\alpha = 1$. The resulting optimal discrete bid levels are shown in figure 3, for three different mean numbers of bidders ($v = 2$, 20 and 40) and over a continuous range from 2 to 100.

In both cases, we use 10 bid levels (i.e. $m = 10$), as this makes clear the differences between the two cases. Note that whilst changing the number of bid levels does affect their value, it does not affect the general form of the distribution seen in the plot.

Now, Rothkopf and Harstad showed that in the case where there were two bidders, the optimal discrete bid level distribution for the uniform distribution is a fixed bid increment with evenly spaced bid levels. In addition, for an exponential distribution, the optimal bid levels with two bidders is an increasing bid increment with bid levels becoming more widely spaced as the auction progresses. Our results show that in the general case, where there is uncertainty over the number of bidders that are participating, the distribution of the optimal discrete bid levels is complex. For the uniform distribution there is a decreasing bid increment whereby the discrete bid levels become closer together as the auction progresses. While, for the exponential distribution, the bid increment initially decreases, reaches a minimum size and then subsequently increases.

We also see that as the number of bidders increases, the value of l_0 increases. Rothkopf and Harstad fixed the values of the first and last bid levels at the extremes of the valuation distribution. However, we make no such restriction and thus the values of l_0 and l_m are optimised at the same time as the other bid levels. Now, since l_0 is equivalent to the reserve price of the auction (i.e. the item will not sell if there are no bidders willing to pay at least l_0) the results indicate that, in contrast to the literature of optimal auctions with continuous bid increments, the optimal reserve price of an auction with discrete bid levels is dependent on the mean number of bidders. In general, we see that when the number of bid levels is large, or the mean number of bidders is small, the value of l_0 tends toward the continuous result (for the uniform distribution, this is $x^* = \max(\underline{x}, \bar{x}/2)$, and for the exponential distribution it is $x^* = 1/\alpha$ [10]).

Intuitively we can understand these effects by the fact that given a fixed number of bid levels, we should position them closer together in areas where they are most likely to differentiate the bidders with the highest valuations. Thus, for the uniform distribution, the bid levels become closer together nearer to the upper limit of the distribution. Whilst in the exponential distribution, they become closer together where we expect to find the bidder with the second highest valuation. This result suggests that it may be possible to describe the optimal bid levels in terms of the distribution of the expected second highest valuation. However, it has not proved possible to describe the revenue of the discrete bid auction in these terms, so at the moment, this shortcut is not available to us.

5   Estimating Auction Parameters

In the previous sections, we showed that the optimal discrete bid levels, and hence the revenue of the auctioneer, are dependent on the number of bidders that participate and their valuation distribution. Now, when the values of the parameters that characterise these distributions are not known, we must estimate their value through observations of previous auctions. Since, in this paper we have derived an expression for the probability of the auction closing at any particular bid level (given these parameter values) it is natural to use Bayesian inference to perform this task. That is, having observed an auction closing at a certain bid level, we calculate our belief that a particular set of parameter values gave rise to this event. This method contrasts with statistical maximum likelihood techniques since rather than simply providing a single 'most likely' parameter value, we derive a distribution that describes our belief over all possible values.

To illustrate this process, we describe a general setting, in which an auctioneer implements a regularly repeating auction, and in each auction a single identical item is sold. As described earlier, we assume that there is a large pool of potential bidders, who have private independent valuations that are drawn from a common distribution. Each potential bidder has a small probability of actively participating in any auction, and thus each repeated auction faces a number of bidders that is described by the Poisson distribution shown in equation 4. Note that whilst their numbers are similar, these bidders are different individuals with different valuations and, since we are explicitly interested in the actions of the auctioneer, we assume that their bidding behaviour is unaffected by their own observations of previous auctions[1]. Thus, our goal is to estimate the typical number of bidders who participate in each auction, v, and also the parameters that describe their common valuation distribution. These estimated parameter values can then be used to calculate optimal discrete bid levels in subsequent auctions.

5.1   Estimating the Mean Number of Bidders

We first consider an example in which the bidders' valuation distribution is known, but, v, the parameter that characterises the Poisson distribution and represents the mean number of bidders participating in each repeated auction, is unknown. Thus, if at time t the auctioneer implemented an auction that used the discrete bid levels $\mathbf{l}^t = \{l_0^t \ldots l_m^t\}$ and closed at bid level l_w^t, we wish to find the value v that best explains this outcome. In other words, we wish to calculate the probability distribution $P(v|l_w^t, F(x), \mathbf{l}^t)$. Now, in equation 6 we have already derived the probability of the auction closing at any bid level, in terms of the mean number of bidders, the bidders' valuation distribution and the actual bid levels implemented. Thus, in the notation we are using here, we have already derived $P(l_w^t|v, F(x), \mathbf{l}^t)$. With this expression, we can use Bayes' theorem in order to calculate the required result:

$$P\left(v|l_w^t, F(x), \mathbf{l}^t\right) = \frac{P\left(l_w^t|v, F(x), \mathbf{l}^t\right) P(v)}{P\left(l_w^t|F(x), \mathbf{l}^t\right)} \tag{9}$$

Now, this described the case where the auctioneer has made an observation of a single auction. In general, if t such auctions have been observed, the auctioneer can use all of this evidence to improve its estimate. Thus if the bid levels used in these auctions were $\mathbf{L} = \{\mathbf{l}^1, \ldots, \mathbf{l}^t\}$, and the observed closing prices were $\mathbf{l_w} = \{l_w^1, \ldots, l_w^t\}$, we have:

$$P(v|\mathbf{l_w}, F(x), \mathbf{L}) = \frac{\prod_{i=1}^{t} P\left(l_w^i|v, F(x), \mathbf{l}^i\right) P(v)}{Z} \tag{10}$$

In this expression, Z is a normalising factor that ensures that $P(v|\mathbf{l_w}, F(x), \mathbf{L})$ sums to one over the range of possible values of v. Now, $P(v|\mathbf{l_w}, F(x), \mathbf{L})$ is a continuous prob-

---

[1] This assumption is reasonable in circumstances where historical auction data is not available to the bidders. However, we intend to investigate the full implications of this assumption in future work.

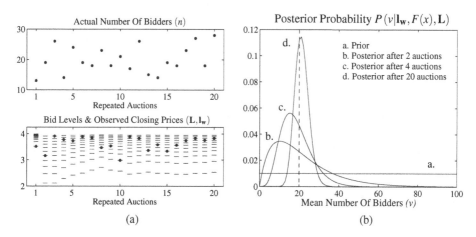

Fig. 4. Plots showing (a) the actual number of bidders that participated in the auction (unknown to the auctioneer) and the actual bid levels and closing prices observed by the auctioneer and (b) the prior and posterior belief distributions of the auctioneer after 2, 4 and 20 repeated auctions

ability distribution. However, for our purposes, we calculate it as a discrete probability distribution over a suitable range. In this example, we calculate $P(v|\mathbf{l_w}, F(x), \mathbf{L})$ for integer values of v from $\underline{v}$ to $\overline{v}$. Thus, this normalising factor is given by:

$$Z = \sum_{v=\underline{v}}^{\overline{v}} \left[\prod_{i=1}^{t} P\left(l_w^i | v, F(x), \mathbf{l}^i\right) P(v) \right] \tag{11}$$

Finally, $P(v)$ represents the auctioneers' prior belief; an initial assumption as to which values of v are most likely to occur, before any observations have been made. If no such intuition is available (as in our simulations here), the prior can simply be initialised as a uniform distribution, and it will have no effect on the estimates generated.

Thus the procedure adopted by the auctioneer is as follows: it first uses its prior belief (i.e. an initial guess) to calculate the bid levels for the first auction. Having observed the closing price of this auction, the expression in equation 10 is used to calculate the probability distribution that describes its updated belief in the parameter v. This probability distribution is then used to choose the value of v for the calculation of the optimal bid levels to be implemented in the next auction. There are two ways in which this choice can be made, either: (i) the most likely value of v can be used (i.e. the value of v where the probability distribution has a maximum), or (ii) a value of v may be sampled from this probability distribution. The first option is identical to a statistical maximum likelihood estimator. However the second option ensures more rapid convergence in cases where the auctions that occur early in the learning process represent extreme events (i.e. when many of the bidders have extremely high or low valuations or the auction happens to have many more or many less bidders than is typical).

Simulation results for this procedure are shown in figure 4. Here, we consider the same uniform valuation distribution as discussed in section 5 (i.e. $\underline{x} = 0$ and $\overline{x} = 4$). The real value of v in this case is 20, whilst the auctioneer's prior belief is that it lies somewhere between 0 and 100 (i.e. $P(v)$ is a uniform distribution over this range). In

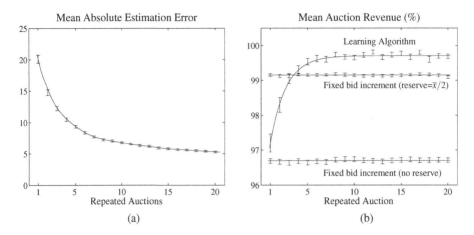

Fig. 5. Plots showing (a) the converging estimates generated by the learning algorithm, and (b) how this results in improvements in the auctioneer's revenue

figure 4a we show the actual number of bidders that participated (unknown to the auctioneer) and the bid levels that were implemented in each repeated auction, along with the actual bid level at which the auction closed (denoted by a filled circle on the appropriate bid level and observed by the auctioneer). In figure 4b, we show the probability distribution, $P(v|\mathbf{l_w}, F(x), \mathbf{L})$, that describes the auctioneers' belief in the values of v (shown after 2, 4 and 20 auctions). The variance in the observed auction closing prices is driven by the stochastic nature of the number of bidders, their valuations and also the changing auction bid levels. However, despite this variance, the auctioneers' belief in the most likely value of v converges rapidly to the true value. Thus the bid levels implemented by the auctioneer also converge to the those that generate the maximum revenue.

To demonstrate the convergence of this algorithm, after each repeated auction we calculate the error in the estimate that it produced (i.e. the difference between the estimated value and the true value). We repeat the process 1000 times using the same parameter values (i.e. $v = 20$ and a uniform bidders' valuation distribution where $\underline{x} = 0$ and $\bar{x} = 4$) and average over the results. Figure 5a shows the mean absolute estimation error plotted against the number of repeated auctions. The plot shows that the estimates improve rapidly after the first few auctions and then converge to the true value.

Figure 5b shows the improvement in revenue that results from more accurately estimating the mean number of bidders who are participating in the auctions, and then use this result to optimise the discrete bid levels used in subsequent auctions. For the same simulation runs presented in figure 5a, we show the efficiency of the auction, calculated in terms of the percentage of the second highest bidder's valuation that the auction was able to extract. We compare this revenue to that which would have been achieved with an auction that used the more commonly implemented fixed bid increment, with and without setting a reserve price. Clearly, as the estimates of the auction parameters improve, so the revenue of the auctioneer increases. Significantly, the greatest improve-

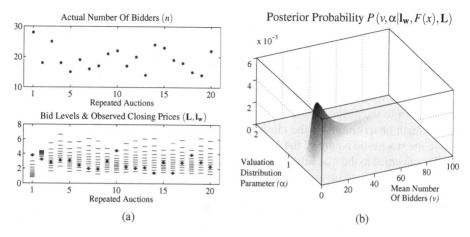

Fig. 6. Plots showing (a) the actual number of bidders that participated in the auction (unknown to the auctioneer) and the actual bid levels and closing prices observed by the auctioneer and (b) the joint posterior belief distributions of the auctioneer after 20 repeated auctions

ment is realised after the first few auction and after this point, the revenue exceeds that generated with fixed bid increments.

5.2 Estimating Multiple Parameters

The algorithm that we have presented here is certainly not restricted to learning single parameters. In figure 6 we present a second example, this time for the exponential valuation distribution presented in section 4.2. In this case we infer both the value of parameter that describes the distribution of the number of bidders, v, and the value of the parameter that describes the bidders' exponential valuation distribution, α. Thus we must calculate the two-dimensional joint probability distribution $P(v, \alpha | \mathbf{l_w}, F(x), \mathbf{L})$. Again, despite the stochastic nature of the auction process, after twenty repeated auctions the probability distribution shows a clear peak around the true values of $v = 20$ and $\alpha = 1$, and thus the bid levels converge toward the true optimal bid levels. Space does not allow us present a full analysis of the convergence, however, in general, increasing the number of parameters that are learnt reduces the convergence rate.

We can extend this method to estimate more parameters, by simply calculating larger joint probability distributions in more dimensions. However, in so doing, the cost of performing this exact calculation increases geometrically. Fortunately Bayesian inference is a well developed field with sophisticated methods that allow us to approximate these distributions. For example, variational methods (which we intend to explore in the future) allow us to approximate the full n-dimensional joint distribution as the product of n independent distributions, with a corresponding computational saving [9].

6   Conclusions

In this paper we considered the optimal design of English auctions with discrete bid levels and our aim was to automate their configuration to generate the maximum revenue for the auctioneer. To this end, we extended earlier work and derived an expression for the revenue of the auction under uncertainty in the number of bidders who are participating in the auction. We used this result to numerically calculate optimal bid levels under this uncertainty and showed that the value and distribution of these optimal bid levels are highly dependent on both the mean number of bidders and the bidders' valuation distribution. Finally, we considered the case in which these environmental parameters are unknown to the auctioneer, and used Bayesian inference to estimate these parameters through observations of the closing price of previous auctions. We showed that despite the stochastic nature of the auctions, the estimates generated by this algorithm rapidly converged to the true values. In addition, we showed that by correctly estimating the true values of these parameters, the auctioneer is able to bid levels that result in an increase in auction revenue.

Our future work in this area consists of extending the auction model to incorporate an explicit expression of the auctioneer's costs (rather than the explicit bound on the maximum number of bid levels that we have presented here). In addition, we intend to extend the inference method that we have presented here, and in particular, we would like to use these techniques to perform model identification and selection. Thus, we would infer the full parameters of several different valuation distributions (using variational methods to minimise the computational cost of this task) and then infer which of these distributions best explains the closing prices that were observed (also considering the effect that an incorrect assumption will have). In so doing, we believe these techniques will significantly contribute toward our goal of automating the mechanism design of optimal discrete bid auctions.

Acknowledgments

This research was funded by the DIF-DTC project on Agent-Based Control and the ARGUS II Defence and Aerospace Research Partnership. This is a collaborative project involving BAE SYSTEMS, QinetiQ, Rolls-Royce, Oxford University and Southampton University, and is funded by the industrial partners together with the EPSRC, Ministry of Defence (MoD) and Department of Trade and Industry (DTI). Sarit Kraus is also affiliated with the University of Maryland Institute for Advanced Computer Studies (UMIACS) and this work was part supported by NSF Grant IIS-0208608.

References

1. P. Bajari and A. Hortacsu. The winners curse, reserve prices, and endogenous entry: empirical insights from eBay auctions. *RAND Journal of Economics*, 34(2):329–355, 2003.
2. M. Bichler and J. Kalagnanam. A non-parametric estimator for setting reserve prices in procurement auctions. In *ACM Conference on Electronic Commerce 2003*, pages 254–255, 2003.
3. M. S.-Y. Chwe. The discrete bid first auction. *Economics Letters*, 31:303–306, 1989.
4. E. David, A. Rogers, J. Schiff, S. Kraus, and N. R. Jennings. Optimal design of english auctions with discrete bid levels. In *Proceedings of ACM Conference on Electronic Commerce*, pages 98–107, 2005.

5. L. A. Hageman and D. M. Young. *Applied Iterative Methods*. Academic Press, 1981.

6. J.-J. Laffont, H. Ossard, and Q. Vuong. Econometrics of first-price auctions. *Econometrica*, 63(4):953–980, 1995.

7. D. Levin and J. L. Smith. Equilibrium in auctions with entry. *American Economic Review*, 84(3):585–99, 1994.

8. D. H. Lucking-Reiley. Auctions on the internet: What's being auctioned, and how? *Journal of Industrial Economics*, 48(3):227–252, 2000.

9. D. J. C. MacKay. *Information Theory, Inference and Learning Algorithms*. Cambridge University Press, 2003.

10. R. Myerson. Optimal auction design. *Mathematics of Operations Research*, 6(1):58–73, 1981.

11. W. H. Press, B. P. Flannery, S. A. Teukolsky, and W. T. Vetterling. *Numerical Recipes: The Art of Scientific Computing*. Cambridge University Press, 1992.

12. J. G. Riley and W. F. Samuelson. Optimal auctions. *American Economic Review*, 71:381–392, 1981.

13. M. H. Rothkopf and R. Harstad. On the role of discrete bid levels in oral auctions. *European Journal of Operations Research*, 74:572–581, 1994.

14. M. H. Rothkopf, T. J. Teisberg, and E. P. Kahn. Why are Vickrey auctions rare? *Journal of Political Economy*, 98(1):94–109, 1990.

15. B. S. Yamey. Why 2,310,000 [pounds] for a Velazquez? An auction bidding rule. *Journal of Political Economy*, 80:1323–1327, 1972.

16. J. Yu. *Discrete Approximation of Continous Allocation Mechanisms*. PhD thesis, California Institute of Technology, Division of Humanities and Social Science, 1999.

Repeated Auctions with Complementarities

P.J. 't Hoen[1] and J.A. La Poutré[2]

[1] Center for Mathematics and Computer Science (CWI)
P.O. Box 94079, 1090 GB Amsterdam, The Netherlands
Phone: +31 20 5929333; Fax: +31 20 5924199
[2] TU Eindhoven
De Lismortel 2, 5600 MB Eindhoven, The Netherlands
{hoen, hlp}@cwi.nl

Abstract. There is an extensive body of literature concerning optimal bidding strategies for agents participating in single shot auctions for single, individually valued goods. However, it remains a largely open question how a bidder should formulate his bidding strategy when there is a sequence of auctions and, furthermore, there are complementarities in the valuation for the bundle of items acquired in the separate auctions. We investigate conditions for which adjusting the bidding horizon beyond the immediate auction is profitable for a bidder. We show how such a strategy, in the limit, reduces agents to zero marginal profits as predicted by the Bertrand economic theory. We support our experimental results by drawing a parallel to the nIPD.

1 Introduction

With the rapid growth of agent-mediated electronic commerce, it is becoming increasingly evident that in a few years the Internet will host large numbers of interacting software agents instead of human bidders and auctioneers. The large-scale application of software agents is becoming inevitable due to the increasing number, complexity, and interactions between available online auctions. In line with this development, there is a growing body of literature on market-based allocation of scarce resources in competitive Multi-Agent Systems (MASs) [2,12,14], where the focus in the research is on sophisticated auction mechanisms and bidding strategies grounded in auction theory [10].

The field of auction theory has intensively explored optimal bidding strategies for single shot auctions, i.e. auctions for individual items. For example, it is well known that the dominant strategy in the second price Vickrey auction [16] for an agent is to bid its true valuation of a good. This property, however, does not carry over in the case of future auctions when, for example, there are substitute goods expected in future auctions. An agent then needs to deliberate the possible value of waiting for a future, possibly cheaper auction. The formulation of a good bidding strategy is even more complex when a bundle of goods is desired, as illustrated in [8] and [15] for the TAC classic[1]. As another example, consider

---

[1] Visit http://www.sics.se/tac for details.

H. La Poutré, N. Sadeh, and S. Janson (Eds.): AMEC and TADA 2005, LNAI 3937, pp. 16–29, 2006.

a software agent shopping for the cheapest possible computer assembled from parts. An incomplete bundle has a large negative impact on utility. The literature investigates two main solutions; simultaneous auctions and combinatorial auctions.

The first solution proposes for agents to participate in parallel auctions, one for each desired item in the bundle [6]. This however is problematical as an agent can have an exposure problem, i.e. how much of a sunk cost is incurred if one or more items of the bundle are not won. This exposure problem is not evident for combinatorial auctions, where the burden has shifted from estimating the value of individual goods to bidding on and estimating the value of complete bundles [14]. Both type of auctions however require availability (or at least knowledge) of all goods for auction at the same time.

This last issue of availability can be infeasible in practice. For example, an agent may have to procure a bundle of items where the items are auctioned at different points in time. Consider also a logistics setting where orders for transport are auctioned online. New opportunities for transport dynamically occur in the course of operations as clients place new orders. It is then an issue as to how well a new order can fit into an existing schedule, as this is a determining cost factor. For example, an agent that is better able to expect future demand has a better bundling of drop off points for cargo and is able to make a higher profit due to a more efficient route.

A characteristic of the above examples is that agents have to incorporate in their bidding strategy an expectation of emerging future items, expected competition, and an estimate of the complementary[2] value of possible items in auctions still to come. Goods with complementarities are items whose value as a bundle is higher than the value of the items considered in isolation. The search for a good bidding strategy for bundles with complementary issues in the items for such a repeated auction setting is still largely an open question, but a growing and essential area of research [5]. Much of this research has been restricted to a limited number of agents, bundles, number of items in the bundles, known order of the auctions, or to specific scenarios.

We extend the previous work by analyzing agents competing for a large number of unknown, individual items still to be auctioned to form profitable bundles. More specifically, we study a set of agents based on a logistics domain. This domain is of interest due to its large-scale application, its competitive nature, and its dynamic setting. These aspects make it a representative setting for evaluating bidding strategies.

The capacitated agents compete for orders by bidding for available cargo as these are offered in consecutive auctions. Each agent, in the face of competition, has to learn to focus on types of bundles, depending on already won orders, in order to maximize expected profit in auctions still to come. We show, using computational experiments, that individual agents have an incentive to bid higher (overbid) than the immediate valuation of a good if this increases probability of

---

[2] This in the literature is also called super-additive or synergy[11], i.e. $u(\{A, B\}) > u(\{A\}) + u(\{B\})$.

winning profitable goods with complementarities in future auctions. We present initial results using a straightforward machine learning technique that is able to learn intuitive bidding strategies that can be interpreted from an economic perspective for this difficult problem. In a strongly competitive scenario with intelligent bidders, the profits of the agents are reduced to near marginal costs. This is in line with economic theory, but our experimental results are a validation for a large-scale, adaptive MAS.

We present a more in-depth analysis from a game theoretical perspective. We link results of our experiments to outcomes of $n \geq 2$ player iterated prisoners' dilemma ($nIPD$). Analytical results are first presented for two players. The dominant strategy of the individual agents is to overbid for items in auctions in order to achieve higher profits in future auctions at the expense of the other agent. We show that the profits of both agents are however lower if both agents follow this strategy. This is in line with the two player prisoners' dilemma game where higher returns are received if both agents cooperate (do not overbid), but the dominant strategy is for both agents to defect (overbid). We generalize these results for $n > 2$ players and show that defection, i.e. strategic overbidding, is the dominant strategy for all agents. Our analysis indicates that the computational results of the experiments are indicative for the properties of the domain with complementarities. More sophisticated learning algorithms for the agents will arrive at similar results in equilibrium. However, we argue, and support through experimental results, that agents can have a first-mover advantage when choosing a more fine-tuned defect strategy, especially under changing circumstances.

The rest of the document is structured as follows: Section 2 formally defines the agents and the auctions. Section 3 discusses how an agent can exploit expectation of future auctions using machine learning techniques. Section 4 presents experimental results where strategically bidding agents compete with opponents for various representative settings. Section 5 presents the game theoretical link to the $nIPD$. Section 6 discusses how bidders, given our results, can still benefit from adaptive bidding strategies. Section 7 discusses and concludes.

2   The Model: Agents and Auctions

In this section we present the model of the agents and auctions. We use a relatively simple model with a limited problem domain. The model is however of sufficient complexity to allow for profitable opportunistic bidding by agents, especially if faced by opposing agents that do not consider the worth of future auctions. We present the agents and auctions from a logistics perspective to facilitate some of the intuitions in the choice of the model. We discuss the agents as representing trucks that transport the won loads.

Each $agent_i$ from the set $Agents$, where $\mid Agents \mid \geq 2$, has an integer $capacity > 0$ constraint. Each auctioned load l has a dimension of 1. The number of the loads won by agent $agent_j$ cannot exceed its capacity. Agents are limited in their capacity and must target the loads that maximize utility. Finally, the agents are homogeneous, except in their bidding strategies, to facilitate analysis of the results.

The $Auctions = \{auction_1, auction_2, \ldots, auction_t\}$ are held sequentially. In each $auction_i$ one separate load l is sold. We let each $auction_i$ be a Vickrey second price auction. This choice is motivated by three reasons. First of all, Vickrey auctions have limited overhead in communication and are straightforward to handle by the auctioneer. Second, for the last known auction $auction_t$, or for an auction that if won fills the agent to capacity, the agents, as derived from auction theory under some mild conditions, have as dominant strategy to bid their true valuation. Thirdly, use of Vickrey auctions gives a basis for a simple bidding strategy to formulate baseline agents to compete against in the computational experiments. These baseline agents, which we call myopic bidders, in each auction simply bid their true valuation for the item for auction (if not full) as if there were no future auctions to be taken into consideration.

We note that the results of Section 4 and the analysis of Section 5 are not dependent on the specific choice of auction. We feel a first price, sealed bid auction will result in comparable equilibrium outcomes. However, the additional strategic deliberations available in an open cry auction, i.e. each agent knows the going price (and the winner), can allow an agent to more quickly adapt and arrive at our predicted equilibrium outcomes.

The loads for auction originate in fruitful regions [9] where $FruitfulRegions = \{F_1, F_2, \ldots, F_n\}$. Each fruitful region represents a cluster of customers that require transport of loads to a central depot D. The fruitful regions are differentiated in the number of loads they offer in one sequence of auctions and are abstract representations of populations.

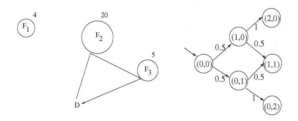

Fig. 1. Fruitful regions (a) and state representations (b)

In Figure 1a, there are three fruitful regions F_1, F_2, and F_3 from which loads originate that have to be delivered to the depot D. An agent can, for example, pick up 2 loads in region F_2 and continue to region F_3 and pick up one more before returning to the depot D.

An $agent_j \in Agents$ has a private valuation function for an auctioned load l. In Figure 1a, the valuation is influenced by the already won loads L in previous auctions, as movement cost is a major factor in calculating the marginal utility of accepting a new load l for transport. For example, the agent above for Figure 1a can cheaply pick up another load at fruitful region F_2 or F_3, as this fits in its current planned route, but it will have to make a costly detour to pick up a load l originating in region F_1.

In our experiments, we consider agents making one round trip starting from the depot D and visiting each fruitful region F_i only if at least one load has been won in an auction. The agents only pick up their cargo after all the auctions are finished. Without taking into account movement costs, the valuation is equal to 1 for every load from each and every region for each and every agent. In this initial setting, there are as yet no complementarity issues.

However, we impose a movement cost of 0.25 from the depot D to any fruitful region and a movement cost of 0.5 between any two fruitful regions. The straightforward valuation for a new load l_1 of fruitful region F_i is hence 0.5 if an agent a has not yet won any loads for that fruitful region. A second load l_2 won from F_i will then yield a straightforward valuation of 1 as no extra movement costs are required to incorporate the pickup of l_2. There is hence a complementary valuation between l_1 and l_2 which can give an incentive for a to bid more than 0.5 for l_1 to increase the changes of winning l_2, and further loads from this same fruitful region. Let agent a have won loads $L = \{L_1, L_2, \ldots, L_n\}$ where L_i are the loads won in fruitful region F_i. We define the immediate valuation of agent a for a new load l from fruitful region F_k as 0.5 if $\mid L_k \mid = 0$ and as 1 otherwise.

The state of the agent $agent_i$ during the auctions is, in part, characterized by the number of auctions won for each fruitful region, limited by the capacity of the agent. In Figure 1b we show the possible states for an agent with capacity 2 bidding in auctions for loads originating in one of $n = 2$ fruitfulregions. The agent starts with 0 loads acquired $((0,0))$ and moves to consecutive states as it wins loads in auctions. The immediate valuation is given for the transitions between states. For a state s and a load l from fruitful region F_i, we call the new state s' a successor of s for l. For example, in Figure 1b, state $(0,1)$ is a successor of state $(0,0)$ for a load l from fruitful region F_2. In a logistics domain, fruitful regions are useful, realistic abstractions that allow us to reduce a large, fine-grained world to a few abstract points of interest. This allows us to define a compact state space as a function of the number of loads acquired per fruitful region.

In each of the sequential auctions $Auctions = \{auction_1, \ldots, auction_t\}$, one load from one of the fruitful regions is sold. Hence the number of auctions $t = \Sigma_i F_i$. For each auction, one random load from any of the remaining loads is chosen. The agents know the number of auctions, they know the initial number of loads available a priori for each fruitful region, but they do not know the bidding strategies of their opponents and the specific order in which the loads will be auctioned. The agents participate in many repeated epochs of such sequential auctions. After each epoch, the order in which the loads are auctioned are randomized anew. At the end of each epoch, agents can adjust their bidding strategy.

The question is whether an agent can formulate a bidding strategy that can exploit the complementary values in the domain. I.e, can an agent formulate a bidding strategy that can increase its chances of exploiting the complementarity gain in utility for the second and following loads won from the same fruitful region? Furthermore, in Section 4, we randomize the number of available loads per fruitful region for each epoch to also quantify the impact of a more stochastic environment.

The focus on complementary values is more fine grained than the seminal work of [5] and the continuous extension in [4]. In these works, an agent is faced with the challenge of participating in a number of sequential auctions, with a known, fixed order of items. An agent only achieves a positive utility if it is able to acquire one of several bundles completely. Our domain is smoother in the sense that *any* bundle of acquired goods is potentially profitable. Furthermore, the agents in [5] have a limited budget where we measure performance only in terms of mean profits. Finally, the agents in [5] model the prices experienced in the previous rounds of auctions. This is less beneficial in our approach due to larger number of agents and the randomness of the order of the auctions. The agents in [5] also assume no correlation in the prices between the auctions, an assumption which we invalidate. However, modeling of the experienced prices can become beneficial for learning a more sophisticated bidding strategy than the approach we propose in Section 3. To apply the dynamic programming techniques of [5,12,8] and approximations of [4] to our domain with an exponential number of possible bundles and budget considerations is a challenging venue of research.

3 Strategic Bidding Behavior

In Section 2, we have introduced the model of the agents and auctions along with the complementary properties of the loads that can be won in the auctions. Here, we discuss how an agent might exploit this property to increase its expected profits and present a possible policy for a strategic bidder.

We stress that we do not aim to devise the best possible strategy or even to analyze all counter strategies. In general, formulating the best possible bidding strategy for this setting is difficult to analyse (for example as Bayes-Nash), let alone learn. It is however sufficient for our purposes that being smarter than other agents gives an added advantage. We can then show that this leads to an arms race. We present a more game-theoretical analysis of the best-response strategy in equilibrium in Section 5. Additionally, in Section 6, we show that more sophisticated learning algorithms can however have a temporary advantage before equilibrium outcomes are reached due to first-mover principle.

We restrict our discussion to a setting with at least a moderate number of agents, i.e $|\ Agents\ | \geq 10$. We hereby largely preclude the modeling of specific opponents and detailed analysis of opponent strategies. We focus on relatively large-scale settings typical for logistics and strongly competitive environments. This also makes many machine learning approaches intractable due to the large state space and the exponentially growing number of possible future states that can be reached. For example, in [7], 4.5 billion decision nodes are needed for a five agent, four item sequential auction with 5 bid choices and random tie breaking for straightforward expansion to the extensive form of this game. In this setting, the agents are only interested in one item, and not even bundles of items.

Furthermore, we focus on experimental settings where the total capacity of the agents exceeds demand, i.e. more loads can be transported than are available for auction ($|$ *Agents* $| *capacity >| Auctions |$). This is in line with the field of logistics where competition is intense and with competitive scenarios where auctions are most appropriate. It forces the agents to formulate an aggressive bidding strategy as items for auction are in high demand. In the design of the bidding strategy, we do not have to explicitly consider the possible scenario of an agent waiting until all other agents are full before trying to win auctions when demand exceeds total capacity. In Section 4, we however do predict outcomes for such scenarios.

We formulate a stochastic bidding strategy for an agent a. For each state s and a successor state s' (i.e. for one extra won load for one of the fruitful regions), we define a local stochastic policy that chooses from a set of three bidding strategies b_i where b_1 is the strategy of bidding the immediate valuation, b_2 is the strategy of overbidding the immediate valuation, and b_3 is the strategy of bidding less than the immediate valuation.

Strategy b_1 acts as if there is no complementary valuation between the current auction and future auctions. An agent using strategy b_1 simply bids the immediate valuation of a good as defined in Section 2. Strategy b_2 has a more aggressive line where a higher bid is submitted than the immediate valuation. This is the bid as dictated by strategy b_1, but increased with a fixed, additive *bidmodifier* $= 0.1$. Strategy b_3 returns the bid as in strategy b_1 but lowered by *bidmodifier*. Intuitively, strategy b_1 is the "naive" or myopic bidder. Strategy b_2 aims to acquire more than one item from the same fruitful region in order to acquire the complementary benefit. Strategy b_3 is also added to allow an agent to back off from an auction. This reduce its chances of winning specific auctions to allow an agent to reserve capacity for more profitable future loads[3]. We discuss the impact of various settings of this bid modifier and the possibility for an agent to learn to set this part of the strategy in Section 6.

For each state s and successor state s', a local strategy vector $sv = < p_1, p_2, p_3 >$ where $\Sigma_i \ p_i = 1$ is maintained where p_i is the probability of playing bidding strategy b_i when entering an auction for a load l from state s. The policy, the bidding strategy, of the agent is hence distributed over the state transitions of the agents and is conditioned on the already won bids and expected future possibilities. If s' is however a state where full capacity has been reached, then the fixed strategy vector is simply $< 1, 0, 0 >$ as there are no future auctions to bid strategically for. All other strategy vectors are initialised to $< 0.9, 0.05, 0.05 >$.

During one sequence of auctions (one epoch), for each agent a, a separate *history* $= < h_1, h_2, \ldots, h_n >$ is recorded where h_i registers the knowledge a has of the results of the *ith* auction. This entails the results for bidding in the *ith* auction (loss or win and paid price), the state of a at that moment, and the

---

[3] Experimental results (not shown) indicated that agents without the option of a lowered bid performed significantly worse than their more versatile opponents.

bidding strategy b_j used. Additionally, the mean $\mu = \frac{1}{N}\Sigma_i\ euro_i$ of the derived profits and variance $\sigma = \frac{1}{N}\Sigma_i\ (\mu - euro_i)^2$ at the end of each sequence of auctions are logged per agent. The *history*, along with the measured performance of a, is used to update the parameters of the bidding strategy to improve expected profits per agent.

Per agent, we adjust the local likelihood for strategies for the participated auctions if, and only if, the derived profits *euros* for a specific *history* if *euros* is not in the $range = [\mu - \sigma, \mu + \sigma]$. This indicates that decisions were made that should be promoted or decreased in likelihood due to the exceptional positive or negative performance. For a derived profits of *euros* after a history of bidding, an *euros* outside of the *range*, then Δ equals the excess in performance outside of *range*. This Δ was caused by the actual strategies used for each state in the entering of auctions. We are however faced with a credit assignment problem, i.e. which of the choices are actually responsible for the change in performance?

We use a Monte Carlo-like approach and distribute the credit (Δ) evenly over all strategy choices at the end of one epoch. Each strategy choice in $h_i \in history$ is assigned $\frac{\Delta}{|history|}$ of the credit. Let s be the state from which the bid in h_i was made for load l and s' the corresponding successor state. Then the likelihood for playing strategy b_k with probability p_k for this transition is updated to $p_{k+1} = p_k + \alpha * \Delta$. To retain unity, the other two strategies are updated to $p_{\widehat{k+1}} = p_{\hat{k}} - 0.5 * \alpha * \Delta$. The variable $\alpha = 0.1$ is the learning rate which, unless stated otherwise, is set low to cope with a highly dynamic environment and to ensure smooth changes in the behavior of an agent in order to not forget good strategies.

4   Experiments

In this section, we illustrate the phenomena encountered when conducting experiments with competitive agents. We note that the presented results are not specific to the chosen settings, but are typical for levels of competition between the agents for available loads and their valuations with complementary values for bundles.

We first consider 10 agents, each with a capacity of 5. There are three fruitful regions with 5, 20, and 10 loads for auction in each epoch respectively. There are hence 35 loads for auction for a total capacity of the agents of 50. In Figure 2a we show the average utility/profits (and variance) of the agents[4] for the above scenario. The first five agents are strategic bidders and the remaining agents (six to ten), use straightforward, myopic bidding as defined in Section 3.

The average profits for all 10 myopic bidders for the above setting is ≈ 1.2 (not shown). The 5 strategic bidders in Figure 2a are evidently able to increase their profits at the cost of the myopic bidders. This is also apparent from a study of the used capacity of the agents. For 10 myopic agents, each agent uses about $\approx 70\%$ of capacity, i.e. an average of $0.7 * 5$ loads is won in the auctions. This is reduced to only 35% use of capacity for the scenario of Figure 2a as the strategic bidders fill their trucks to near capacity at the cost of the myopic bidders.

---

[4] Results are averaged over a 100 runs that ran to a $100,000$ epochs.

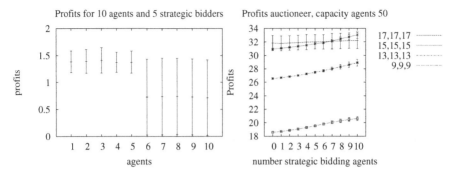

Fig. 2. Profits bidders (a) and auctioneers (b)

The strategic bidders use the possibility to overbid in auctions with good effect. Results for one strategic bidder competing with 9 myopic bidders are even more skewed as the strategic bidder is able to achieve an average profit of 1.8 and is filled to capacity. For 10 strategic bidders, agents are however at the same level of capacity use as for all myopic bidders and loads are distributed evenly. However, the average profit of the agents has dropped to 0.7. This is worse than in the all myopic case (≈ 1.2), as agents strongly compete for the items.

In Figure 2b, we show the total average profit of the auctioneers as a function of the number of agents using a speculative bidding strategy. We present various settings of the number of loads available in fruitful regions $< F_1, F_2, F_3 >$. Clearly, the auctioneers profit from the agents trying to outthink and outbid each other in competitive settings. The slope of the curve is determined by the *bidfactor* employed by the agents and bounded by the total complementary value of all loads for the agents. The added profits of the auctioneers are reduced as the number of loads offered in the auctions approaches the total capacity of the agents. For such scenarios it becomes more useful for agents to wait for cheap resources in auctions and not bid strategically. Plots of the profits of the agents like in Figure 2a for the $< 17, 17, 17 >$ scenario show that agents with strategic bidding perform near identical to myopic players.

In Figure 3a, we compare the profits of the auctioneers as function of the number of strategic bidders in a more stochastic setting. We have plotted the curve as usual for the traditional case of 10 agents as above for 9 loads per 3 fruitful regions ($< 9, 9, 9 >$). We also present results for the same number of fruitful regions, but with a random number of loads of 8, 9, or 10 equiprobably and independently available for each of the three fruitful regions each epoch ($< 9, 9, 9 > S$(tochastic)). The agents therefore are faced not only with competition, but also with a varying supply of loads for sale per fruitful region.

The agents react by optimizing for the worst case scenario, that of least available supply. We also observed that competition between the agents can be more varied for a larger number of fruitful regions. The agents experience a varied level of competition as the agents oscillate in their choice of targetting the fruitful regions, and hence the competition between the agents induces stochasticity in the supply.

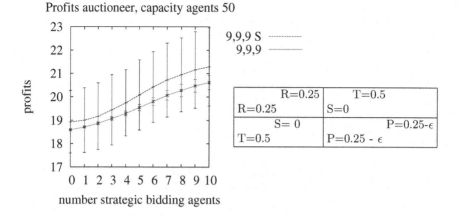

Fig. 3. Stochastics (a) and Payoffs PD (b)

Based on Figures 2a and 2b, it is of increasing importance for an agent to bid aggressively in situations where the supply of loads for transport are increasingly scarce. In such settings, a myopic bidder is vulnerable to exploitation by strategic bidders. We also expect that uncertainty in the environment will intensify the need of profit seeking agents to use an aggressive bidding strategy.

5   A Prisoners' Dilemma

Section 4 presented results where agents, though learning, are able to exploit myopic bidders that do not consider the complementary value of future auctions. However, if all agents bid strategically, results show learning is detrimental from the viewpoint of the bidders, but positive from the viewpoint of the auctioneers. In this section, we argue that the model of Section 2 contains settings that lead to prisoners' dilemma (PD) [3] type outcomes. The decreasing returns for strategic bidders in Section 4 are natural in these settings.

In the classic PD, each player has a choice of two operations: either cooperate (C) with the other player or defect (D). If both players cooperate, they both receive a given payoff. However, a higher payoff is received by the one player that defects while the other player receives as "sucker" payoff for cooperating. This leads both players to pursue the defect strategy and to arrive at the suboptimal outcome of both players receiving a low reward.

In Figure 3b, we have given the average payoff for 2 players either playing as myopic bidders (cooperating), or using an overbidding strategy as defined in Section 3 with a *bidmodifier* of value $0 < \epsilon < 0.5$. We consider the case when there are 2 loads for auction from the same, and only, fruitful region. For a joint action of (C,C), both players 50% of the time win the first load for auction and then win the second load for a marginal profit of 0.5. By overbidding, one of the players for situation (C,D) or (D,C), can win both loads by overbidding and thereby clinching the win for the second load. If both players however defect,

(D,D), then once again both loads are won by one agent. A loss in profit of ϵ is however incurred due to the aggressive bidding of the opponent.

According to the classic definitions of the PD, the payoff matrix must meet the strict conditions $T > R > P > S$ and $R > \frac{S+T}{2}$. According to [13], it is however a sufficient condition for one player to fulfill the condition that $((0.25 - \epsilon) - 0)(0.5 - 0.25) > 0$ for this player to have as dominant strategy to play defect. As the payoff matrix is symmetrical, both players will converge to the (D,D) equilibrium.

More generally, the n-player Prisoners' Dilemma game can be defined as in [17]:

1. each player faces two choices between cooperation (C) and defection (D);
2. the D option is dominant for each player, i.e. each has a better payoff choosing D than C no matter how many of the other players choose C;
3. the dominant D strategies intersect in a deficient equilibrium. In particular, the outcome if all players choose their non-dominant C-strategies is preferable from every player's point of view to the one in which everyone chooses D, but no one is motivated to deviate unilaterally from D.

More formally, the conditions used in [17] are: (1) $D_i > C_i$ for $0 \leq i \leq n - 1$; (2) $D_{i+1} > D_i$ and $C_{i+1} > C_i$ for $0 \leq i < n - 1$; (3) $C_i > \frac{(D_i + C_{i-1})}{2}$ for $0 \leq i \leq n - 1$. The payoff matrix is symmetric for each player. Here C_i denotes the reward for cooperating with C_i cooperators and D_i the reward for defecting with i cooperators and $n - i - 1$ other defectors[5].

In Figure 4a we give the (average) payoff of one agent playing with 10 agents for 3 fruitful regions of value $< 9, 9, 9 >$ as given by experimental results. We show the expected payoffs for selecting a cooperative (myopic bidding) or a defect strategy (an overbidding strategy) as function of the total number of cooperators in the game.

Analysis of a 2 player situation with a payoff matrix of the form of Table 4b with the rest of the agents invariant and of which $0 \leq n \leq 8$ choose to cooperate, shows that each individual agent, when deliberating in isolation, will converge to defect. The conditions of [13] are again met. Furthermore, [17] showed in computational experiments that coalitions of cooperators with 8 or more players were extremely difficult to realize. In [1], these results are improved by allowing tagging of individuals to enable agents to track defectors, but still cooperation is extremely tenuous. The auction mechanism as currently defined in Section 2 anonymises the individual agents and precludes tagging. Lastly, the payoffs for a choice of defect in Figure 4a greatly exceed the bounds of the third condition, $C_i > \frac{(D_i + C_{i-1})}{2}$, of the $nIPD$ as used in the above work, leading to a stronger preference for a defect strategy by the agents.

For new domains, and novel settings, it is worthwhile to compare the performance of a simple bidding strategy, like the one in Section 3, to a myopic bidder

---

[5] Note that these constraints do not reduce to the classic PD for two players, but thankfully do meet the weaker constraints derived from [13]. The used payoff table for the experiments of [17] however do meet the 3 criteria given.

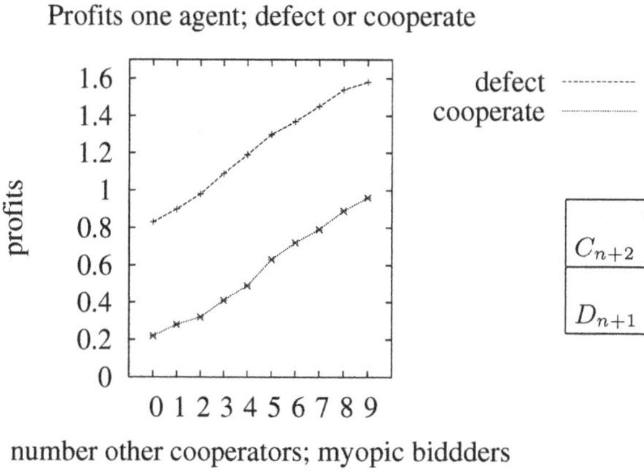

Profits one agent; defect or cooperate

Fig. 4. Profits cooperate or defect (a) and generalized payoff table (b)

and to verify whether the conditions of the $nIPD$ hold like above. If this is the case, then there is a strong indication of the equilibrium outcome for more advanced strategic bidding.

6   Perspectives for the Bidders

In Section 5, we have argued that, in the limit, agents attempting to exploit the complementary value of future auctions will lead to suboptimal profits due to the prisoners' dilemma type nature of the domain. Does this however mean that agents ultimately cannot benefit from (machine) learning?

The results of Section 4 are presented for *bidmodifier* = 0.1. This is a reasonable first choice, but agents can individually benefit from a better choice. In Figure 5(a), we show results for the first 7 agents using a strategic bidding strategy and the last three agents using a myopic bidding strategy as usual. However, the first two strategic agents use a bid modifier of *bidmodifier* + 0.1. The non-strategic bidders are, of course, worse off but the first two most aggressive bidders outperform their more conservative rivals.

In Figure 5(b) we again present results for 10 agents. Of these, 8 use an aggressive bid strategy with the standard *bidmodifier* = 0.1 (overbid) and one uses a higher *bidmodifier* of 0.2 (rampant). The last agent is a myopic bidder. Results give the mean profits as function of the number of epochs learned. We plot results for the usual learning rate $\alpha = 0.1$ and a high(er) learning rate of $alpha = 0.2$.

Study of Figure 5(b) learns that more aggressive overbidding, as expected from Figure 5(a), is a profitable strategy. Additionally, a better choice in the learning rate (in this case higher), results in higher aggregate profits as agents more quickly adapt towards the equilibrium strategy.

The above two results are of great importance in real-life models or more stochastic domains. We claim in Section 5 that we can predict the equilibrium

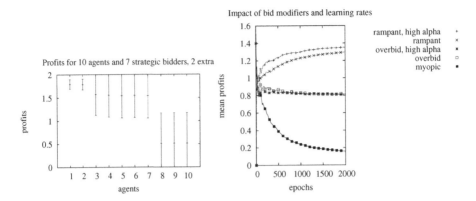

Fig. 5. More speculative bidders (a) and better learning (b)

outcome for smart agents competing in scenarios where resources are scarce. The perfect tuning of the strategy will however depend on how scarce the resources currently are and how tactical the opponent agents are. Furthermore, an agent that is more quickly able to adapt to changing circumstances, i.e. a change in the number of sold goods in the auctions, or has a better learning algorithm/model, can likely temporarily exploit the other bidders until the next equilibrium is reached.

7   Discussion and Conclusion

The application of software agents bidding in online auctions is of increasing importance. In this work, we contributed to the understanding of bidding strategies for domains where bundles of items are bought in a unknown sequence of auctions where there are complementarities between the items of the bundle. We show, through experiments and a game theoretical analysis link to the $nIPD$, that agents in competitive settings converge to near marginal utility as they attempt to exploit the super additive value in their bids for the individual items. This is beneficial from the viewpoint of the auctioneers.

References

1. F. Alkemade, D.D.B. van Bragt, and J.A. La Poutré. Stabilization of tag-mediated interaction by sexual reproduction in an evolutionary agent system. *Journal of Information Sciences*, 170(1):101–119, 2005.
2. P. Anthony, W. Hall, V. D. Dang, and N. R. Jennings. Autonomous agents for participating in multiple on-line auctions. In *Proceedings of the International Joint Conference on Artificial Intelligence (IJCAI) Workshop on E-Business and the Intelligent Web*, pages 54–64, 2001.
3. R. Axelrod. *The Evolution of Co-operation*. Basic Books, Inc., New York, 1984.

4. C. Boutilier, M. Goldszmidt, and B. Sabata. Continuous value function approximation for sequential bidding policies. In *Proceedings of the Fifteenth Annual Conference on Uncertainty in Artificial Intelligence (UAI-99)*, pages 81–90, 1999.

5. C. Boutilier, M. Goldszmidt, and B. Sabata. Sequential auctions for the allocation of resources with complementarities. In *Proceedings of the Sixteenth International Joint Conference on Artificial Intelligence (IJCAI-99)*, pages 527–534, 1999.

6. A. Byde, C. Preist, and N. R. Jennings. Decision procedures for multiple auctions. In *Autonomous Agents & Multiagent Systems*, pages 613–622, part 2. ACM press, 2002.

7. G. Cai and P. R. Wurman. Monte Carlo approximation in incomplete-information, sequential-auction games. *Decision Support Systems*, 39(2):153–168, 2005.

8. A. Greenwald and J. Boyan. Bidding under uncertainty: Theory and experiments. In *Proceedings of the Twentieth Conference on Uncertainty in Artificial Intelligence*, pages 209 – 216, 2004.

9. J.I Van Hemert and J.A. La Poutré. Dynamic routing problems with fruitful regions: Models and evolutionary computation. In *in proceedings of the eigth conference on Parallel Problem Solving from Nature (PPSN VIII)*, Lecture Notes in Computer Science, pages pages 690–699. Springer, 2004.

10. P. Klemperer. Auction theory: A guide to the literature. *Journal of Economic Surveys*, 13(3):227–286, July 1999.

11. V. Krishna and R. W. Rosenthal. Simultaneous auctions with synergies. *Games and Economic Behavior*, 17(1):1–31, 1996.

12. J. MacKie-Mason, A. Osepayshvili, D. Reeves, and M. Wellman. Price prediction strategies for market-based scheduling. In *Proceedings of the 14Th International Conference on Automated Planning and Scheduling, (ICAPS'04)*, pages 244–252. AAAI press, 2004.

13. F. Redondo. *Game Theory and Economics*. Cambridge University Press, 2001.

14. T. Sandholm. IJCAI computers and thought award 2003, award talk writeup: Making markets and democracy work: A story of incentives and computing. In *in Proceedings of the International Joint Conference on Artificial Intelligence (IJCAI-03)*, pages 1649–1671, 2003.

15. P. Stone, R. E. Schapire, M. L. Littman, J. A. Csirik, and D. McAllester. Decision-theoretic bidding based on learned density models in simultaneous, interacting auctions. *Journal of Artificial Intelligence Research*, 19:209–242, 2003.

16. W. Vickrey. Counterspeculation, auctions and competitive sealed tenders. *Journal of Finance*, 16:8–37, 1961.

17. X. Yao and P. J. Darwen. An experimental study of n-person iterated prisoner's dilemma games. In *Evo Workshops*, pages 90–108, 1994.

An Analysis of Sequential Auctions
for Common and Private Value Objects

Shaheen S. Fatima[1], Michael Wooldridge[1], and Nicholas R. Jennings[2]

[1] Department of Computer Science,
University of Liverpool, Liverpool L69 7ZF, U.K.
{S.S.Fatima, M.J.Wooldridge}@csc.liv.ac.uk
[2] School of Electronics and Computer Science,
University of Southampton, Southampton SO17 1BJ, U.K.
nrj@ecs.soton.ac.uk

Abstract. Sequential auctions are an important mechanism for buying/selling multiple objects. Now existing work in the area has studied sequential auctions for objects that are exclusively either common value or private value. However, in many real-world cases an object has both features. Also, in such cases, the common value depends on how much each bidder values the object. Moreover, a bidder generally does not know the true common value (since it may not know how much the other bidders value it). Given this, our objective is to study settings that have both common and private value elements by treating each bidder's information about the common value as *uncertain*. Each object is modelled with two signals: one for its common value and the other for its private value. The auctions are conducted using English auction rules. For this model, we first determine equilibrium bidding strategies for each auction in a sequence. On the basis of this equilibrium, we find the expected *revenue* and the *winner's expected profit* for each auction. We then show that even if the common and private values of objects are distributed identically across all objects, the revenue and the winner's profit are not the same for all of them. We show that, in accordance with Ashenfelter's experimental results [1], the revenue for our model can decline in later auctions.

1 Introduction

Market-based mechanisms such as auctions are now being widely studied as a means of buying/selling resources in multiagent systems. This uptake is occurring because auctions are both simple and have a number of desirable properties (typically the most important of which are their ability to generate high revenues to the seller and to allocate resources efficiently) [18,4,20]. Now, in many cases the number of objects to be auctioned is greater than one. There are two types of auctions that are used for multiple objects: *combinatorial auctions* [17] and *sequential auctions* [7,3,11]. The former are used when the objects for sale are available at the same time, while the latter (which are the main focus of this paper) are used when the objects become available at different points in time. In the sequential case, the auctions are conducted at different times, therefore a bidder may participate in more than one auction. In such a scenario, it has been shown that although there is only one object being auctioned at a time, the bidding

H. La Poutré, N. Sadeh, and S. Janson (Eds.): AMEC and TADA 2005, LNAI 3937, pp. 30–42, 2006.

behaviour for any individual auction strongly depends on the auctions that are yet to be conducted [7,3]. For example, consider sequential auctions for oil exploration rights. In this scenario, the price an oil company will pay for a given area is affected not only by the area that is available in the current round, but also by the areas that will become available in subsequent rounds of leasing. Thus, it would be foolish for a bidder to spend all the money set aside for exploration on the first round of leasing, if potentially even more favourable sites are likely to be auctioned off subsequently.

Against this background, a key problem in the area is to study the strategic behaviour of bidders in each individual auction. To date, considerable research effort has been devoted to this problem, but an important shortcoming of existing work on sequential auctions is that it focuses on objects that are either exclusively private value (different bidders value the same object differently) or exclusively common value (an object is worth the same to all bidders) [15,21,16,10,7]. Furthermore, some of this work also makes the complete information assumption [16,2]. However, most auctions are neither exclusively private nor common value, but involve an element of both [12]. Again, consider the above example of auctioning oil-drilling rights. This is, in general, treated as a common value auction. But private value differences may arise, for example, when a superior technology enables one firm to exploit the rights better than others. Also, in such cases, the common value (which is the same for all the bidders) depends on how much each bidder values the object. Moreover, generally speaking an individual bidder does not know the true common value, since it is unlikely to know how much the other bidders value it. On the other hand, the private value of a bidder is independent of the other bidders' private values.

Given this, our objective is to study sequential auctions for the general case where there are both common and private value elements. We do this by modelling each object with a two-dimensional signal: one for its common value and the other for its private value component. Each bidder's information about the common value is *uncertain*. Also, each bidder needs at most one object. The auctions are conducted using English auction rules. For this model, we first determine equilibrium bidding strategies for each auction in a sequence. On the basis of this equilibrium, we find the *expected revenue* and the *winner's expected profit* for each auction. We show that even if the common and private values are distributed identically across all objects, the revenue and the winner's profit are not the same for all of them[1]. Specifically, we consider an example scenario and show that in accordance with Ashenfelter's empirical result [1], the revenue for our model can decline in later auctions.

Our paper therefore makes two important contributions to the state of the art in multi-object auctions. First, we determine equilibrium bidding strategies for sequential auctions that involve both common and private value elements. Second, we show that, in accordance with Ashenfelter's experimental results [1], the revenue can decline in later auctions.

---

[1] This study is important because Ashenfelter [1] showed a *declining price anomaly*: in real-world sequential auctions mean sale prices for identical objects decline in later auctions. In contrast, for objects that are exclusively common/private value, the theoretical results of Milgrom and Weber [19,14], and McAfee and Vincent [13] show a completely opposite effect. Our objective is therefore to show that, for our model, the revenue can decline in later auctions.

The remainder of the paper is organised as follows. Section 2 describes the auction setting. Section 3 determines equilibrium bidding strategies. In Section 4, we present an example auction scenario to illustrate a decline in the revenue of later auctions. Section 5 provides a discussion of how our result relates with existing work on sequential auctions. Section 6 concludes. Appendix A to C provide proofs of theorems.

2   The Sequential Auctions Model

Single object auctions that have both private and common value elements have been studied in [9]. We therefore adopt this basic model and extend it to cover the multiple objects case. Before doing so, however, we give an overview of the basic model.

Single object. A single object auction is modelled in [9] as follows. There are $n \geq 3$ risk neutral bidders. The *common value* (V_1) of the object to the n bidders is equal, but initially the bidders do not know this value. However, each bidder receives a signal that gives an estimate of this common value. Bidder $i = 1, \ldots, n$ draws an estimate (v_{i1}) of the object's true value (V_1) from the probability distribution function $Q(v)$ with support $[v_L, v_H]$. Although different bidders may have different estimates, the true value (V_1) is the same for all bidders and is modelled as the average of the bidders' signals: $V_1 = \frac{1}{n} \sum_{i=1}^{n} v_{i1}$. Furthermore, each bidder has a *cost* which is different for different bidders and this cost is its *private value*. For $i = 1, \ldots, n$, let c_{i1} denote bidder i's signal for this private value which is drawn from the distribution function $G(c)$ with support $[c_L, c_H]$ where $c_L \geq 0$ and $v_L \geq c_H$. Cost and value signals are independently and identically distributed across bidders. Henceforth, we will use the term *value* to refer to common value and *cost* to refer to private value.

If bidder i wins the object and pays b, it gets a utility of $V_1 - c_{i1} - b$, where $V_1 - c_{i1}$ is i's surplus. Each bidder bids so as to maximize its utility. Note that bidder i receives two signals (v_{i1} and c_{i1}) but its bid has to be a single number. Hence, in order to determine their bids, bidders need to combine the two signals into a *summary* statistic. This is done as follows. For i, a one-dimensional summary signal, called i's surplus[2], is defined as:

$$S_{i1} = v_{i1}/n - c_{i1} \tag{1}$$

which allows i's optimal bids to be determined in terms of S_{i1} (see [9] for more details about the problems with two signals and why a one-dimensional surplus is required). In order to rank bidders from low to high valuations, $Q(v)$ and $G(c)$ are assumed to be log concave[3]. Under this assumption, the conditional expectations $E(v|S = x)$ and $E(v|S \leq x)$ are non-decreasing in x. Furthermore, $E(c|S = x)$ and $E(c|S \leq x)$ are non-increasing in x. In other words, the bidders can be ranked from low to high values on the basis of their surplus. We now extend this model to $m > 1$ objects.

---

[2] Note that i's true surplus is $V_1 - c_{i1}$ which is equal to $v_{i1}/n - c_{i1} + \sum_{j \neq i} v_{j1}/n$. But since $v_{i1}/n - c_{i1}$ depends on i's signals while $\sum_{j \neq i} v_{j1}/n$ depends on the other bidders' signals, the term 'i's surplus' is also used to mean $v_{i1}/n - c_{i1}$.

[3] Log concavity means that the natural log of the densities is concave. This restriction is met by many commonly used densities like uniform, normal, chi-square, and exponential, and it ensures that optimal bids are increasing in surplus. Again see [9] for more details.

Multiple objects[4]. For each of the $m > 1$ objects, the bidders' values are independently and identically distributed and so are their costs. There are m distribution functions for the common values, one for each object. Likewise, there are m distribution functions for the costs, one for each object. For $j = 1, \ldots, m$, let $Q_j : R_+ \rightarrow [0, 1]$ denote the distribution function for the value of the jth object and $G_j : R_+ \rightarrow [0, 1]$ that for its cost. Thus, each bidder receives its value signal for the jth object from Q_j and its cost signal from G_j.

The m objects are sold one after another in m auctions that are conducted using English auction rules. Furthermore, each bidder receives the cost and value signals for an auction just before that auction begins. The signals for the jth object are received only after the $(j - 1)$ previous auctions have been conducted. Consequently, although the bidders know the distribution functions from which the signals are drawn, they do not know the actual signals for the jth object until the previous $(j - 1)$ auctions are over.

Each bidder can win at most one object. The winner for the jth object cannot participate in the remaining $m - j$ auctions. Thus, if n agents participate in the first auction, the number of agents for the jth auction is $(n - j + 1)$. For objects $j = 1, \ldots, m$ and bidders $i = 1, \ldots, n$, let v_{ij} and c_{ij} denote the common and private values respectively. The true common value of the jth object (denoted V_j) is:

$$V_j = \frac{1}{n - j + 1} \sum_{i=1}^{n-j+1} v_{ij} \tag{2}$$

For objects $j = 1, \ldots, m$ and bidders $i = 1, \ldots, n$, let $S_{ij} = v_{ij}/n - c_{ij}$ denote i's surplus for object j.

Note that the values/costs for our model are not correlated. Such correlations occur across objects, if for a bidder (say i) the value/cost of object $j = 2, \ldots, m$ can be determined on the basis of i's value/cost signal for the first object. However, in many cases such a direct relation between the objects may not exist. Hence, we focus on the case where different objects have different distribution functions. Furthermore, although each bidder knows the distribution functions from which the values/costs are drawn before the first auction begins, it receives its signals for an object only just before the auction for that object begins. In the following section, we determine equilibrium bidding strategies for this multi-object model.

3   Equilibrium Bidding Strategies

The m objects are auctioned in m separate English auctions that are conducted sequentially. The English auction rules are as follows. The auctioneer continuously raises the price, and bidders publicly reveal when they withdraw from the auction. Bidders who drop out from an auction are not allowed to re-enter that auction. A bidder's strategy for

---

[4] Our model for multiple objects is a generalisation of [3]. While [3] studies sequential auctions for two private value objects, we study sequential auctions for $m \geq 2$ objects that have both private and common values.

the jth (for $j = 1, \ldots, m - 1$) auctions depends on how much profit it expects to get from the $(m - j)$ auctions yet to be conducted. However, since there are only m objects there are no more auctions after the mth one. Thus, a bidder's strategic behaviour during the last auction is the same as that for a single object English auction. Equilibrium bidding strategies for a single object of the type described in Section 2 have been obtained in [9]. We therefore briefly summarize these strategies and then determine equilibrium for our m objects case.

Single object. For a single object with value V_1, the equilibrium obtained in [9] is as follows. A bidder's strategy is described in terms of its surplus and indicates how high the bidder should go before dropping out. Since $n \geq 3$, the prices at which some bidders drop out convey information (about the common value) to those who remain active. Suppose k bidders have dropped out at bid levels $b_1 \leq \ldots \leq b_k$. A bidder's (say i's) strategy is described by functions $B_k(S_i; b_1 \ldots b_k)$, which specify how high it must bid given that k bidders have dropped out at levels $b_1 \ldots b_k$ and given that its surplus is S_i. The n-tuple of strategies $(B(\cdot), \ldots, B(\cdot))$ with $B(\cdot))$ defined in Equation 3, constitutes a symmetric equilibrium of the English auction.

$$B_0(x_{i1}) = E(v_{i1} - c_{i1} | S_{i1} = x_{i1})$$

$$B_k(x_{i1}; b_1 \ldots b_k) = \frac{n - k}{n} E(v_{i1} | S_{i1} = x_{i1}) + \frac{1}{n} \sum_{y=0}^{k-1} E(v_{i1} | B_y(S_{i1}; b_1, \ldots, b_y) = b_{y+1})$$

$$- E(c_{i1} | S_{i1} = x_{i1}) \tag{3}$$

where x_{i1} is i's surplus. The intuition for Equation 3 is as follows. Given its surplus and the information conveyed in others' drop out levels, the highest a bidder is willing to go is given by the expected value of the object, assuming that all other active bidders have the same surplus. For instance, consider the bid function $B_0(S_{i1})$ which pertains to the case when no bidder has dropped out yet. If all other bidders were to drop out at level $B_0(S_0)$, then i's expected payoff ($ep = V_1 - c_{i1} - B_0(S_0)$) would be:

$$ep = S_{i1} + \frac{n - 1}{n} E(v | S = S_0) - B_0(S_0)$$

$$= S_{i1} + \frac{n - 1}{n} E(v | S = S_0) - E(v - c | S = S_0)$$

$$= S_{i1} - S_0$$

Using strategy B_0, i remains active until it is indifferent between winning and quitting. Similar interpretations are given to B_k for $k \geq 1$; the only difference is that these functions take into account the information conveyed in others' drop out levels.

Let f_1^n denote the first order statistic of the surplus for the n bidders and let s_1^n denote the second order statistic. f_1^n and s_1^n are obtained from the distribution functions Q_1 and G_1. For the above equilibrium, it has been shown that the bidder with the highest surplus wins and the expected revenue (denoted ER) is [9]:

$$ER = E(V) - E(c | s = f_1^n) - E(\pi_w) \tag{4}$$

where $E(\pi_w)$ is the winner's expected profit. This profit is:

$$E(\pi_w) = E(f_1^n) - E(s_1^n) \qquad (5)$$

On the basis of the above equilibrium for a single object, we determine equilibrium for sequential auctions for the m objects defined in Section 2 as follows.

Multiple objects. We first introduce some notation and them derive the equilibrium. We will denote the first order statistic of the surplus for the jth (for $j = 1, \ldots, m$) auction as f_j^{n-j+1} and the second order statistic as s_j^{n-j+1}. Also, we denote a bidder's cumulative ex-ante expected profit from auctions j to m (where $1 \le j \le m$) as α_j. Finally, we denote the winner's expected profit for the jth auction as $E(\pi_{wj})$. Given this, the following theorem characterises the equilibrium for $m > 1$ objects.

Theorem 1. *For $1 \le j \le m$ and $j \le y \le m$, let β_j^y and α_j be defined as:*

$$\beta_j^y = [\prod_{k=j}^{y-1}(1 - 1/(n - y + k + 1))][1/(n - j + 1)] \qquad (6)$$

$$\alpha_j = \sum_{y=j}^{m}(\beta_j^y[E(f^{n-j+1}) - E(s^{n-j+1}) + \alpha_{j+1}]) \qquad (7)$$

where $\alpha_{m+1} = 0$. Then the n-tuple of strategies $(B(\cdot), \ldots, B(\cdot))$ with $B(\cdot)$ defined in Equation 8 constitutes an equilibrium for the jth (for $j = 1, \ldots, (m-1)$) auction at a stage where k bidders have dropped out:

$$B_0^j(x_{ij}) = E(v_{ij} - c_{ij}|S_{ij} = x_{ij}) - \alpha_{j+1}$$
$$B_k^j(x_{ij}; b_1, \ldots, b_k) = \frac{n - j + 1 - k}{n - z + 1}E(v_{ij}|S_{ij} = x_{ij}) - E(c_{ij}|S_{ij} = x_{ij})$$
$$+ \frac{1}{n - j + 1}\sum_{y=0}^{k-1}E(v_{ij}|B_y(S_{ij}; b_1, \ldots, b_y) = b_{y+1})$$
$$-\alpha_{j+1} \qquad (8)$$

For the last auction, the equilibrium is as given in Equation 3 with n replaced with $(n - m + 1)$.

For the above equilibrium, the winner for the jth (for $j = 1, \ldots, m$) auction is the bidder with the highest surplus for that auction (see proof of Theorem 3 in the appendix for details). The following two theorems characterise the expected revenue and the winner's expected profit.

Theorem 2. *For the jth (for $j = 1, \ldots, m - 1$) auction, the winner's expected profit (denoted $E(\pi_{wj})$) is:*

$$E(\pi_{wj}) = E(f_j^{n-j+1}) - E(s_j^{n-j+1}) + \alpha_{j+1} \qquad (9)$$

and for the last auction, the winner's expected profit is:

$$E(\pi_{wm}) = E(f_m^{n-m+1}) - E(s_m^{n-m+1}) \qquad (10)$$

Theorem 3. *For the jth (for $j = 1, \ldots, m$) auction, the expected revenue (denoted ER_j)) is:*

$$\forall_{j=1}^{m} ER_j = E(V) - E(c|s = f_j^{n-j+1}) - E(\pi_{wj})$$

$$(11)$$

In the following section, we use the above equilibrium to show how the expected revenue and the winner's expected profit vary from auction to auction.

4   Revenue and Winner's Profit

In Section 3, we determined equilibrium for the case where the distribution function for the value (cost) was different for different objects. In this section, our objective is to show that even if these distribution functions are identical across objects, the expected revenue is not the same for all objects. We present an example auction scenario which shows that in accordance with Ashenfelter's empirical result [1], the revenue for our model can decline in later auctions.

It must be noted that our objective here is not to provide a comprehensive study of how the expected revenue varies, but only to illustrate (with an example) that there exist cases where the variation predicted by our theoretical analysis accords with the experimental results of Ashenfelter [1].

Example auction scenario. This example in intended to show that:

- the revenue declines in later auctions (this result corresponds with Ashenfelter's empirical results [1]), and
- the winner's expected profit declines in later auctions.

In more detail, the setting for our analysis is as follows. The bidders' values are identically distributed across objects and so are their costs. The common values of all m objects are drawn from a single distribution function. This function (say $Q : R_+ \to [0, 1]$) is used to draw the common value of the jth ($j = 1, \ldots, m$) object. Also, there is a single distribution function (say $G : R_+ \to [0, 1]$) for the cost of the jth ($j = 1, \ldots, m$) object. As before, each bidder receives a value signal (from Q) and a cost signal (from G) for an auction just before that auction begins.

Since there is a single distribution function for all objects, we drop the subscripts (for the order statistics) in Equations 9 and 11 for profit and revenue and rewrite them as:

$$E(\pi_{wj}) = E(f^{n-j+1}) - E(s^{n-j+1}) + \alpha_{j+1}$$

$$(12)$$

$$ER_j = E(V) - E(c|s = f^{n-j+1}) - E(\pi_{wj})$$

$$(13)$$

We determine the expected revenues for the case where the values and costs are distributed normally. Recall that the normal distribution satisfies the log concavity assumption mentioned in Section 2. Both value and cost signals are distributed normally. The

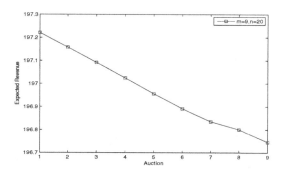

Fig. 1. A varying revenue in a series of auctions for the normal distribution

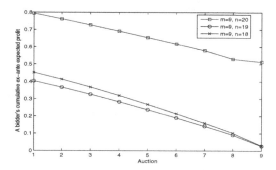

Fig. 2. A bidder's cumulative ex-ante expected profit (α_j) for the normal distribution

normal distribution is denoted $\mathcal{N}(\mu, \nu)$ where μ is the mean and ν is the variance. Let μ_v, μ_c, and μ_s denote the mean for the value, cost and surplus respectively. Also, let ν_v, ν_c, and ν_s denote the variance for the value, cost, and surplus respectively. We took $\mu_v = 200$, $\mu_c = 2$, $\nu_v = 0.5$, and $\nu_c = 0.5$. These values ensure that $c_L > 0$ and $v_L > c_H$ for more than 99.8 percent of the population. Given this, for the jth auction, we get the mean and variance for the surplus as $\mu_s = \mu_v/(n - j + 1) - \mu_c$ and $\nu_s = 1.0$ [6].

Let $F(x)$ and $f(x)$ denote the distribution and density function for the surplus where:

$$f(x) = \frac{1}{\nu_s \sqrt{2\pi}} e^{-(x-\mu_s)^2/2\nu_s^2}$$

From a continuous distribution with cumulative distribution function $F(x)$, if n random samples are drawn, then the expectation of the second highest order statistic of these n samples between limits $\bar{x}$ and $\underline{x}$ is [5]:

$$E(s^n) = n(n-1) \int_{\underline{x}}^{\bar{x}} x[F(x)]^{n-2}[1 - F(x)]f(x)dx \qquad (14)$$

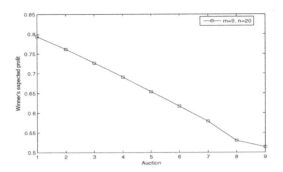

Fig. 3. The winner's expected profit for the normal distribution

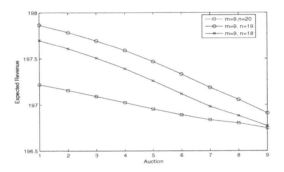

Fig. 4. Revenue for a varying competition

and the difference between the first and second highest order statistics is [5]:

$$E(f^n) - E(s^n) = n \int_{-\infty}^{\infty} [F(x)]^{n-1}[1 - F(x)]dx \qquad (15)$$

We substitute these values for $E(s^n)$ and $E(f^n) - E(s^n)$ to find the expected revenue and the winner's expected profit for each individual auction in a series.

The variation in the revenue for different auctions is shown in Figure 1. As shown in the figure, the expected revenue decreases from one auction to the next. A bidder's cumulative ex-ante expected profit from auctions j to m (i.e., α_j) is shown in Figure 2. This profit decreases from one auction to the next. The winner's expected profit also drifts downward as shown in Figure 3.

The effect of competition. In order to study the effect of competition, we fix the number of objects (m) and vary the number of bidders (n) for the example scenario described above. Figure 4 is a plot of the expected revenue for different n. As seen in the figure, for all the three values of n (i.e., $n = 20$, $n = 19$, and $n = 18$) the seller's revenue declines from one auction to the next. Figure 5 is a plot of the winner's expected profit

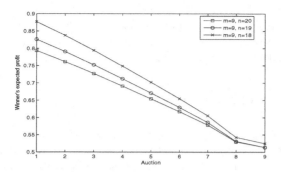

Fig. 5. The winner's expected profit for a varying competition

for different n. As seen in the figure, for all the three values of n, the winner's expected profit also decreases from one auction to the next.

5 Related Work

Existing work has studied the dynamics of the revenue of objects for sequential auctions [15,19,14,3]. However, a key limitation of this work is that it focuses on objects that are either exclusively private value or exclusively common value. For instance, Ortega-Reichert [15] determined the equilibrium for sequential auctions for two private value objects using the first price rules. Weber [19] showed that in sequential auctions of identical objects with risk neutral bidders who hold independent private values, the expected revenue is the same for each auction. On the other hand, Milgrom and Weber [14] studied sequential auctions in an interdependent values model with affiliated[5] signals. They showed that expected revenues have a tendency to drift upward. This may be because earlier auctions release information about the values of objects and thereby reduce the winner's curse problem.

In contrast to the above theoretical results, there has been some evidence in real-world sequential auctions for identical objects – for art and wine auctions in particular – that the prices tend to drift downward [1,13]. Because the theoretical models mentioned above predict either a stochastically constant or increasing price, this fact has been called the *declining price anomaly*. Mc Afee and Vincent [13] consider two identical private value objects and using the second price sealed bid rules, they show that the declining price anomaly cannot be explained even if the bidders are considered to be risk averse. Bernhardt and Scoones [3] show a decline in the sale price by considering two private value objects. Here, we generalise this model to $n > 2$ objects with both common and private values[6]. Although the objects we consider have both common and

---

[5] Affiliation is a form of positive correlation. Let $X_1, X_2, \ldots, X_n$ be a set of positively correlated random variables. Positive correlation roughly means that if a subset of X_is are large, then this makes it more likely that the remaining X_js are also large.

[6] Multi-object auctions for common and private value objects have been studeied in [8]. This work focusses on the efficiency of these auctions, while our present work focusses on the variation in the revenue of such auctions.

private values, each bidder receives its signals for an auction just before the auction begins. In other words, during an auction, the information that bidders obtain about the others' value signals does not carry forward to subsequent auctions. Hence, as in the case of [3], our model too shows a decline in the revenue.

6   Conclusions and Future Work

This paper has analyzed a model for sequential auctions for objects with private and common values in an uncertain information setting. We first determined equilibrium strategies for each auction in a sequence. Then we showed that even if the value and cost signals are distributed identically across objects, then in accordance with Ashenfelter's result [1], the expected revenue can decline in later auctions.

There are many interesting directions for future work. First, our present focus was on determining how the expected revenue varies in a series of English auctions. However, in order to generalize our results, we intend to extend the analysis to other auction forms. Second, we studied the case where bidders received the cost and value signals for an object just before the auction. In future, we will extend the analysis to the case where the values and costs for the last $(m - 1)$ objects can be determined from the signals for the first object (i.e., values and costs are perfectly correlated).

References

1. O. Ashenfelter. How auctions work for wine and art. *Journal of Economic Perspectives*, 3(221):23–36, 1989.
2. J. P. Benoit and V. Krishna. Multiple-object auctions with budget constrained bidders. *Review of Economic Studies*, 68:155–179, 2001.
3. D. Bernhardt and D. Scoones. A note on sequential auctions. *The American Economic Review*, 84(3):653–657, 1994.
4. P. Dasgupta and E. Maskin. Efficient auctions. *Quarterly Journal of Economics*, 115:341–388, 2000.
5. H. David. *Order Statistics*. Wiley, New York, 1969.
6. M. Dwass. *Probability and Statistics*. W. A. Benjamin Inc., California, 1970.
7. W. Elmaghraby. The importance of ordering in sequential auctions. *Management Science*, 49(5):673–682, 2003.
8. S. S. Fatima, M. Wooldridge, and N. R. Jennings. Sequential auctions for objects with common and private values. In *Proceedings of the Fourth International Conference on Autonomous Agents and Multi-Agent Systems*, pages 635–642, Utrecht, Netherlands, 2005.
9. J. K. Goeree and T. Offerman. Competitive bidding in auctions with private and common values. *The Economic Journal*, 113(489):598–613, 2003.
10. B. Katzman. A two stage sequential auction with multi-unit demands. *Journal of Economic Theory*, 86:77–99, 1999.
11. V. Krishna. *Auction Theory*. Academic Press, 2002.
12. J. Laffont. Game theory and empirical economics: The case of auction data. *European Economic Review*, 41:1–35, 1997.
13. R. P. McAfee and D. Vincent. The declining price anomaly. *Journal of Economic Theory*, 60:191–212, 1993.

14. P. Milgrom and R. J. Weber. A theory of auctions and competitive bidding II. In P. Klemperer, editor, *The Economic Theory of Auctions*. Edward Elgar, Cheltenham, U.K, 2000.
15. A. Ortega-Reichert. Models of competitive bidding under uncertainty. Technical Report 8, Stanford University, 1968.
16. C. Pitchik and A. Schotter. Perfect equilibria in budget-constrained sequential auctions: An experimental study. *Rand Journal of Economics*, 19:363–388, 1988.
17. T. Sandholm and S. Suri. BOB: Improved winner determination in combinatorial auctions and generalizations. *Artificial Intelligence*, 145:33–58, 2003.
18. W. Vickrey. Counterspeculation, auctions and competitive sealed tenders. *Journal of Finance*, 16:8–37, 1961.
19. R. J. Weber. Multiple-object auctions. In R. Engelbrecht-Wiggans, M. Shibik, and R. M. Stark, editors, *Auctions, bidding, and contracting: Uses and theory*, pages 165–191. New York University Press, 1983.
20. M. P. Wellman, W. E. Walsh, P. R. Wurman, and J. K. McKie-Mason. Auction protocols for decentralised scheduling. *Games and Economic Behavior*, 35:271–303, 2001.
21. R. E. Wiggans and C. M. Kahn. Multi-unit pay your-bid auctions with variable rewards. *Games and Economic Behavior*, 23:25–42, 1998.

Appendix

A   Proof of Theorem 1

Proof. We consider each of the m auctions by reasoning backwards.

- **mth auction.** To begin, consider the mth auction for which there are $(n - m + 1)$ bidders. Since this is the last auction, an agent's bidding behaviour is the same as that for the single object case. Hence, the equilibrium for this auction is the same as that in Equation 3 with n replaced with $(n - m + 1)$. For $j = 1, \ldots, m$, let α_{ij} denote an agent's cumulative ex-ante expected profit from auctions j to m. Recall that although the bidders know the distribution (from which the cost and value signals are drawn) before the first auction begins, they draw the signals for the jth auction only after the $(j - 1)$ earlier auctions end. Since α_{ij} is the ex-ante expected profit (i.e., it is computed before the bidders draw their signals for the jth auction), it is the same for all participating bidders. Thus, we will simplify notation by dropping the subscript i and denote α_{ij} simply as α_j We know from Equation 5 that:

$$\alpha_m = \frac{1}{n - m + 1}(E(f_m^{n-m+1}) - E(s_m^{n-m+1})) \qquad (16)$$

  This is because all the $(n - m + 1)$ agents that participate in the mth auction have ex-ante identical chances of winning it. Note that the right hand side of Equation 16 does not depend on i. In other words, since bidders receive their signals for the mth auction after the $(m - 1)$th auction, the ex-ante expected profit for the mth auction (before the $(m - 1)$th auction ends) is the same for all the $(n - m + 1)$ bidders.
- **$(m - 1)$th auction.** Consider the $(m - 1)$th auction. During this auction, a bidder bids b if $(V_{m-1} - c_{m-1} - b \geq \alpha_m)$ or $(b \leq V_{m-1} - c_{m-1} - \alpha_m)$. Hence, a symmetric equilibrium for the $(m - 1)$th auction is obtained by substituting $j = m - 1$ in

Equation 8. We know from Equation 4, that the expected revenue for the single object case is the second order statistic of the surplus. The difference between the equilibrium bids for the single object case and the $(m-1)$th auction of the m objects case is α_m (see Equations 3 and 8). Hence, the expected revenue for the $(m-1)$th auction is $E(s_{m-1}^{n-m+2}) - \alpha_m$. This implies that the winner's expected profit for the $(m-1)$th auction is:

$$E(\pi_{w(m-1)}) = E(f_{m-1}^{n-m+2}) - E(s_{m-1}^{n-m+2}) + \alpha_m \tag{17}$$

- **First** $(m-2)$ **auctions.** We now find $\alpha_1, \ldots, \alpha_m$. For $1 \le j \le m$ and $j \le y \le m$, let β_j^y denote the ex-ante probability that a bidder wins the yth auction in the series from jth to the mth auction. This probability is

$$\beta_j^y = [\prod_{k=j}^{y-1}(1 - 1/(n-y+k+1))][1/(n-j+1)] \tag{18}$$

Also, let α_j denote a bidder's cumulative ex-ante expected profit for all the auctions from the jth to the mth. This profit is:

$$\alpha_j = \sum_{y=j}^{m}(\beta_j^y[E(f^{n-j+1}) - E(s^{n-j+1}) + \alpha_{j+1}]) \tag{19}$$

where $\alpha_{m+1} = 0$. Generalising Equation 17 to the first $(m-1)$ auctions, we get the winner's expected profit $(E(\pi_{wj}))$ as:

$$E(\pi_{wj}) = E(f_j^{n-j+1}) - E(s_j^{n-j+1}) + \alpha_{j+1} \tag{20}$$

In other words, a bidder's optimal bid for the jth auction is obtained by discounting the single object equilibrium bid by α_{j+1}. Hence, we get the equilibrium bids in Equation 8.

B Proof of Theorem 3

Proof. For the jth (for $j = 1, \ldots, m$) auction, the total expected surplus that gets split between the auctioneer and the winning bidder is $E(V) - E(c|s = f_j^{n-j+1})$. From this surplus, the winning bidder gets a share of $E(\pi_{wj})$. Hence, the seller's revenue is $ER_j = E(V) - E(c|s = f_j^{n-j+1}) - E(\pi_{wj})$.

C Proof of Theorem 2

Proof. The mth auction is identical to the single object case. Hence, the expected profit for this auction is:
$$E(\pi_{wm}) = E(f_m^{n-m+1}) - E(s_m^{n-m+1})$$
Since the difference between the expected revenue for the single object case and the jth (for $j = 1, \ldots, m-1$) auction of the m objects case is α_{j+1}, the winner's expected profit for the jth auction is $E(\pi_{wj}) = E(f_j^{n-j+1}) - E(s_j^{n-j+1}) + \alpha_{j+1}$.

Algorithms for Distributed Winner Determination in Combinatorial Auctions

Muralidhar V. Narumanchi and José M. Vidal

Computer Science and Engineering
University of South Carolina
Columbia, SC. 29208
narumanc@cse.sc.edu, vidal@sc.edu

Abstract. The problem of optimal winner determination in combinatorial auctions consists of finding the set of bids that maximize the revenue for the sellers. Various solutions exist for solving this problem but they are all centralized. That is, they assume that all bids are sent to a centralized auctioneer who then determines the winning set of bids. In this paper we introduce the problem of distributed winner determination in combinatorial auctions which eliminates the centralized auctioneer. We present a set of distributed search-based algorithms for solving this problem and study their relative tradeoffs.

1 Introduction

In a combinatorial auction the buyers bid on bundles of items. After clearing, each buyer receives either the entire bundle he bid on or nothing. Combinatorial auctions are often preferred over sequential auctions because bidders can express complementarity and substitutability of their choices within the bids. The optimal winner determination problem in a combinatorial auction involves finding the set of bids that maximizes the revenue generated. This problem is known to be an $\mathcal{NP}$-Hard problem [1]. Various centralized approaches using A^* [2], dynamic programming [1], integer programming [3], linear programming [4], and approximation techniques [5] have been proposed for determining the optimal and approximately-optimal solution. All these algorithms assume the existence of a centralized auctioneer who collects all the bids and computes the set of winning bids. All these algorithms also fail to address the question of revenue division amongst the winning goods. In this paper we investigate the problem of distributed winner determination, that is, the determination of the set of winning bids in the absence of a centralized auctioneer. We provide some distributed search-based solutions as well as a negotiation-based approach which also performs revenue division.

Our research is motivated by a vision of a future Internet-based distributed electronic marketplace. The system would be a peer-to-peer system, without the need for a centralized auctioneer, and would have to provide the proper incentives for selfish agents to participate and perform their duties as required. For such a system to exist we will need, among other technologies, protocols that distribute

H. La Poutré, N. Sadeh, and S. Janson (Eds.): AMEC and TADA 2005, LNAI 3937, pp. 43–56, 2006.

the computational task of winner determination. But, since the agents performing the computation have an interest in the outcome of the computation and might try to manipulate it, we need protocols that provide the correct incentives to agents and prevent them from manipulating the outcome. As such, our problem is an instance of a distributed algorithmic mechanism design problem [6,7]. Hence it is also essential that we address the issue of revenue distribution among the sellers in each winning combinatorial bid, an issue that has not been addressed by any of the centralized winner determination algorithms we have found.

Specifically, we assume that each agent has a good for sale and receives combinatorial bids from prospective buyers. The agents must then implement some protocol which will lead to the distributed calculation of the set of winning bids. We consider both the case where the agents are cooperative and when they are selfish. A system with cooperative agents could arise if all the agents are owned by the same entity or if the participants have previously arrived at an off-line agreement. Selfish agents more closely simulate the selfish interests of their human counterparts who want to maximize their profit.

We start by covering some of the past work on combinatorial auctions in section 2. Section 3 formally defines the distributed combinatorial auctions problem. Sections 4, 5 and 6 give a complete algorithm, a simple hill-climbing algorithm and a partitioning-based algorithm, respectively. Section 7 provides a negotiation based approach. Finally, section 8 shows our test results and section 9 discusses the future work.

2   Related Work

Sandholm [2] has given an algorithm for calculating the optimal set of bids in a combinatorial auction using an implementation of A^*. Hoos and Boutilier have provided a solution using stochastic local search [8]. Rothkopf et al. provides a solution using dynamic programming [1]. Fujishima et al. proposes one method to speed up the search by structuring the search space and a heuristic method that lacks optimality guarantees but performs well on average [9]. All these algorithms are centralized.

In the area of multiple agents operating simultaneously in a market setting, Preist provides an algorithm for agents that participate in multiple English auctions [10,11]. Wellman *et. al.* [12] use a market mechanism to solve a decentralized scheduling problem. Both solve different problems from ours. The reader new to combinatorial auctions can read the survey provided by [13].

3   Problem Description

A distributed combinatorial auction is defined as a set goods G where $g_i \in G$ and $|G| = n$, a set of consumers C where $c_i \in C$ and $|C| = k$, and a set of bids B where $b_i \in B$. Each bid b_i is a tuple $\{c, g, p\}$ where c is the consumer who placed the bid, $g \subseteq G$ is the set of goods being bid on, and p is the bid price. There is no centralized auctioneer who collects these bids. We will use b_i^g to refer to the set of goods for bid b_i, b_i^p to refer to the price of bid b_i and g_i^b to refer to the list of bids in which good g_i is present.

Each consumer can place any number of bids[1]. The bid can be for either a single good or a combination of goods. For example, consumer c_i can place a bid b_k on the bundle $\{g_1, g_4, g_7\}$ for a value of v_1 and another bid b_j on bundle $\{g2\}$ for value v_2.

Definition 1 (Feasible Allocation). *An allocation A of goods is a feasible allocation if and only if no two bids in the allocation share a good.*

The set of all feasible allocations, given B, is given by F which is

$$F \equiv \{b \subseteq B \,|\, \forall_{b_i, b_k \in A, i \neq k} b_i^g \cap b_k^g = \emptyset\}. \tag{1}$$

The value of an allocation A is given by

$$V(A) = \sum_{b \in A} b^p. \tag{2}$$

The revenue maximizing solution A^* is the feasible allocation that maximizes the total price paid for all the goods, that is $A^* = \arg\max_{A \subseteq F} V(A)$.

In distributed combinatorial auctions there is no centralized auctioneer who collects all the bids. Instead, we assume that each good for sale is represented by an agent. When a consumer places a bid b_i, the bid is passed on to b_i^g which are the agents representing the goods present in the bids[2]. Any agent g_i can communicate with any other agent. Thus each agent has the list of bids in which it is present.

We further assume that a bid can be cleared if and only if all the agents in the bid agree to clear it. The final agreement reached by the agents is final and binding. We also assume that the agents don't have a reservation price for their goods and that goods can be sold only once. Finally, some of the algorithms we will introduce make use of $w(b)$ which is the average price per good for bid b. That is, $w(b) = \frac{b^p}{|b^g|}$.

The question we try to answer is: *How can the agents determine the set of winning bids in the absence of the centralized controller?*

4   Complete Search Algorithm

In a complete search the agents search over the space of all the possible allocations to determine the optimal allocation. Since there is no centralized auctioneer that has global information, the agents must pass messages to each other and perform the search in a distributed manner.

In this algorithm we assume that the agents possess a linear ordering such that every agent has a *child* variable which points to its child, except for the leaf node who sets this variable to $\emptyset$. Each agent also maintains the following variables:

---

[1] In our paper, we assume that each consumer places a single bid.
[2] We use the terms "agent" and "good" interchangeably.

COMPLETE-SEARCH(*allocation-from-parent*)

1   *global-utility* ← 0
2   *final-allocation* ← ∅
3   *cleared-goods* ← $\bigcup_{b \in allocation\text{-}from\text{-}parent} b^g$
4   *valid-bid-pool* ← {$b \in bid\text{-}pool \mid \forall_{g \in b^g} b \notin cleared\text{-}goods$}
5   **if** *child* = ∅   ▷ I am leaf.
6   **then** *final-allocation* ← *allocation-from-parent* ∪ arg max$_{b \in valid\text{-}bid\text{-}pool}$ $w(b)$
7   **return** *final-allocation*
8   **if** *valid-bid-pool* = ∅
9   **then** *final-allocation* ← *child* .COMPLETE-SEARCH(*allocation-from-parent*)
10   **else**
11   **for** *bid* ∈ *valid-bid-pool*
12   **do** *new-allocation* ← *allocation-from-parent* ∪ *bid*
13   *allocation-from-successor* ← *child* .SUCCESSOR(*new-allocation*)
14   **if** $V(allocation\text{-}from\text{-}successor) > V(global\text{-}utility)$
15   **then** *global-utility* ← $V(allocation\text{-}from\text{-}successor)$
16   *final-allocation* ← *new-allocation*
17 **return** *final-allocation*

Fig. 1. Complete search algorithm. It is started by calling the root agent with COMPLETE-SEARCH(∅).

- *bid-pool* is the list of bids in which it is present,
- *final-allocation* is the best allocation encountered thus far in the execution,
- *global-utility* is the utility of the final-allocation,

Each agent adds zero-valued singleton bid for itself, even if a singleton bid is present in the list of bids. This bid enables the agent to search for the allocations where the agent is not cleared in any bid. The head agent (whose execution is initiated by the controller[3]) does not have any parent. Similarly the last agent in the ordering does not have a child agent so it does not send a message to child or wait for a reply. The agents search all the possible allocations to determine the optimal winner, see Figure 1.

We can prove the correctness of this algorithm by observing that the algorithm is performing a linear search of all the feasible allocations[4]. The agents simply implement a depth first search over all possible bid sets except that they only check feasible bid sets. As such, this algorithm sequentializes the agents' execution so it has a long running time.

5   Individual Hill-Climbing Algorithm

We now present an algorithm that creates a feasible allocation using a simple hill-climbing approach. In this approach, the agents simply clear bids in a greedy

---

[3] The controller does not control any agents, it simply initiates the execution of the head agent.

[4] Proofs omitted due to lack of space.

CLEARED($sender$)

1    $list\text{-}of\text{-}bids \leftarrow \{b \in list\text{-}of\text{-}bids \mid sender \notin b^g\}$
2   **if** $list\text{-}of\text{-}bids = \emptyset$
3   **then** Exit   ▷ We are done. I did not sell my good.
4   SEND-ACCEPT()

ACCEPT($sender, bid$)

1    $accepted[bid] \leftarrow accepted[bid] \cup sender$
2   **if** $accepted[best\text{-}bid] = best\text{-}bid^g$ ▷ Everyone has accepted it.
3   **then for** $agent \in neighbors$
4   **do** $agent$.CLEARED(g_i)
5   Exit   ▷ We are done. I sold my good.

SEND-ACCEPT()

1   **if** $best\text{-}bid \notin list\text{-}of\text{-}bids$
2   **then** $best\text{-}bid \leftarrow \arg\max_{b \in list\text{-}of\text{-}bids} w(b)$
3            $accepted[best\text{-}bid] = accepted[best\text{-}bid] \cup g_i$
4   **for** $agent \in best\text{-}bid^g$
5   **do** $agent$.ACCEPT($g_i, best\text{-}bid$)

HILL-CLIMBING()

1    $list\text{-}of\text{-}bids \leftarrow g_i^b$
2    $neighbors \leftarrow \bigcup_{b \in g_i^b} b^g$
3    $best\text{-}bid \leftarrow \emptyset$
4   SEND-ACCEPT()

Fig. 2. Hill-Climbing algorithm. It is started by having all agents execute HILL-CLIMBING.

fashion ordered by $w(b)$, the average value per good until there are no more bids that can be cleared. In fact, this algorithm is but a variation of the algorithm given in [14] for coalition formation.

The algorithm proceeds as follows: Each agent finds the bid in its *list-of-bids* which has the highest average value. The agent then sends an ACCEPT message to the goods that are present in this bid. The agent clears this bid only when it receives an ACCEPT message from all the goods in this bid. This ensures that a bid is cleared if and only if all the goods in the bid agree to clear it. When an agent clears a bid, it sends a CLEARED to all its neighbors—the set of agents with which it shares some bid—telling them that it has cleared and all bids including the agent should be dropped from consideration. The agents that receive a CLEARED message from agent *sender* delete the bids *sender*[b]. The agents stop execution when they clear a bid or the *list-of-bids* is empty. See Figure 2 for the complete algorithm.

It is easy to show that this algorithm always finds a feasible allocation and never enters a deadlock as it only considers feasible solutions. However, the algorithm is not guaranteed to converge to the global optimal allocation as it can get stuck at a local maxima by clearing a bid that has high $w(b)$ but is not to be found in the optimal allocation.

6   Partitioning Based Search

The greedy algorithm produces a non-optimal solution in polynomial time and the complete search provides the optimal solution in exponential time. Although the complete algorithm determines the optimal winner in a distributed manner, there is no parallelism as only one agent is active at any instant. The agents in the hill-climbing algorithm execute in parallel but they can get stuck at local maxima. Hence we now present a partitioning based approach. Our main motivation for proposing this approach is to obtain solutions whose quality is better than solutions produced by greedy approach but where the execution is comparable to the time taken by the greedy algorithm. In this approach, we partition the goods and the agents perform a complete search within the group (while ignoring the bids outside the partition). The algorithm proceeds as follows:

1. The controller partitions the agents into different groups. The controller also selects the *headAgent* of every group.
2. Each agent is provided with its partition information (the linear ordering in its partition).
3. Each agent deletes the bids that contain any good not present in its partition.
4. The controller initiates the COMPLETE-SEARCH algorithm in every partition.

In order to explain how the controller partitions the agents, we first define the following:

Definition 2 (Graphical representation of Combinatorial Auction). *A combinatorial auction can be represented as a graph $G = (N, E)$, where N is the set of nodes and E is the set of edges. Each node corresponds to a good on sale. An edge exists between any two nodes if they are present in the same bid.*

It is not always possible to divide the goods into disjoint partitions (where there is no edge between partitions). There could be bids on goods in different partitions. Currently, we use a greedy approach to address this issue. The agents do not consider the bids that have a good that is not present in its partition. This approach will result in an optimal solution only if the ignored bids are not part of the optimal allocation.

7   Negotiation Based Approaches

The search-based approaches provided in the earlier sections ignored the issue of splitting revenue among multiple sellers. That is unrealistic in cases where, for example, one agent has a good that is in much more demand than all the other goods in the combinatorial bids that it is in. This problem has been identified

CLEARED(j)

1   $list\text{-}of\text{-}bids \leftarrow \{b \in list\text{-}of\text{-}bids \mid j \notin b\}$
2   UPDATE-BEST-BID

READY(j, bid)

1   $ready[j] \leftarrow bid$
2   **if** $\forall_{g \in bid^g} ready[g] = bid$
3   **then for** $g \in neighbors$
4   **do** g.CLEARED(i)
5   Exit   ▷ Cleared my good with bid.

TELL-ASK-VALUE(j, val)

1   $ask\text{-}value[j] \leftarrow val$
2   UPDATE-BEST-BID()

Fig. 3. Modified MCP message receiving procedures

for a long time by sociologists studying social networks [15], and by economics studying social networks [16] (note that their networks are different, even if they refer to them by the same name). We use two approaches for addressing the issue of revenue division. The first technique is inspired from the well-studied monotonic-concession protocol [17] and in the second approach we borrow results from sociological network exchange theory [15].

7.1   Modified Monotonic Concession Protocol

In this section we propose a modified version of the Monotonic Concession Protocol (MCP). In MCP the two negotiating nodes alternately propose a deal that allocates the revenue between the agents. A deal d consists of the tuple (p_1, p_2) such that $p_1 + p_2 = b^p$, where p_1 is the amount agent 1 gets and p_2 is what agent 2 gets. If the receiving node gets an offer where it gets more than or equal to what it had asked for in the last round the protocol terminates. If the receiving node does not agree to the offer, in next round it should propose a new deal, subject to the condition that its payment for the other agent must be strictly higher than in the previous deal. This protocol will either converge to a solution or terminate without agreements if time runs out. Unfortunately, MCP can only be used for bi-party negotiation.

We propose a modified-MCP (mMCP) that can be used for simultaneous multi-party negotiation for the division of the revenue. In it, each agent maintains an *ask-value* which is initialized to the maximum the agent can expect to get given the bids it is involved in. The algorithm then proceeds as follows:

1. At each time-step, the agents send their *ask-value* to other agents with which it is involved in negotiation. As in MCP, the agents have to reduce their *ask-value* from what they demanded in the previous round.

2. Upon receiving the *ask-value* of its neighbors the agent checks if it can still get its *ask-value* for the bids in which it is present, that is, $\sum_{i \in b^g} ask\text{-}value_i \leq b^p$.

UPDATE-BEST-BID()

1 **for** $b \in$ *list-of-bids*
2   **do** *demand*[b] $\leftarrow \sum_{g \in b^g}$ *ask-value*[g]
3 *ready-to-clear* $\leftarrow \{b \in$ *list-of-bids* $\mid$ *demand*[b] $\leq b^p\}$
4 **if** *ready-to-clear* $\neq \emptyset$
5   **then**
6   Sort *ready-to-clear* first by *demand* and second by bid id.
7   *best-bid* $\leftarrow$ first(*ready-to-clear*)
8   **for** *agent* $\in$ *best-bid*^{g}
9   **do** *agent*.READY(i, *best-bid*)
10

MMCP()

1 **for** $j \in G$
2   **do** *ask-value*[j] $\leftarrow \infty$
3 *neighbors* $\leftarrow \bigcup_{b \in g_i^b} b^g$
4 *list-of-bids* $\leftarrow g_i^b$
5 **for** *ask-value*[i] $\leftarrow \max_{b \in g_i^b} b^p$ **to** 0 **step** 1
6   **do for** *agent* $\in$ *neighbors*
7   **do** *agent*.TELL-ASK-VALUE(i, *ask-value*[i])
8   Wait for all *neighbors* to tell me their *ask-value*
9 Exit $\triangleright$ Unable to clear my good.

Fig. 4. Modified MCP main procedures. The algorithm starts by having all agents execute MMCP

3. If the agent can get its *ask-value* on any bid, it clears the bid and it informs the other agents with which it is negotiating that it is out of negotiations.

Just like in MCP, since every node has to lower its *ask-value* in successive iterations, the nodes converge to a solution. However, a problem with the mMCP is that it can cause some revenue to be left unallocated, which happens when the revenue is not evenly divisible by the number of participants given the decrement step (which is 1 in the algorithm as shown but can be set to any positive constant). See Figures 3 and 4 for the detailed algorithm.

7.2 Sociological Network Exchange Theory

Sociological Network Exchange Theory (NET) studies the effects of power on the outcomes of exchanges between people in power relation-networks. In a network, the nodes are the participants and any two nodes can negotiate (for dividing a resource or exchanging goods) if they have an edge between them. The edges represent the amount the agents are trying to divide. Based on extensive studies with human subjects, Sociologists have been able to identify equations that can predict the outcome of human negotiations in particular networks.

Specifically, in [15, Chapter 2] Willer presents an equation which predicts that an exchange occurs on any relation between two nodes at equi-resistance. For

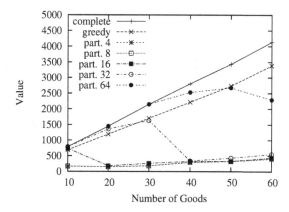

Fig. 5. Value of the winning set of bids

example, if nodes A and B want to divide some resource between them then the amounts that A and B will agree on (P_A and P_B respectively) can be obtained by solving equations (3) and (4) for P_A and P_B. In these equations, P_A^{con} is the amount that A makes if it has a confrontation with B (i.e., it doesn't exchange with B) and P_A^{max} is the maximum that A can make from exchange with B.

$$\frac{P_A^{max} - P_A}{P_A - P_A^{con}} = \frac{P_B^{max} - P_B}{P_B - P_B^{con}} \tag{3}$$

$$P_A + P_B = TotalRevenue \tag{4}$$

Equation (3) tells us that the resistance of A must be equal to the resistance of B. Equation (4) tells us that the sum of the payments must be equal to the total revenue. We can easily generalize these equations to n agents by simply adding another resistance equation for each agent and insisting that all resistances must be the same[5]. In all cases we end up with $n + 1$ equations of n variables, so we can solve for the payments.

The iterated equi-resistance method [15] tells us to start out with initial payments for the agents equal to an even distribution of the total revenue and then iteratively solve the resistance equations for each agent in order to find its payment given those of the other agents. We are to continue doing this for several rounds or until the system stabilizes. At some point, the agents decide to take the deal (bid) for which they are to receive the highest payment.

This method is easy to implement in a simulator. All we need to do is at each time step calculate the agents' payments by solving the equi-resistance equations. We can then continue to do this until either the payments stabilize or we detect

---

[5] However, we must stress that studies with human subjects only consider binary negotiations. As such, there is no empirical evidence to suggest that human behavior can be predicted using the equi-resistance equation for negotiations among three or more agents.

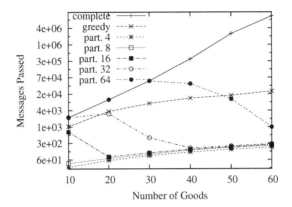

Fig. 6. Total number of messages sent

that they have entered a cycle. This type of implementation is the one we have used for the test results in section 8.

We do not yet have a distributed algorithm that can implement this method. One problem is the fact that the calculation of an agent's payments requires knowledge of the P^{con} values for all the agent's neighbors. It is unclear to us how an agent might come to acquire this knowledge if we assume that all agents are selfish. Still, since this method is predicts the behavior of humans, who do not know their opponents' P^{con} values, we are confident that we will come up with an appropriate distributed algorithm in the near future.

8   Preliminary Results

The input data for our algorithms was generated using CATS [18] using random distribution. Figure 5, compares the value of allocation for the three search algorithms. The first point on x-axis consists of 10 goods and 50 bids (thereafter the goods and bids increment by 5 and 50 respectively). The values shown in the figure are the average of 25 runs. As expected, the complete algorithm computes the solution with best revenue. Similarly, figures 6 and 7 compare the messages passed and the execution time (in clock ticks[6]) respectively for the three search algorithms. The complete search algorithm takes exponential time $O(n^{|b|})$ to provide the optimal allocation. The greedy algorithm takes linear time $O(|b|)$, where n is the number of goods and $|b|$ is the number of bids.

Figure 8 shows the value of the allocations produced by mMCP and iterated-resistance equations. The simulations were run on randomly generated data on NetLogo [19]. In each run, the protocol and the iterations were run for 10 cycles. Even though our solution using resistance equations is not guaranteed to converge, the results are very promising because the algorithm seems to produce

---

[6] The clock tick was chosen to be long enough for the agents to process and execute a single iteration of the search algorithm.

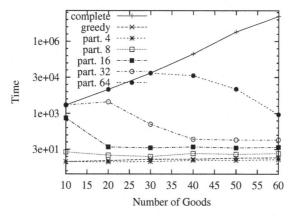

Fig. 7. Total time spent by algorithm

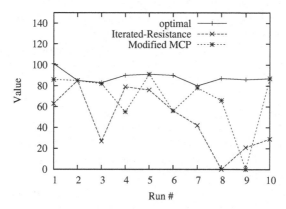

Fig. 8. Value of the solution found by MMCP, iterated-resistance equations, and the global optimum

high-valued allocations (even though suboptimal) for many cases and always in a short period of time.

9   Discussion and Future Work

We have presented the new problem of distributed winner determination in combinatorial auctions which is an instance of a distributed search problem and, when selfish agents are assumed, is an instance of a distributed algorithmic mechanism design problem. We presented and compared several algorithms for solving the problem under various circumstances. Our results are summarized in Table 1.

The complete algorithm performs a linear search to determine the optimal winner. This algorithm works in the absence of a centralized auctioneer. However, the running time will be of the order of total number of feasible allocations. This is because, even though it is distributed, the agents do not execute in parallel. At

Table 1. Algorithm Comparison

Algorithm	Optimal?	Agents	Time	Revenue Split?	Always Converges?
Complete Search	Yes	Cooperative	Exponential	No	Yes
Hill Climbing	No	Cooperative	Linear: $O(|b|)$	No	Yes
Partitioning	No	Cooperative	Dependent on partition size	No	Yes
mMCP	No	Selfish	Linear: $O(|b|)$	Yes	Yes
Equiresistance	No	Selfish	Not defined	Yes	No

any given time only one agent is performing the computation. The hill climbing algorithm on the other hand does not guarantee an optimal solution but performs much faster. More tests need to be done in order to determine the expected quality of the solution found by the hill climbing algorithm.

The partitioning based approach ignores the bids outside partitions. This results in sub-optimal solution if the ignored bids are part of the optimal solution. One of the reasons our partitioning approach performed worse than hill-climbing (fig. 5) is that the goods were randomly partitioned. One way to improve the quality of solution in the general case would be to partition the strongly connected goods together, i.e., try to put goods that have lot of common bids in one partition. We intend to extend our work to create dynamic distributed partitioning algorithms that can tailor their partitioning strategy to the characteristics of the set of bids under consideration.

The MMCP that we proposed is again similar to a greedy approach. It can converge to a local maximum and is always guaranteed to converge. We are currently testing it to see if we can predict what are the characteristics of the solution that it converges to. We are also studying modifications of the algorithm that force convergence to optimal as well as the tradeoffs associated with using different step sizes and other shortcuts for faster convergence.

Our study of the applicability of the NET equations is preliminary. We note that these equations can be applied only if agents' know their neighbors' P_{con} values—an unrealistic assumption in most cases. Another problem we face is the fact that the algorithm does not always converge. We are studying possible ways of either forcing convergence or determining a priori if the problem is one that will converge. Still, we are attracted to the fact that the equi-resistance equations have been shown to model the behavior of humans. We believe that the widespread adoption of a peer-to-peer agent-based marketplace requires agents that behave as humans. That is, if a user notices his agent either gives up negotiation too soon or is too aggressive in its negotiations then the user will likely not use that system. We see the possibility of a whole research program dedicated to building agents that negotiate, not necessarily optimally, but as humans would.

In summary, the problem of distributed winner determination in combinatorial auctions is an important problem whose solution will enable the construction of sophisticated peer-to-peer marketplaces. It is also an interesting combination of distributed computation and distributed algorithmic mechanism design. Our algorithms and analysis are a first step towards the understanding of this problem and its ramifications.

References

1. Rothkopf, M.H., Pekec, A., Harstad, R.M.: Computationally manageable combinational auctions. Management Science 44 (1998) 1131–1147
2. Sandholm, T.: An algorithm for winner determination in combinatorial auctions. Artificial Intelligence 135 (2002) 1–54
3. Andersson, A., Tenhunen, M., Ygge, F.: Integer programming for combinatorial auction winner determination. In: Proceedings of the Fourth International Conference on MultiAgent Systems, IEEE (2000) 39–46
4. Nisan, N.: Bidding and allocation in combinatorial auctions. In: Proceedings of the ACM Conference on Electronic Commerce. (2000) 1–12
5. Zurel, E., Nisan, N.: An efficient approximate allocation algorithm for combinatorial auctions. In: Proceedings of the ACM Conference on Electronic Commerce. (2001)
6. Nisan, N., Ronen, A.: Algorithmic mechanism design. Games and Economic Behavior 35 (2001) 166–196
7. Feigenbaum, J., Shenker, S.: Distributed algorithmic mechanism design: Recent results and future directions. In: Proceedings of the 6th International Workshop on Discrete Algorithms and Methods for Mobile Computing and Communications, ACM Press, New York (2002) 1–13
8. Hoos, H.H., Boutilier, C.: Solving combinatorial auctions using stochastic local search. In: Proceedings of the Seventeenth National Conference on Artificial Intelligence and Twelfth Conference on Innovative Applications of Artificial Intelligence, AAAI Press / The MIT Press (2000) 22–29
9. Fujishima, Y., Leyton-Brown, K., Shoham, Y.: Taming the computational complexity of combinatorial auctions: Optimal and approximate approaches. In: Proceedings of the Sixteenth International Joint Conference on Artificial Intelligence, Morgan Kaufmann Publishers Inc. (1999) 548–553
10. Preist, C., Bartolini, C., Phillips, I.: Algorithm design for agents which participate in multiple simultaneous auctions. In: Agent-Mediated Electronic Commerce III, Current Issues in Agent-Based Electronic Commerce Systems (includes revised papers from AMEC 2000 Workshop), Springer-Verlag (2001) 139–154
11. Preist, C., Byde, A., Bartolini, C.: Economic dynamics of agents in multiple auctions. In: Proceedings of the fifth international conference on Autonomous agents, ACM Press (2001) 545–551
12. Wellman, M.P.: Market-oriented programming: Some early lessons. In Clearwater, S., ed.: Market-Based Control: A Paradigm for Distributed Resource Allocation. World Scientific (1996)
13. de Vries, S., Vohra, R.V.: Combinatorial auctions: A survey. INFORMS Journal on Computing 15 (2003) 284–309
14. Shehory, O., Kraus, S.: Methods for task allocation via agent coalition formation. Artificial Intelligence 101 (1998) 165–200
15. Willer, D., ed.: Network Exchange Theory. Praeger Publishers, Westport CT (1999)

16. Kakade, S.M., Kearns, M., Ortiz, L.E., Pemantle, R., Suri, S.: Economic properties of social networks. In Saul, L.K., Weiss, Y., Bottou, L., eds.: Advances in Neural Information Processing Systems 17. MIT Press, Cambridge, MA (2005)
17. Rosenschein, J.S., Zlotkin, G.: Rules of Encounter. The MIT Press, Cambridge, MA (1994)
18. Leyton-Brown, K., Pearson, M., Shoham, Y.: Towards a universal test suite for combinatorial auction algorithms. In: Proceedings of the 2nd ACM conference on Electronic commerce, ACM Press (2000) 66–76 http://cats.stanford.edu.
19. Wilensky, U.: NetLogo: Center for connected learning and computer–based modeling, Northwestern University. Evanston, IL (1999) http://ccl.northwestern.edu/netlogo/.

Market-Based Allocation with Indivisible Bids*

L. Julian Schvartzman and Michael P. Wellman

University of Michigan
Computer Science & Engineering
Ann Arbor, MI 48109-2121 USA
{lschvart, wellman}@umich.edu

Abstract. We study multi-unit double auctions accepting bids with indivisibility constraints. We propose different price-quote policies and study their influence on the efficiency of market-based allocation. Using a reconfigurable manufacturing scenario where agents trade large quantities of multiple goods, we demonstrate potential benefits of supporting indivisibility constraints in bidding. These benefits are highly sensitive to the form of price quote provided, indicating interesting tradeoffs in communication and allocation efficiency.

1 Introduction

Consider a scenario with N manufacturing facilities with capabilities to produce various industrial parts. The facilities are controlled by different agents (e.g, firms, or profit-center divisions within the same large firm), and may vary in capacity, fixed and variable costs for producing the different part types, time for reconfiguring to switch between parts, transportation costs, and perhaps other factors. Each facility also has a set of customer orders, each representing a promise to pay a fixed amount contingent on delivery of a specified quantity of a particular type of part in the current period.

Since the facilities face heterogeneous cost structures, they stand to achieve significant gains in efficiency by exchanging orders among themselves. We can formulate the order allocation problem as a global optimization, but of course the agents may not have the appropriate incentives to reveal their private information about costs and orders, or comply with the resulting order exchanges. Economic mechanisms such as combinatorial auctions [1] can address these incentives problems, and provide an elegant solution when in fact they can be instituted. However, there are several organizational and computational impediments to holding large-scale (measured in numbers of goods and agents, and units per good) two-sided combinatorial auctions, and these are as yet uncommon in practice. It is substantially simpler to deploy individual two-sided multi-unit auctions for each of several goods, and these more ad hoc markets can address the allocation problem to a useful degree. For example, idealized models of such configurations as general-equilibrium systems demonstrate the potential of computational markets to achieve efficient allocations in convex, competitive environments [2,3].

---

* This work was supported by the NSF Engineering Research Center for Reconfigurable Manufacturing under Award EEC-9529125 of the National Science Foundation. An extended report is available from the authors.

H. La Poutré, N. Sadeh, and S. Janson (Eds.): AMEC and TADA 2005, LNAI 3937, pp. 57–70, 2006.
© Springer-Verlag Berlin Heidelberg 2006

However, realistic versions of this scenario vary from the idealization in several ways.[1] One particularly important characteristic of this application domain is nonconvexity in preferences and production technology, as manifest (for example) in fixed costs, reconfiguration switching costs, and preset order sizes. The most straightforward multi-unit auction mechanisms assume divisibility of offers: an agent willing to buy q units at some price would also be willing to accept $q' \leq q$ units at that price. This assumption will not generally hold given nonconvex preferences and costs, and therefore agents with these characteristics may be hesitant to bid at all absent some condition that its offer be accepted in whole or not at all.

We investigate the design of multi-unit auctions accommodating such indivisibility constraints. Our focus is on how such auctions can be operated in a computationally efficient manner, and on the auctions' *price quote* policies for revealing information to agents to guide their bidding. We evaluate our designs experimentally, employing a version of the manufacturing scenario sketched above. Our main finding is that supporting indivisibility constraints can in fact improve the quality of global allocations achieved through trading, but that this improvement does depend pivotally on the form of the price quote. In the full version of this paper we also show how the computational costs of optimizing bid matching and producing meaningful quotes can be amortized over the auction's operation, calculated incrementally throughout the dynamic bidding process.

2   Auction Mechanisms

We consider two-sided auctions for multiple units of a single good. The auctions clear periodically at predefined intervals, and thus implement a *call market*. We distinguish two major versions of this auction, differing in their treatment of offer quantities. In the first (called "standard" for purposes of this paper), quantities appearing in bids are assumed divisible, and so the bidder effectively expresses a willingness to trade any amount up to the specified quantity at the associated unit price. In the second, offers are considered "all-or-none" (AON), and so agents explicitly specify the payment at which they would be willing to trade any acceptable discrete quantity. We refer to this version as the "AON" auction henceforth.

In both auctions, agents may submit *bid schedules*, indicating the prices offered to trade various quantities (with negative quantities indicating amounts offered to sell). The points on the schedule are exclusive (i.e., treated as "XOR" [4]), in that the resulting allocation will employ at most one of them. For divisible (standard) bids, the prices are per unit, and consistency requires that unit prices be nonincreasing in quantity. For indivisible (AON) bids, the prices represent total payments for the associated quantity, and these totals (not the per-unit payments) must be nondecreasing in quantity. Assuming only free disposal, with AON bids, agents can express arbitrary valuations for the good [5,4]. Standard divisible bids can express only convex valuations.

Operation of the standard auction is relatively simple, as described, for example, by Wurman et al. [6]. Mechanisms resembling the AON auction have been described in the

---

[1] Our work does not address all important variations from the ideal. In particular, we maintain the assumption of competitiveness, modeling our agents essentially as price takers.

literature, and employed in practice.[2] For example, van Hoesel and Müller [7] consider the special case of combinatorial auctions where all goods are the same, and point out that optimal allocations can be found by dynamic programming. This corresponds to a one-sided, one-shot version of the AON auction. Kothari et al. [8] present a one-sided, one-shot auction that supports AON bidding in the form of a minimum trade quantity, but then assumes divisibility for quantities beyond this minimum. Several other authors have considered indivisibility constraints in multi-unit auctions [9,10,5], and have also identified the connection to knapsack methods for matching bids. We describe details of the allocation algorithm, as well as other AON auction policies, in the sections below.

2.1 Bids Matching Algorithm

As pointed out most explicitly by Kelly [5], optimal winner determination for single-good, two-sided, multi-unit auctions with indivisible XOR bids (i.e., our AON auctions) reduces to the *Multiple Choice Knapsack Problem* (MCKP) [10]. Here we present a formulation of MCKP specialized (slightly) to the auction setting.

Consider a set of N agents, with agent i submitting bid B_i. Each B_i is comprised of m_i *bid points*, (p_{ij}, q_{ij}), specifying a payment p_{ij} offered to exchange quantity q_{ij}. Each bid includes a dummy point $(0,0)$. Offers to buy are expressed as positive payment-quantity pairs, and offers to sell as negative payment-quantity pairs. Because the standard MCKP requires positive coefficients, we define transformed bid points $(p'_{ij}, q'_{ij}) = (p_{ij} + \bar{p}_i, q_{ij} + \bar{q}_i)$, where $\bar{p}_i \equiv -\min_{j \in B_i} p_{ij}$, and $\bar{q}_i \equiv -\min_{j \in B_i} q_{ij}$. (Note that this transformation affects only bids with sell points; for buy-only bids, $\bar{q}_i = \bar{p}_i = 0$.) We then define the knapsack *capacity* $c \equiv \sum_i \bar{q}_i$. Conceptually, the capacity c is equivalent to the total number of units that are offered for sale. We denote by C the maximum number of units that could be traded. In order to ensure that C is bounded, we assume agents have a limited ability to take short positions in the goods traded. The MCKP is formulated as:

$$\text{maximize: } \sum_{i=1}^{N} \sum_{j=1}^{m_i} p'_{ij} x_{ij}$$

$$\text{subject to: } \sum_{i=1}^{N} \sum_{j=1}^{m_i} q'_{ij} x_{ij} \leq c,$$

$$\sum_{j=1}^{m_i} x_{ij} = 1, i \in A, x_{ij} \in \{0, 1\}.$$

We assume free disposal of units, reflected in allowing the auction to match bids with more sales than purchases. Excess units are allocated arbitrarily among sellers. Note that formulating and implementing the same problem without the assumption of free disposal is straightforward.

---

[2] Our understanding is that practical trading mechanisms admitting AON bids typically handle them in an ad hoc manner. For example, such bids might be matched in a greedy manner, as in common electronic stock trading systems, which just pass over AON bids if the entire quantity cannot be fulfilled.

Solving MCKP is NP-hard, which is shown by reduction to a basic knapsack problem [10] (p. 318). Using dynamic programming, however, the problem can be solved in pseudopolynomial time [11]. Let $Z_l(d)$ be the value of the optimal solution to the MCKP defined to include only the first l agents, $1 \leq l \leq N$, and with restricted capacity $0 \leq d \leq c$. We further define $Z_0(d) = 0$ for $0 \leq d \leq c$, and $Z_l(d) = -\infty$ for $d < 0$.

We can characterize $Z_l(d)$, $1 \leq l \leq N$, $0 \leq d \leq c$, using the following recursion:

$$Z_l(d) = \max_{1 \leq j \leq m_l} Z_{l-1}(d - q'_{lj}) + p'_{lj}. \tag{1}$$

The optimal solution is obtained when $l = N$ and $d = c$. Given N bids of maximum size $m = \max_i m_i$, the running time to solve MCKP using dynamic programming is $O(mNc)$ [10]. If agents choose to submit full demand curves (i.e., with up to C bundles each), the running time becomes $O(NC^2)$.

Many different methods exist to solve MCKP, including a number of branch-and-bound techniques and hybrid algorithms (see Kellerer et al. [10] for an extensive review). Our implementation is customized for the dynamic auction context, which may call for repeated solution of the MCKP for small changes in the set of bids. We therefore developed an incremental version of the clearing algorithm, designed to minimize the average solution time over a sequence of auction operations. Space constraints preclude a description of the algorithm here; see the full paper for details.

2.2   Clearing and Pricing

Clearing the auction is the process of identifying the subset of bids that match and produce the highest possible surplus. The outcome of a clear operation is to determine the deals resulting from this matching, and removing the matched bids from the order book. Given our incremental algorithm, most of the work is performed when bids are inserted into the order book. Once this is done, identifying the match takes constant time. Extracting the deals takes time linear in the number N' of bids matched. Modifying the order book to include only unmatched bids requires N' deletions or $(N - N')$ insertions.

Matching bids with indivisibility constraints and three or more agents requires non-uniform pricing [12]. It is easy to understand the impossibility of having uniform pricing through an example. Consider the bids in Table 1. In such example, the auction would match all four bids. However, it is impossible to make all buyers pay at most what they offered while making all sellers receive at least what they requested with a single price.

Table 1. Matching these bids requires non-uniform prices

(13 @ 26)	buy 13 units at \$2 each
(2 @ 1)	buy 2 units at \$0.5 each
(-11 @ -11)	sell 11 units at \$1 each
(-4 @ -10)	sell 4 units at \$2.5 each

There are many ways to determine non-uniform prices consistent with a given set of bids and an allocation. For a fixed allocation of goods, monetary transfers do not affect overall efficiency. Therefore, since we are not addressing strategic issues in this work, the choice is not pivotal for our experimental analysis. Nevertheless, to fully specify the mechanism one must identify a pricing rule. Ours starts with Vickrey prices and adjusts them proportionally to ensure budget balance.[3] The Vickrey calculation requires that we compute the total surplus with each agent's bid excluded, for which $O(N')$ deletion and insertion operations need to be performed.

2.3 Quoting

After each bid, the auction issues a *price quote*, providing to the agents some information regarding the state of the order book, intended as a guide to future bidding. In the standard auction, the quote comprises a BID-ASK pair, representing the prices at which an agent could successfully trade at least one unit. The BID quote defines the price at which an agent could sell one unit, and the ASK quote the corresponding price to buy. For standard (divisible-bid) auctions, we can incrementally maintain the order book so that price quotes can be provided in constant time once the bids are inserted [6].

For the AON auction, it is not immediately apparent how the auction should define its price quotes. We identified four candidate quoting policies, described here and compared experimentally in Section 4 below.

Standard Quote. One possibility is for the AON auction to provide a "standard" quote, defined as the BID-ASK pair reflecting the order book interpreted *as if the bids were divisible*. Constructing this interpretation requires some care, since simply treating each bid point as a divisible offer may violate the standard auction's consistency condition requiring that quantity be nonincreasing in unit price. To ensure this monotonicity, we transform each bid B_i by first sorting the bid points (p_{ij}, q_{ij}) (not including the dummy point with $p_{ij} = q_{ij} = 0$) in decreasing order of unit price. We then traverse the list, translating each to a unit-price bid point, skipping any that would violate the monotonicity condition with respect to those already seen. These translated bids can then be handled by the order book and quoting algorithm of the standard auction.

Marginal Unit Quote. A second quote candidate attempts to maintain the interpretation of the standard quote as a price threshold sufficient to trade one unit, but respecting the indivisibility constraints of AON bids. Calculating this quote requires solving the MCKP for the bids in the order book. Under this interpretation, the ASK quote is always defined as long as there is any sell offer in the order book. The same is not true for the BID quote, however, because it could be the case that no existing offer or combination of offers can be satisfied by contributing a single additional unit. The marginal unit quote takes the same form as the standard quote, but provides more conservative values. Indeed, it is even possible (and consistent) that the ASK price quoted be lower than the BID price, something that cannot happen in the divisible case. It would also be possible to define this quote with any particular quantity defined as "marginal" (e.g., ten units

---

[3] Intuitively, this should tend toward reducing the incentive to behave strategically, though we know this is not strictly true. Of course, no budget-balanced mechanism can achieve this exactly. A serious treatment of strategic concerns in this context is a subject of future work.

instead of one). Given our incremental computation (detailed in the full version of the paper), these quotes can be extracted from the order book in constant time.

Anonymous Full Schedule Quote. The third quote we consider provides to all agents a full schedule of payments that would be required to exchange any feasible quantity given the current state of the order book. This can be viewed as a collection of marginal unit quotes, one for each feasible quantity. The quote is anonymous because the same values are provided to every agent. Note that only relevant payment-quantity pairs need to be communicated to an agent: for a given payment, a quote for the minimum number of units the agent needs to sell to get such payment, and the maximum number of units the agent can buy with such payment. As for the marginal unit quote, the schedule may not be monotone: the unit price to exchange various quantities may be increasing or decreasing or mixed along the schedule.

Also like the marginal unit quote, the full schedule quote can be extracted directly from the order book given our incremental computation scheme, though of course extracting and communicating it will take time proportional to its size, $O(C)$.

Non-Anonymous Full Schedule Quote. The final quote we consider is similar to the previous one, but each agent is provided with personalized values based on its existing bid. More specifically, this quote provides agent i the schedule of payments calculated by excluding from the order book the bid sent by i.

Quote Discussion. The four candidate quotes present distinct tradeoffs. The standard and marginal-unit quotes are compact, but the more accurate one may be excessively conservative when used as a guide for quantities greater than a single unit. The full schedule quotes provide high-fidelity information, but may be too large to be reasonably communicated in some applications.

We explore the implications of the various quote policies in our experiments below. (Results for non-anonymous quotes are pending from ongoing experiments, not reported here.) Of course, the worth of a quote is intimately tied to how the agents use this information in their bidding. We discuss our assumptions about agent behavior in Section 4.2 below.

2.4   Implementation

We implemented the AON auction as an extension of AB3D, a configurable auction and market-game server developed at the University of Michigan [13]. AB3D provides a flexible bid-processing architecture, with a rule-based scripting language to specify particular auction policies and temporal control structure. The standard call market was already supported by AB3D. To handle indivisible bidding, we added a new bid language specifying quantity-payment schedules, and new matching, pricing, and quoting modules implementing the algorithms and policies described above. In particular, we implemented all four quoting candidates as selectable options. Parameters in the auction script determine whether to allow AON bids, and if so, which of the available quoting and pricing policies to employ.

3   Manufacturing Domain

We evaluate the AON auction in a market-based allocation problem based on the manufacturing scenario sketched in the Introduction. The setting comprises a set of N manufacturing *modules*, defined as arrangements of manufacturing machines, with capabilities for producing a variety of parts. Each module is controlled by an agent, whose objective is to maximize profit by operating the module to produce parts fulfilling customer orders over an L-day production period. In our market-based model, agents may increase their individual and collective profit by exchanging orders among themselves, thus exploiting their comparative advantages and configuration decisions.

We provide a full specification of the model below, describing the goods traded, utility and cost functions of the manufacturing modules, and the market configuration. Specific parameter settings for the model, and trading policies implemented by agents in our simulations, are described in Section 4.

3.1   Goods Traded

The core allocation problem in this domain is deciding which manufacturer will produce what quantity of each of M types of parts in the current period. The total quantity demanded of part type r is D_r, and initially each agent is given orders for some share of that demand. Producing part r entitles the manufacturer to a fixed income of I_r per unit, up to the number of units for which it holds orders.

The purpose of the market is to enable trading of orders among manufacturing modules. The goods traded are the rights to produce parts for orders. A unit of good r, therefore, entitles the holder to produce a unit of the corresponding part and receive the corresponding payment I_r from the customer.

Note that the parameter D_r bounds the maximum quantity of good r that can be exchanged at one time, and thus plays the role of C in the definition of the AON auction.

3.2   Agent Objectives

Agents aim to maximize profit, defined as

$$\text{income} - \text{production costs} + \text{trading cash flow}.$$

Income is simply the total payment for producing parts. Trading cash flow represents the balance of payments from trading orders with other agents. Production costs include several components, depending on the quantity and types of parts produced. These are defined by a set of agent-specific parameters:

- FC_i: Fixed cost, a one-time payment if module i produces one or more parts.
- LC_i: Labor cost, paid for every day in which the module is in production.
- $VC_{i,r}$: Variable cost, be paid for each unit of part r that gets produced.
- CF_i: Set of possible *configurations*. Each manufacturing configuration provides distinct production capabilities. Only one configuration can be used in any given day. For each configuration $f \in CF_i$, each module has:

- $PC_{f,r}$: Production capacity per part type, the quantity of parts of type r that the module produces per day.
- RC_f: Reconfiguration cost to be paid if the configuration is used.
- RT_f: Reconfiguration time (in days) that it takes to set up configuration f, during which no part can be produced.

The configuration capacities and times, along with the period length L, define the production possibilities for module i. The various cost parameters define the total cost for any feasible production plan.

Although complicated, the foregoing determines well-defined optimization problems for the agent:

- Determining an optimal production plan given holdings of goods r.
- Determining optimal demand for goods r given current holdings and market prices.

3.3   Market Configuration

The overall market system comprises the agents representing manufacturing modules, plus one auction for each part type. We simulate an instance of this setup by generating parameter values from prespecified probability distributions, and communicating these values to the respective agents. Each agent is initially allocated customer orders corresponding to equal shares, D_r/N, of the overall demand for each part r.

The simulations are implemented using our configurable market game server, AB3D [13]. Each game instance lasts twenty minutes, with each auction clearing periodically every 48 seconds. The auctions are staggered, so that the initial clears occur at multiples of $48/M seconds$.

The agents operate asynchronously, submitting bids to the auctions according to the policy described in Section 4.2. Agents can request price quotes reflecting the latest auction state, and retrieve notices of any transactions from prior bids.

At the end of a game instance, the server calculates final holdings based on cumulative transactions, and determines a score for each agent. The score depends on an agent's production plan given its total available orders, which entails solving an optimization problem for each agent. AB3D solves these using a commercial optimization package (AMPL/CPLEX), given an integer linear programming (ILP) formulation specified as part of the game description.

The overall value of the resulting allocation is simply the sum of the scores over the N agents. For comparison, we can also calculate (offline if necessary) the global optimum of the system without trading, assuming a central planner that can allocate orders across manufacturing modules.

4   Experiments

We ran a set of 58 paired trials with both standard and AON auctions. For AON auctions, we tested *standard*, *marginal*, and *full schedule* quotes. The following sections describe the specific problem instance we chose for our manufacturing scenario, the behavior of the agents, and the results obtained.

4.1 Manufacturing Problem Setting

For each of the 58 trials run, we obtained a new set of randomly chosen parameter values, as specified in Table 2. Each paired trial used the same set of parameter values, and compared standard auctions and AON auctions with the quoting alternatives discussed.

Table 2. Settings of the manufacturing scenario used for our experiments. Parameters specifying a range are drawn from a uniform distribution. (*) parameter specifies total for all parts in a configuration, each part getting a random proportion.

Parameter		Values
General	# of agents (N)	4
	# of parts (M)	4
Public information	I_r	[1000, 2000]
	D_r	[2000, 6000]
	L	[250, 300]
Private information for agent i	FC_i	[300000, 400000]
	LC_i	[15000, 20000]
	VC_i	[250,350]
	$|CF_i|$	2
For each $f \in CF_i$	PC_f	[20,60] (*)
	RC_f	[400000, 800000]
	RT_f	[5,15]

4.2 Agent Bidding

Agents bid in a set of auctions G, each corresponding to a different good r. Each agent follows an incremental bidding approach similar to the one described by Cheng and Wellman [2]. The main loop that controls an agent's behavior is as follows.

```
1: repeat
2:    Get price quotes.
3:    Get transactions (i.e., matching bids).
4:    for each auction g ∈ G do
5:       Select a new point to be added to the bid in g.
6:       Fix inconsistencies in bid.⁴
7:       Submit updated bid to g.
8:    end for
9: until Timeout {allocation process is over}
```

The results described in Section 4.4 were obtained by using the same agent structure, with some variations in terms of selection of new bidding points which are explained below.

---

⁴ Make smallest possible changes to the old points in the bid in order to maintain divisible prices nonincreasing in quantity and indivisible payments nondecreasing in quantity.

4.3   Selection of New Bidding Points

In each iteration a of the main loop, an agent updates its bid for good in auction g with one new point $(p_{g,a}, q_{g,a})$, taking into account current holdings and assuming other goods (not in auction g) could be freely bought or sold at the most recent quote. We used two different methods for picking incremental points, one for dealing with divisible bids and another for indivisible ones.

DIVISIBLE: For divisible bids, an agent selects a new bidding point for the good in auction g by picking a price $p_{g,a}$ and calculating the quantity $q_{g,a}$ the agent would be willing to buy or sell at such price in order to maximize its profit. Calculation is done using an ILP model that encodes the agent's utility function as explained in Section 3.2. Prices $p_{g,a}$ are selected in the following arbitrary order:

1. $p_{g,a} = \text{BID}$
2. $p_{g,a} = \text{ASK}$
3. If the bid in g already contains prices for 1 and 2 above, $p_{g,a}$ is selected from a normal distribution $N(\mu, 1)$,

$$
\mu = \begin{cases}
(hb + \text{ASK})/2 & \text{if } q_{a-1} > 0 \vee (q_{a-1} = 0 \wedge pr < .25) \\
(ls + \text{BID})/2 & \text{if } q_{a-1} < 0 \vee (q_{a-1} = 0 \wedge pr < .5) \\
lb & \text{if } (q_{a-1} = 0 \wedge pr < .75) \\
hs & \text{otherwise}
\end{cases}
$$

where hb (hs) and lb (ls) are the highest buy (sell) and lowest buy (sell) offers already in the bid and pr is a random value uniformly distributed between 0 and 1.

(Note that BID and ASK refer to the most recent quote obtained by the agent.)

The basic idea behind the approach described above is to help agents find feasible trades by gradually making them place their highest buy and their lowest sell offer. We empirically tested other alternatives to ensure that our comparison of divisible versus indivisible bidding was not biased by an unreasonable point-selection approach. Specifically, we compared the procedure described with a random selection of points, and also with another in which prices are picked by finding the maximum possible gap between any two consecutive pairs of (sorted) prices already in the bid and selecting their average. Our results indicated that the approach chosen provided the best average performance among the alternatives we evaluated.

INDIVISIBLE: For indivisible bidding, the agent selects a new bidding point for the good in auction g by picking a quantity $q_{g,a}$. The payment $p_{g,a}$ is given by the maximum (minimum) value at which the agent is willing to buy (sell) $q_{g,a}$ units, which is calculated using an ILP model that encodes the agent's utility function as explained in Section 3.2. Quantities $q_{g,a}$ are selected in the following order:

1. $q_{g,a} = -H_{g,a}$ (sell all holdings available in iteration a)
2. $q_{g,a} = D_g - H_{g,a}$ (buy all available items, i.e., demand minus holdings)
3. $q_{g,a} = $ random value uniformly distributed in the range $[-H_{g,a}, D_g - H_{g,a}]$ (excluding 0)

4. If the bid already contains quantities for 1, 2, and 3 above:

$$q_{g,a} = \begin{cases} -H_{g,a} & \text{with probability .1} \\ D_g - H_{g,a} & \text{with probability .1} \\ \text{average between any two} \\ \text{consecutive (sorted) quantities} \\ \text{that are further apart} & \text{with probability .8} \end{cases}$$

The method described gradually fills the largest gaps in the bid being constructed, and "refreshes" each extreme occasionally with a 0.1 probability.

4.4   Results

The average performance relative to a global optimal allocation (i.e., assuming a central planner) as calculated from our 58 trials is given in Table 3. Results show that AON auctions quoting an anonymous full schedule provided the best performance, and that AON auctions using either a standard or marginal unit quote performed worse than standard auctions with divisible bids. Using AON auctions with standard quotes provided the worst average performance, although the differences with AON auctions quoting marginal units are not statistically significant at reasonable levels.

Table 3. Results of 58 paired trials calculated as average performance in terms of global optimal. Differences between 1 and 2 are significant at the 10^{-7} level, 2 and 3 at the .03 level, but 3 and 4 only at the 0.07 level.

#	Auction	Quote	Average performance
1	AON	Full schedule	91.3 %
2	Standard	Standard	79.2%
3	AON	Marginal unit	70.7 %
4	AON	Standard	61.7%

We are not suggesting based on this particular experiment that the differences shown in Table 3 are an indicator of the differences to be found under any possible parameter configuration of our scenario or other settings. Before we ran the systematic paired tests described above, we informally experimented with other parameter settings. Even though we observed that AON auctions quoting full schedules always provided the best average performance, in several settings the differences detected were not as stark.

4.5   Influence of Quoting

Quoting marginal prices with standard auctions makes sense from two perspectives. First, it provides an accurate value for marginal units in order for agents to construct their bids. Second, it provides a lower (upper) bound on both the unit price and total payment to be paid (received) when bidding to buy (sell) an arbitrary number of units.

On the contrary, marginal values for AON auctions do not contain similarly valuable information. By assuming divisibility with AON auctions, the marginal value provided is neither accurate for the marginal nor a bound on the price for additional units. In this case, the quote provides a very loose approximation of value. Similarly, if we took into consideration indivisibility constraints when quoting marginal values with AON auctions, the result would be such very conservative. It is often undefined for the BID (we need an agent or combination of them intending to buy a single unit), and the ASK can often be excessively high (when the auction matches bids with sell quantities much larger than the marginal). Moreover, this quote provides no information about the unit price beyond the marginal, showing only that the total payment for more units will be at least the price for a single unit.

The effects described above were confirmed in part by measurements applied to our simulation results. We define a trade as *desired* (A) with respect to agent i, if, once executed, it increases or maintains the profit (i.e., income minus costs plus cashflow) of i assuming that no further trades occur. We identified three possible reasons for agent i to engage in undesired trading: *outdated information* (B1), *misleading non-anonymous quotes* (B2), or *misleading anonymous quotes* (B3). A bid can contain outdated information because its points were calculated incrementally or due to the asynchronous nature of the bidding process. Outdated information (B1) thus refers to the case in which i engaged in a trade that it would have rejected had it reevaluated its bid using the most up-to-date information (i.e., current holdings and quotes). Misleading non-anonymous (B2) or anonymous (B3) quotes are those that made i believe that it could buy or sell goods at the quote, when that was actually not possible. Non-anonymous quotes are those calculated by excluding from the order book the bid sent by agent i. Finally, every transaction that decreased utility and cannot be otherwise explained must have occurred because of a *dependency on other auctions* (C). Such dependencies exist because agents construct their bids in an auction assuming they could trade in other auctions at the quote. Since communication is asynchronous and auctions clear at different times, some intermediate decreases in utility are normal and expected.

Suppose we had T transactions, and transaction t occurred in auction g for quantity q_t and payment p_t. We perform two different optimizations for each agent i:

- $R^*(H)$ is the profit achieved by i when calculating its optimal production plan based on holdings H, assuming that i cannot trade further.
- $P^*(H,Q)$ is the highest payment that i is willing to offer to trade quantity q_t in auction g, assuming it holds goods H and that it could freely trade goods in auctions other than g at the prices given by quotes Q.

We further define Q_i and Q as the most up-to-date non-anonymous and anonymous quotes, respectively. Holdings H^t are the goods held by i in all auctions right after t occurred; holdings H^0 are initial endowments; holdings $H^{t'}_i$ and $H^{t'}$ are the goods held right after t and an hypothetical clear of all auctions other than g occurred, assuming that i bid to achieve optimal holdings as calculated for $P^*(H^{t-1},Q_i)$ and $P^*(H^{t-1},Q)$, respectively; and p'_t is the lowest hypothetical payment that i could have bid in order to trade q_t in g. Negative coefficients for payments and quantities are used for sell offers. Given these definitions, we can classify transaction t for agent i as follows.

- (A) Desired   If $R(H^{t-1}) \leq R(H^t)$
- (B1) Occurred due to outdated information   If $P^*(H^{t-1}, Q_i) < p'_t$
- (B2) Occurred due to a misleading non-anonymous quote If $R(H^{t'_i}) < R(H^{t-1})$
- (B3) Occurred due to a misleading anonymous quote   If $R(H^{t'}) < R(H^{t-1})$
- (C) Necessary due to auction dependencies   If $t \notin A, B1, B2, B3, C$

Using the same data obtained for the experiments reported in Table 3, we measured the percentage of transactions in (A), (B1), (B2), (B3), or (C) for the different quoting mechanisms we tested with AON auctions. The results are shown in Table 4. Note that the Full Schedule quote was the least misleading. Had we used a non-anonymous full schedule quote for decision making, we would have entirely avoided (by definition) misleading quotes, potentially increasing the overall performance even further. The marginal unit and standard quotes were similarly misleading, providing comparable results regardless of quote anonymity. Thus, personalizing these two quotes for decision making does not seem likely to help. Marginal unit quotes appeared to provide a relatively high percentage of desired trades (but poor overall results), which is somewhat expected given such a highly conservative quote.

Table 4. Analysis of transactions in AON auctions. (*) Offline simulation only.

#	Quoting	(A)	(B1)	(B2)*	(B3)	(C)
1	Full schedule	62.1%	20.7%	0%	17.8%	16.1%
2	Marginal unit	64.8%	17.6%	26.2%	25.2%	3.5%
3	Standard	57.4%	22.8%	24.8%	23.1%	7.1%

5 Discussion and Future Work

Our study of the AON auction provides evidence for the viability and potential benefits of accounting for indivisibility constraints in market-based allocation, without resorting to fully combinatorial auction designs. Whether one should adopt an AON auction or standard divisible auction depends on the specific setting. Relevant factors include:

1. Expressivity. Divisible bids allow expressing only convex valuations, whereas indivisible ones do not have such limitation. Would agents with nonconvex valuations refrain from participating in auctions with mandatory divisibility?
2. Undesired trades. If agents with nonconvex valuations do participate in a divisible auction, they risk loss-producing transactions. How much they suffer as a result depends on the degree of nonconvexity.
3. Computation. Our incremental algorithms provide a relatively efficient way to operate AON auctions, which should be fast enough for several practical applications. Standard auctions, however, are still faster to operate, and more predictable since performance is less dependent on the number of units offered for sale.
4. Quote communication. Our experiments showed that the level of detail in price-quote information can play an important role in overall efficiency, and in particular that simple marginal quotes were not enough for AON auctions to improve on the

performance of a standard auction. Even though much work remains to be done in this area, it is obvious that the communication burden of the quote used should be evaluated when choosing an auction mechanism over the other.

Further work will refine our comparisons and evaluate additional quoting policies. For example, it would be interesting to measure the potential benefit of providing full schedule quotes in standard auctions, as we have for AON auctions. It would be particularly beneficial to identify intermediate quoting policies for AON auctions that provide much of the benefit of full schedule quotes without the full expense. Understanding this tradeoff remains an important goal. Finally, we are interested in exploring the strategic bidding issues posed by indivisibility constraints as well as alternative quoting policies.

References

1. Cramton, P., Shoham, Y., Steinberg, R., eds.: Combinatorial Auctions. MIT Press (2005)
2. Cheng, J.Q., Wellman, M.P.: The WALRAS algorithm: A convergent distributed implementation of general equilibrium outcomes. Computational Economics **12** (1998) 1–24
3. Ygge, F., Akkermans, H.: Decentralized markets versus central control: A comparative study. Journal of Artificial Intelligence Research **11** (1999) 301–333
4. Nisan, N.: Bidding and allocation in combinatorial auctions. In: Second ACM Conference on Electronic Commerce, Minneapolis (2000) 1–12
5. Kelly, T.: Generalized knapsack solvers for multi-unit combinatorial auctions: Analysis and application to computational resource allocation. In: AAMAS-04 Workshop on Agent-Mediated Electronic Commerce (AMEC-VI), New York (2004)
6. Wurman, P.R., Walsh, W.E., Wellman, M.P.: Flexible double auctions for electronic commerce: Theory and implementation. Decision Support Systems **24** (1998) 17–27
7. van Hoesel, S., Müller, R.: Optimization in electronic markets: Examples in combinatorial auctions. Netnomics **3** (2001) 23–33
8. Kothari, A., Parkes, D.C., Suri, S.: Approximately-strategyproof and tractable multi-unit auctions. In: Fourth ACM Conference on Electronic Commerce, San Diego, CA (2003) 166–175
9. Kalagnanam, J.R., Davenport, A.J., Lee, H.S.: Computational aspects of clearing continuous call double auctions with assignment constraints and indivisible demand. Electronic Commerce Research **1** (2001) 221–238
10. Kellerer, H., Pferschy, U., Pisinger, D.: Knapsack Problems. Springer Verlag (2004)
11. Dudzinski, K., Walukiewicz, S.: Exact method for the knapsack problem and its generalizations. European Journal of Operations Research (1987) 28:3–21
12. Wurman, P.R., Wellman, M.P., Walsh, W.E.: A parametrization of the auction design space. Games and Economic Behavior **35** (2001) 304–338
13. Lochner, K.M., Wellman, M.P.: Rule-based specification of auction mechanisms. Third International Joint Conference on Autonomous Agents and Multi-Agent Systems (AAMAS-04), New York (2004) 818–825

Achieving Allocatively-Efficient and Strongly Budget-Balanced Mechanisms in the Network Flow Domain for Bounded-Rational Agents

Yoram Bachrach and Jeffrey S. Rosenschein

Hebrew University, Jerusalem, Israel
(yori, jeff)@cs.huji.ac.il

Abstract. Vickrey-Clarke-Groves (VCG) mechanisms are a well-known framework for finding a solution to a distributed optimization problem in systems of self-interested agents. VCG mechanisms have received wide attention in the AI community because they are efficient and strategy-proof; a special case of the Groves family of mechanisms, VCG mechanisms are the *only* direct-revelation mechanisms that are allocatively efficient and strategy-proof. Unfortunately, VCG mechanisms are only weakly budget-balanced.

We consider self-interested agents in a network flow domain, and show that in this domain, it *is* possible to design a mechanism that is both allocatively-efficient and almost completely budget-balanced. This is done by choosing a mechanism that is not *strategy-proof* but rather *strategy-resistant*. Instead of using the VCG mechanism, we propose a mechanism in which finding the most beneficial manipulation is an NP-complete problem, and the payments from the agents to the mechanism may be minimized as much as desired. This way, the mechanism is virtually strongly budget-balanced: for any $\epsilon > 0$, we find a mechanism that is ϵ-budget-balanced.

1 Introduction

Mechanisms face the problem of finding a system-wide solution to an optimization problem based on private information given by self-interested agents. As mechanism designers, we want to build a mechanism that would encourage agents to report their information truthfully, so that we can implement a desirable social choice function and maximize social welfare. A well-known solution to this problem in the case of quasi-linear preferences is that of Groves mechanisms. A special case of the Groves family of mechanisms are VCG mechanisms, which are budget-balanced, allocatively-efficient and strategy-proof.

Thus, in many cases, by using VCG we get a mechanism that operates with no outside subsidy (weakly budget-balanced) and maximizes the agents' utility. We maximize the agents' utility by choosing the outcome that maximizes the total utility according to the agents' reported types. Since VCG mechanisms are strategy-proof, the agents report their true preferences, and the mechanism maximizes their true utility. Also, VCG mechanisms are individually rational.

H. La Poutré, N. Sadeh, and S. Janson (Eds.): AMEC and TADA 2005, LNAI 3937, pp. 71–84, 2006.

Although in VCG mechanisms the agents pay the mechanism, they never pay more than they value the chosen outcome; the agents always have positive utility, and voluntarily participate.

A significant disadvantage of VCG mechanisms is that they are only *weakly* budget-balanced. We would in principle prefer a *strongly* budget-balanced mechanism, where the total sum of payments to the mechanism is zero: $\sum_i t_i(\theta) = 0$. Impossibility results ([1] and [2]) show that in a quasi-linear environment, it is impossible to achieve a mechanism that is strategy-proof, allocatively-efficient, and strongly budget-balanced. Given this fact, we are faced with a grim future. Giving up allocation-efficiency means we would no longer maximize the sum of agents' utilities, which was our goal in the first place. Giving up strategy-proofness means agents may have an incentive to try and manipulate the mechanism by not reporting their true preferences, which may lead us to a sub-optimal result. However, without sacrificing one of the two, we will not be able to achieve strong budget-balance.

We propose addressing this problem by relaxing the strategy-proof requirement, replacing it with *strategy-resistance*. A mechanism is strategy-proof if the dominant strategy of each agent is to reveal its true type to the mechanism. Strategy-resistance only requires that even if an agent is given the reported types of the other agents, it still faces a computationally intractable problem to solve if it wishes to find a beneficial manipulation (i.e., report a false type to the mechanism in order to gain higher utility). We here consider a scenario in which it is an NP-hard problem for an agent to find a useful manipulation. NP-hardness is a worst case notion of computational difficulty, in the sense that it only indicates that a certain problem has *some* hard instances. A stronger notion of strategy-resistance could also require the manipulation problem to have no approximation methods, or require it to be in some harder computational complexity class. Also, a stronger sense of strategy resistance could require it to be hard to find *any* beneficial manipulation, not just the *optimal* manipulation. This paper constitutes a first step in establishing the notion of strategy-resistance.

In this paper we consider the network flow domain. In this domain, the edges of a network flow belong to several self-interested agents. Each agent reports its edges to the mechanism. The mechanism is then required to choose a flow from the source vertex to the target vertex. Agents gain utility from flow units on their edges. A reasonable choice for the mechanism would be selecting the flow that maximizes the total flow on all of the agents' edges. In the case of a layer graph, this can easily be done by finding the maximal flow, and we get a simple and tractable algorithm for implementing the mechanism, assuming each of the agents *truthfully* reports its subset of edges. However, in some cases it is beneficial for these agents to hide some of their edges. A VCG mechanism to overcome this problem would be strategy-proof, but only weakly budget-balanced.

We show that in the domain of network flow, it *is* possible to achieve a mechanism that is strategy-resistant (and thus agents have an incentive to be truthful), efficient when agents are truthful, and as budget-balanced as we want it to be (i.e., we can minimize the sum of agent payments, $\sum_i t_i(\theta')$, as much as we want). A mechanism is ϵ-budget-balanced if $0 \leq \sum_i t_i(\theta') < \epsilon$. We analyze a general multiagent flow problem, and show that for every $\epsilon > 0$ we can create a strategy-resistant, allocatively efficient, and ϵ-budget-balanced mechanism. This result indicates that at least for some domains, it is possible to use the fact that agents have computational limitations and are not unboundedly rational, so as to construct mechanisms with beneficial properties.

2   Related Work

The main focus of research on bounded-rational mechanism design is on the problems that computational complexity poses for mechanism designers. Relatively little research has been dedicated to *using* the bounded-rationality of realistic agents to build better mechanisms. This approach was taken in [3] (building on the work in [4]), which used computational complexity to show that common voting protocols are hard to manipulate. A similar approach was taken in [5], where coalition games were analyzed. It was shown there that manipulating a marginal-contribution based value distribution scheme, similar to the standard solution of the Shapley value [6], is an NP-complete problem. [7] considered coalitions among computationally bounded agents. It suggested some bounded rational concepts for coalition games, and indicated that computational complexity considerations may lead us to extend the set of acceptable stable solutions. [8] analyzed VCG auctions, and showed that manipulating VCG auctions using false name bids is NP-hard; it also analyzed approximate VCG auctions. [9] showed that using an approximation method to find the optimal allocation in combinatorial auctions can lead to the loss of strategy-proofness.

3   Preliminaries

In this article, we propose an alternative to VCG mechanisms in quasi-linear domains. In such domains, we have a set I of agents. The mechanism needs to choose one of a set of possible alternatives K. Each agent reports a type $\theta_i \in \Theta_i$ to the mechanism. This type represents the agent's preferences over the different alternatives in K. Each agent has a different valuation of the mechanism's chosen alternative $k \in K$, $v_i(k, \theta_i)$. The mechanism chooses the outcome according to a choice rule $k : \Theta_1 \times ... \times \Theta_I \to K$. Each agent is also required to make a payment p_i to the mechanism. The mechanism chooses the payment of each agent according to a payment rule $t_i : \Theta_1 \times \Theta_I \to \mathbb{R}$. If the agents have quasi-linear utility functions, then the agents have utility $u_i(k, p_i, \theta_i) = v_i(k, \theta_i) - p_i$. An agent might not report its true type, but can choose a type to report to the mechanism. Thus, agent i (A_i) reports a type $\theta'_i = s_i(\theta_i)$, according to its own strategy.

3.1   Groves and VCG Mechanisms

In Groves mechanisms, the mechanism's choice rule given the reported types $\theta' = (\theta'_1, ..., \theta'_I)$ maximizes the sum of the agents' utilities, according to their reported types:

$$k^*(\theta') = arg \max_{k \in K} \sum_i v_i(k, \theta'_i). \tag{1}$$

The payment rule in Groves mechanisms is

$$t_i(\theta') = h_i(\theta'_{-i}) - \sum_{j \neq i} v_j(k^*, \theta'_j) \tag{2}$$

where $h_i : \Theta_{-i} \to \mathbb{R}$ may be any function that only depends on the reported types of agents other than i. Groves mechanisms are allocatively-efficient, and maximize the total utility of the agents. They are also strategy-proof, and for each agent the dominant strategy is to reveal its true type (or preferences) to the mechanism, no matter what the other agents report. Groves mechanisms are known to be the only direct revelation mechanisms that are allocatively-efficient and strategy-proof. Another advantage of Groves mechanisms is that in many cases they are weakly budget-balanced: $\sum_i t_i(\theta) \geq 0$.

A special case of Groves mechanisms is that of the VCG mechanism, when

$$h_i(\theta'_{-i}) = \sum_{j \neq i} v_j(k^*_{-i}(\theta'_{-i}), \theta'_j). \tag{3}$$

Under quite general settings, agents would voluntarily participate in VCG mechanisms, and we say that under these conditions the mechanism is individual-rational. The VCG mechanism also achieves weak budget-balance in quite general settings.

3.2   Main Contribution of the Paper

We approach the problem of designing a mechanism for bounded rational agents by building a mechanism for a distributed flow problem. We will demonstrate that for this domain, we can find a mechanism that is allocatively-efficient, ϵ-budget-balanced, and strategy-resistant. This means that if we assume the agents are bounded-rational and would not try to manipulate the mechanism if such manipulation is an NP-complete problem, they would all truthfully report their preferences. Once the mechanism gets their true preferences, it chooses the outcome that maximizes total utility of the agents. To achieve this truthfulness, the mechanism requires side payments; however, the total sum of these payments can be minimized as much as required. In other words, for every $\epsilon > 0$ we can build such a strategy-resistant, allocatively-efficient mechanism, that would also be ϵ-budget-balanced.

We restrict ourselves to the case where maximizing the graph's flow also maximizes the agents' total utility, since this allows us to choose a tractable mechanism. However, although the mechanism itself performs a polynomial calculation, finding the optimal manipulation for an agent remains NP-complete. The payments we demand from the agents to the mechanism makes finding this manipulation hard, while leaving the mechanism's calculation simple and tractable.

The mechanism we suggest for the self-interested layered-graph network flow problem indicates that for some problems we can devise *tractable* allocatively-efficient, strategy-resistant, and ϵ-budget-balanced solutions. It remains an open problem to characterize the domains in which such a solution is achievable. Also, as explained above, this paper considers a domain in which finding a beneficial manipulation is NP-hard to be a strategy-resistant domain. It also remains an open problem to find domains in which we can achieve a stronger notion of strategy-resistance.

4   Self-interested Network Flow

We now present the self-interested layered-graph network flow problem. Consider a flow network on a layered graph. We have a graph $G = < V, E >$, with source vertex s and target vertex t. The vertices of the graph are partitioned into $n+1$ layers, $L_0 = \{s\}, L_1, ..., L_n = \{t\}$. The edges only run between consecutive layers. We have a capacity function $c : E \to \mathbb{R}$ which is the maximal flow allowed on the edges. We also have a set I of agents. Each agent controls a subset $E_i \subset E$ of the graph's edges. No two agents control the same edge: $\forall_{i \neq j} E_i \cap E_j = \phi$.

The mechanism chooses a valid flow from s to t. A valid flow is a function $f : E \to R$ such that the following hold: $\forall_{(u,v) \in E} f(u,v) \leq c(u,v)$, $\forall_{(u,v) \in E} f(u,v) = -f(v,u)$, and $\forall_{u \in V - \{s,t\}} \sum_{v \in V} f(u,v) = 0$. We denote the positive flow as follows: if $f(u,v) > 0$ then $f^+(u,v) = f(u,v)$, otherwise $f^+(u,v) = 0$. We denote the size of the flow $|f| = \sum_{v \in V} f(s,v)$. The flow the mechanism chooses may only go through edges that belong to some agent. The mechanism knows the capacity constraints of the edges, but must treat edges not reported by an agent as edges whose capacity is 0. Each agent values the flow chosen by the mechanism according to the total flow going through its edges. Let f be the valid flow chosen by the mechanism, and E_f the set of edges in f through which there is a positive flow: $E_f = \{e \in E \mid f(e) > 0\}$. We denote the set of A_i's edges used in the flow f by: $E_{f,i} = E_f \cap E_i$. The agent's valuation of the flow is

$$v_i(f) = \sum_{e \in E_{f,i}} f(e). \tag{4}$$

A direct revelation implementation for the self-interested network flow problem would require each agent to state its valuation of all possible flows, which is not tractable. An alternative tractable implementation is to simply make the type of an agent the set of its declared edges $E_i' \in E_i$. Given this information, the mechanism could compute the agents' valuations of any possible flow. We will assume agents can only declare edges they actually own.

When the mechanism is given the agents' true types, $\theta = E_1, E_2, ..., E_I$, we want it to choose the flow that maximizes the total utility of the agents. The mechanism would be allocatively-efficient if it chooses

$$f^*(\theta) = arg \max_f \sum_i \sum_{e \in E_{f,i}} f(e). \tag{5}$$

4.1   Layered Graphs and Mechanisms for Network Flow

Consider a self-interested network flow problem in a *layered* graph. If each agent truthfully declares its subset of edges, the mechanism can easily compute $f^*(\theta)$ by running a maximal flow algorithm, such as the Edmonds-Karp algorithm.

Proof. Suppose the mechanism chooses a flow f. The total flow exiting s ends up in vertices in L_1. All the flow from L_1 ends up in vertices in L_2, and so on. Since flow may only go through edges owned by some agent, the total utility obtained by the flow f is

$$\sum_{e\in E} f^+(e) = \sum_{u\in L_1, v\in L_2} f^+(u,v)+...+ \sum_{u\in L_{n-1}, v\in L_n} f^+(u,v)= |f|+...+|f| = (n-1)|f$$

(6)

A naive mechanism for the self-interested flow problem, with no payments to the mechanism, is not strategy-proof. An agent may declare only a subset of the edges it controls, to change the flow that the mechanism chooses to a flow that the agent values more. Figure 1 shows two agents on a certain network flow (A_1 and A_2). A_1's edges are marked with dashed lines, and A_2's edges are marked with full lines. A_2 truthfully declares all its edges. Assuming the mechanism favors A_1 and chooses the specific maximal that maximizes A_1's utility among all maximal flows, A_1 can do better by not declaring its topmost edge (v_1, v_4), gaining a utility of 2 instead of 1.

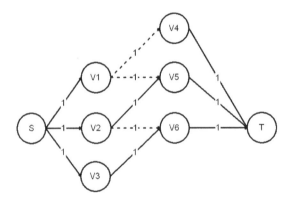

Fig. 1. Manipulations in self-interested flow problems

5   A Mechanism for the Self-interested Network Flow Problem

We assume quasi-linear utility. Each agent pays the mechanism a payment p_i, and its utility is $u_i(f) = v_i(f) - p_i$. We now show that by using a straightforward payment rule, we make finding a beneficial manipulation NP-hard. The payment rule we use is simple: each agent pays the mechanism a constant of c for each edge it declares it owns. Let $E_i' \subset E_i$ be the subset of edges an agent declares it owns. Then $p_i(E_i') = c|E_i'|$. To make sure the mechanism is individual rational, the payment p_i should give the agent a utility of 0 when the agent's valuation of the given flow is less than $c|E_i'|$. Thus, the payment rule is: if $v_i(f^*) > c|E_i'|$ then $p_i = c|E_i'|$, otherwise $p_i = v_i(f^*)$.

Assume that A_i knows E_j' for all $j \neq i$. It can easily calculate the utility it would get by truthfully declaring all its edges. How hard is it for i to find a subset of edges it could declare to the mechanism so as to gain a higher utility? First, note that the question itself is under-constrained. Even given E_j' for all j, including i, there may be several maximal flows; the mechanism is free to choose any of them. However, we will show that even if A_i can decide *which* maximal flow the mechanism chooses, it would still remain an NP-hard problem for that agent to find a better subset of edges.

We now define the problem of *finding* the optimal manipulation in the self-interested network flow domain.

FLOW-EDGE-SUBSET: We are given a layered graph flow network, with the capacity function $c : E \to \mathbb{R}$, E_{-i} the declared edges of the other agents, and E_i, the set of our edges. We are also given the constant c of the payment, and we know that if we declare that we have k edges, our payment to the mechanism would be $p_i = ck$. We assume the mechanism prefers a maximal flow that maximizes *our* utility: if we report a subset of edges $E_i' \subset E_i$ the mechanism would choose the maximal flow f^* to be the flow that maximizes $\sum_{e \in E_{f^*, i}} f(e)$ from among all the possible maximal flows. We are also given a constant k, the target utility for A_i. We are asked if there is a subset of A_i's edges $E_i' \subset E_i$, such that the maximal flow chosen by the mechanism, $f^*(E_1, ..., E_{i-1}, E_i', E_{i+1}, ..., E_I)$ gives A_i a utility of at least k:

$$u_i(f^*, p_i) = v_i(f^*) - p_i = \sum_{e \in E_{f^*, i}} f(e) - c|E_i'| \geq k. \tag{7}$$

5.1   NP-Completeness of FLOW-EDGE-SUBSET

First, we note that FLOW-EDGE-SUBSET is in NP, because given a subset of edges $E_i' \subset E_i$ we can easily compute the maximal flow. We show that FLOW-EDGE-SUBSET is NP-complete by reducing a general VERTEX-COVER problem to a FLOW-EDGE-SUBSET problem. The reduction shows that FLOW-EDGE-SUBSET is NP-complete even if the inputs are restricted to problems where there are only two agents, and the graph has only 5 layers.

VERTEX-COVER: We are given a graph $G = < V, E >$ and a constant n and are asked if there is a subset of n vertices $V' \subset V, |V'| = n$ that covers all the edges $\forall_{(u,v) \in E}$ *either* $u \in V'$ *or* $v \in V'$.

The reduction is done as follows. From the VERTEX-COVER input, we build inputs for the FLOW-EDGE-SUBSET problem. Given the original VERTEX-COVER graph G, we build a layer graph G'. All the inputs to FLOW-EDGE-SUBSET are built with this layer graph G', and in all of them there are two agents, and we are asked about the utility of A_1. In all of these inputs we have the same set of A_1's edges E_1, the same list of declared edges of the other agent, and the same payment constant, c. This payment constant is chosen such that the payment from A_1 to the mechanism is always less than 1, even if A_1 declares all its edges.

The only difference between the inputs is the target utility k. These inputs are constructed such that A_1 has $|V|$ edges, where $|V|$ is the number of vertices in G. The inputs are constructed so that the maximal utility A_1 can achieve is obtained by declaring some set of edges, E_1^*, and in this case, A_1's utility is $u_1(E_1^*) = v_1(E_1^*) - p_1(E_1^*) = |E| - c|E_1^*|$, where $|E|$ is the number of edges in the VERTEX-COVER graph G, and $|E_1^*|$ is the number of vertices in the *minimal vertex-cover* of G. We abuse notation a bit here, and denote $u_1(E_1')$ and $v_1(E_1')$ as the utility and valuation A_1 has when declaring the E_1' subset of edges, since the declared edges of all the other agents are known. Thus the flow chosen by the mechanism only depends on A_1's chosen subset of edges, E_1'.

5.2   The Process of the Reduction

Since the payment from A_1 to the mechanism is always a multiple of c, we can easily check how many vertices are used in the minimal vertex-cover of G. We construct G' from G, and use FLOW-EDGE-SUBSET to check if we can achieve a utility of at least $|E| - |V|c$, then check the possibility of achieving $|E| - (|V| - 1)c$, then $|E| - (|V| - 2)c$, and so on. The answer would initially be 'yes', since due to the construction, A_1 can achieve a utility of $|E| - |V|c$ by declaring all its edges. A_1 can decide to declare any number of edges between 0 and $|V|$. The questions are asked regarding higher and higher requested utilities, so eventually, for some $x \in \mathbb{N}, 0 \le x \le |V|$, the answer for $|E| - xc$ would be 'no'. We would then know the best utility that A_1 can achieve is $|E| - (x+1)c$, and thus the minimal vertex-cover of G is of size $x + 1$. This process involves running FLOW-EDGE-SUBSET $|V|$ times, so if FLOW-EDGE-SUBSET can be done in polynomial time, then this process can also be performed in polynomial time.

5.3   Constructing the FLOW-EDGE-SUBSET Inputs

We now describe how the inputs for FLOW-EDGE-SUBSET are constructed from the VERTEX-COVER input. We build a 5-layer network flow graph, G'. The L_0 layer contains the single source vertex s, and the L_4 layer contains the single target vertex t. Layer L_1 contains a vertex v_{e_i} for each edge $e_i \in E$ in the original VERTEX-COVER graph. Layer L_2 contains a vertex $v_{i,b}$ for each vertex $v_i \in V$ in the original VERTEX-COVER graph. Layer L_3 contains a single vertex $v_{i,a}$ for each vertex $v_i \in V$ in the original VERTEX-COVER graph.

The edges between the layers are constructed as follows. The source vertex s is connected to all the vertices in L_1, and then we mark the edge (s, v_{e_i}) as e_{e_i}. Every vertex v_{e_i} in L_1 is connected to exactly two vertices in L_2. If edge $e_i \in E$ in G connects vertices v_i and v_j in it, then v_{e_i} is connected to $v_{v_i,b}$ and

$v_{v_j,b}$ in the constructed graph G'. Every vertex in L_2 is connected to exactly one vertex in L_3. Vertex $v_{v_i,b}$ in L_2 is connected to $v_{v_i,a}$ in L_3. All the vertices in L_3 are connected to the sink vertex t in L_4. All the edges between L_0 and L_1 and all the edges between L_1 and L_2 have a capacity of 1. All the other edges have capacity of $|E|$.

As explained above, all inputs for FLOW-EDGE-SUBSET are given with regard to A_1. The set of A_1's edges E_1 is $(v_{v_i,b}, v_{v_i,a})$, for all possible i. All of the other edges belong to A_2, and in the input given to FLOW-EDGE-SUBSET, A_2 declares all its edges. The payment constant c is chosen such that $c < \frac{1}{|V|+|E|}$. We demonstrate building the layer graph in Figure 2. The graph on the left of Figure 2 is the input for the VERTEX-COVER, while the graph on the right is the generated FLOW-EDGE-SUBSET layer graph.

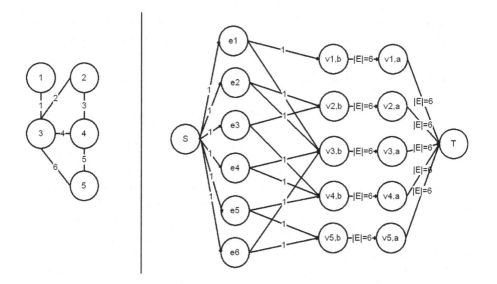

Fig. 2. Reducing VERTEX-COVER to FLOW-EDGE-SUBSET

The intuition behind this construction is simple. A_1's edges in the constructed graph represent vertices in the original graph G. A_1 must choose a subset of edges to report to the mechanism. Let $E_1' \subset E_1$ be the subset of edges that A_1 chooses to declare. Each such choice can also be seen as a choice of a subset of vertices in G. These vertices cover certain edges in the original graph. We later refer to these edges as $EC_{G,E_1'}$. The v_{e_i} vertices in L_1 represent the edges in G.

The construction makes sure that the mechanism can only send flow from s to v_{e_i} if e_i is an edge covered by E_1' ($e_i \in EC_{G,E_1'}$). In fact, a flow going through one of A_1's edges $(v_{v_i,b}, v_{v_i,a})$ can only originate from a v_{e_j} vertex that represents an edge e_j that covers v_i.

Thus A_1's valuation is limited by the number of edges covered by his chosen set of vertices, or in other words by $|EC_{G,E_1'}|$. Therefore, A_1 would choose E_1'

to be edges representing a set of vertices that covers all the edges in G; it would choose E_1' such that $E = EC_{G,E_1'}$.

However, A_1 also realizes it must give the mechanism payments for declaring his edges. Since he pays a constant c per each edge he declares, A_1 would want to minimize the number of edges he declares. This conflicts with A_1's wish to choose E_1' so that $E = EC_{G,E_1'}$, since fewer vertices cover fewer edges.

By choosing a low enough payment constant c, we make sure that A_1's top priority is to cover all the edges in G. It is only his second priority to minimize the number of edges he declares. Thus, A_1 actually wishes to choose E_1' so that the set of vertices E_1' represents is the minimal vertex cover of G.

The following sections formally prove the intuitive claims above.

5.4   Properties of the Constructed Inputs

Lemma 1. *If G had $|E|$ edges, then in the generated network flow graph, A_1's valuation cannot exceed $|E|$. If A_1 can get a valuation of $|E|$, its utility is in the range $|E| - 1 \leq u_1(f) \leq |E|$.*

Proof. The maximal flow cannot exceed $|E|$, because there are only $|E|$ edges between L_0 and L_1, each with a capacity of 1. All of A_1's edges are between L_2 and L_3, so the maximal flow through them also cannot exceed $|E|$. Thus, A_1's valuation of any flow f, $v_1(f)$, cannot exceed $|E|$. A_1's utility when a flow f is chosen is $u_1(f, p_1) = v_1(f) - p_1 = v_1(f) - c|E_1'|$. Due to the choice of c, $p_1 = |E_1'| \cdot \frac{1}{|V|+|E|} < 1$, so $0 \leq p_i \leq 1$.

Let $E_1' \subset E_1$ be the subset of edges that A_1 chooses to declare. We denote $EC_{G,E_1'} = \{e_i \in E \mid e_i = (v_x, v_y)$ and at least one of the following holds: $(v_{v_x,b}, v_{v_x,a}) \in E_1'$ or $(v_{v_y,b}, v_{v_y,a}) \in E_1'\}$. Similarly, we denote $EC_{G',E_1'} = \{e_{e_i} \mid e_i \in EC_G\}$. Intuitively, we identify the edge e_{e_i} with the edge e_i in the original graph. We identify the edge $(v_{v_x,b}, v_{v_x,a}) \in E_1$ with *vertex* v_x in the original graph G, and a subset of edges $E_1' \subset E_1$ with a subset of vertices $V_{E_1'} \subset V$ in G. Such a set of vertices in G covers a subset of the edges in it. EC_G is the set of edges covered by these vertices $V_{E_1'}$, and $EC_{G'}$ is the set of edges in G' corresponding to the covered edges.

Lemma 2. *Let $E_1^* \subset E_1$ be an optimal choice of edges for A_1 to declare. Then $EC_{G,E_1^*} = E$.*

Proof. Let E_1^* be an optimal choice of A_1's edges, f be the flow chosen by the mechanism in this case, and EC_{G,E_1^*} be the subset of E, as explained above. Assume by negation that there *is* some $e = (x, y) \in E$ that $e \notin EC_{G,E_1^*}$. There cannot be any flow on e_e in G', since having such a flow $f(s, v_e) > 0$ would require having either flow $f(v_e, v_{x,b}) > 0$ or $f(v_e, v_{y,b}) > 0$, since v_e is connected only to these two vertices. However, this would require having either a flow $f(v_{x,b}, v_{x,a}) > 0$ or $f(v_{y,b}, v_{y,a}) > 0$, both of which cannot occur, since $e \notin EC_{G,E_1^*}$, and $(v_{x,b}, v_{x,a}) \notin E_1^*$, and $(v_{y,b}, v_{y,a}) \notin E_1^*$. Thus, there cannot be any flow on e_e, and the maximal flow between L_0 and L_1 cannot exceed $|E| - 1$.

Suppose we add to E_1^* the edge $(v_{x,b}, v_{x,a})$. This would allow the mechanism to increase the flow in the following path by exactly 1: $s, v_e, v_{x,b}, v_{x,a}, t$, resulting in a flow f'. The flow through A_1's edges is exactly the same as before, except there is now a flow of 1 through $(v_{x,b}, v_{x,a})$, so $v_1(f') = v_1(f) + 1$. Since the payment to the mechanism is always less than 1, the total utility of A_1 has increased, so E_1^* was not an optimal choice for A_1 to begin with.

Lemma 3. *If A_1 declares $E_1' \subset E_1$ such that $EC_{G,E_1'} = E$, the mechanism can choose a flow f such that $|f| = |E|$.*

Proof. We can fill the capacities of all the edges between L_0 and L_1, having the vertices of L_1 with a total incoming flow of $|E|$. Since $EC_{G,E_1'} = E$, we also have $EC_{G',E_1'} = \{e_{e_i} \mid e_i \in E\}$, and every vertex v_{e_i} in L_1 is connected to at least one vertex $v_{x,b}$ in layer L_2 that is connected (in turn) to $v_{x,a}$ in layer L_3 by an edge $e \in E_1'$. We choose the flow $f(v_{e_i}, v_{x,b}) = 1$. We then continue the flow by sending the incoming flow of vertex $v_{x,b}$ to $v_{x,a}$, by choosing

$$f(v_{x,b}, v_{x,a}) = \sum_{v_{e_i} \in L_1} f(v_{e_i}, v_{x,b}). \tag{8}$$

We can do this since the capacity of the edges between L_2 and L_3 is $|E|$, so $c(v_{x,b}, v_{x,a}) = |E|$, and there is no danger of having a flow coming into a vertex $v_{x,b}$ higher than the total capacity of its outgoing edges. The flow is then continued by sending all the incoming flow of vertex $v_{x,a}$ to the target vertex: $f(v_{x,a}, t) = f(v_{x,b}, v_{x,a})$. Again, this is possible since the capacity of the edges between L_3 and L_4 is $|E|$.

Therefore, the optimal subset of edges that A_1 can declare, $E_1^* \subset E_1$, allows the mechanism to achieve the maximal possible flow f^*, of size $|f^*| = |E|$.

Lemma 4. *The optimal subset of edges for A_1, $E_1^* \subset E_1$, gives A_1 a valuation of $v_1(f^*) = |E|$.*

Proof. From Lemma 2 and Lemma 3 we know that if A_1 declares E_1' in the optimal solution, the mechanism can choose a flow f such that $|f| = |E|$. By Lemma 1 this is a maximal flow that maximizes the utility of A_1. Since A_1 controls all the edges between L_2 and L_3 and has no other edges, we have a total flow of $|E|$ through A_1's edges.

As a private case of Lemma 4, we get that A_1 can get a valuation of $|E|$ by declaring all of its edges, since $EC_{G,E_1} = E$. This case gives A_1 a utility of $|E| - c|E_1|$, since we have declared $|E_1|$ edges.

Lemma 4 shows that the optimal subset of edges for A_1, $E_1^* \subset E_1$, gives A_1 a valuation of $v_1(f^*) = |E|$. However, to calculate A_1's utility in this case, we must also know the payment that A_1 gives the mechanism. This payment only depends on the number of edges in E_1^*.

5.5   Proof of the Reduction

We now prove the validity of the reduction, by showing that the the maximal utility A_1 can achieve in the constructed network flow graph is determined by the size of the minimal vertex cover in the original graph.

Theorem 1. *The size of the minimal vertex-cover of G is k if and only if the maximal utility of A_1 in the constructed inputs to FLOW-EDGE-SUBSET is $|E| - kc$.*

Proof. Assume the maximal utility A_1 can achieve is $|E| - kc$. Due to Lemma 4, in order to obtain this optimal utility A_1 has to declare $E_1' \subset E_1$, a subset of edges with size $|E_1'| = k$. Consider the set $V_{E_1'} = \{v_x \in V \mid (v_{x,a}, v_{x,b}) \in E_1'\}$. From Lemma 2 we have $EC_{G,E_1'} = E$, so this set is a vertex-cover of G. Its size is $|V_{E_1'}| = k$, since the payment A_1 made to the mechanism is kc. Assume by negation that this is not the *minimal* vertex-cover of G. Then there exists a vertex cover VC' with a smaller size of $|VC'| = k'$. Consider $E_{VC'} = \{(v_{x,b}, v_{x,a}) \in E_1 \mid v_x \in VC'\}$. This is a subset of A_1's edges that (by definition of $EC_{G,X}$), $EC_{G,E_{VC'}} = E$. Thus, $v_1(E_{VC'}) = |E|$. However, since $|VC'| = k' < k = |V_{E_1'}|$, the payment from A_1 to the mechanism for declaring $E_{VC'}$ is only $p_1(E_{VC'}) = k' < k$. Thus the utility of A_1 when using $E_{VC'}$ is $u_1(E_{VC'}) = v_1(E_{VC'}) - p_1(E_{VC'}) = |E| - k'c > |E| - kc = u_1(E_1')$, and we would have a subset of edges giving a better utility than the optimal solution.

On the other hand, if we have a vertex-cover VC for G with size $|VC| = k$, consider $E_{VC} = \{(v_{x,b}, v_{x,a}) \in E_1 \mid v_x \in VC\}$. Again, this is a subset of A_1's edges that (by definition of $EC_{G,X}$) makes $EC_{G,E_{VC}} = E$. Thus, $v_1(E_{VC'}) = |E|$. The utility of A_1 when using E_{VC} is $u_1(E_{VC}) = v_1(E_{VC}) - p_1(E_{VC}) = |E| - kc$, so a utility of $|E| - kc$ is achievable.

It remains to show that this is the *maximal* utility achievable. Suppose, by negation, that we have a choice of edges $E_1' \subset E_1$ that gives A_1 a higher utility. The valuation of E_1' must also be $v_1(E_1') = |E|$, since a higher valuation is not possible, and a lower valuation would result in a utility that is below $u_1(E_{VC})$ (since the payment to the mechanism is less than 1). This means that the payment for E_1' is less than the payment for E_{VC}, or $|E_1'| < |E_{VC}|$. As explained above, in order to achieve a utility of $|E|$, E_1' must be a set such that $EC_{G,E_1'} = E$, so $V_{E_1'} = \{v_x \in V \mid (v_{x,b}, v_{x,a}) \in E_1'\}$ must be a vertex-cover of G. However, since $|V_{E_1'}| = |E_1'| < |E_{VC}|$, this would be a vertex-cover of a size smaller than the size of the minimal vertex-cover.

Due to Theorem 1, the process of the reduction as described above is valid, and FLOW-EDGE-SUBSET is NP-complete.

6   Conclusions and Future Directions

We have presented a mechanism for the distributed network flow problem with self-interested agents. With a proper choice of the payment constant c, finding a beneficial manipulation is an NP-complete problem. If most instances of the manipulation problem are indeed computationally intractable, we expect agents would truthfully report their preferences. In this case, the mechanism would choose the result maximizing the sum of agents' utilities, and we have an allocatively-efficient mechanism.

Given some $\epsilon > 0$, we can make the mechanism ϵ-budget-balanced, by choosing a constant $c = \frac{\epsilon}{n(|E|+|V|)}$, so that all of the agents together pay less than ϵ. The mechanism we have described is also individual rational. The mechanism's calculation is tractable, and only involves a polynomial algorithm for finding the maximal network flow. This indicates that the agents' difficulty in finding a beneficial manipulation is not caused by any difficulty in simulating the mechanism, but is instead caused by the difficulty of trying exponentially many options of untruthful declarations to the mechanism.

Therefore, in the domain of network flow, it is possible to achieve an individually-rational, allocatively-efficient, ϵ-budget-balanced, and strategy-resistant mechanism. The standard VCG solution in this domain would be only weakly budget-balanced, but strategy-proof. Impossibility results [1] and [2] indicate that no direct-revelation mechanism can achieve strong budget-balance without sacrificing either allocative-efficiency or strategy-proofness. We believe that in many cases, trading strategy-proofness for strategy-resistance is a fair price to pay for achieving strong budget-balance.

There has been much work dedicated to overcoming the intractability of mechanisms, since in building a real-world mechanism we cannot assume unbounded computation. However, if we are not willing to accept unbounded-rationality on the *mechanism's* part, we must also consider the implications of the bounded-rational nature of the *agents*.

We believe that strategy-proofness should not be the only criteria when considering the susceptibility of a mechanism to manipulations. In fact, we believe it is found on one end of a *scale* of susceptibility. On the other end of this scale are mechanisms where there exists a poly-time algorithm for finding the optimal manipulation. Such mechanisms probably cannot be used in practice, since they are so easy to manipulate. Between these two extremes is the region of strategy-resistant mechanisms. In this paper we have implicitly defined a strategy-resistant mechanism as one in which it is NP-hard to find the optimal manipulation. As we have commented above, this is a rather weak notion of strategy resistance. A preferable solution would be one in which it is computationally intractable to find *any* manipulation. NP-hardness is not sufficient for a problem to be computationally intractable. For example, we can require the manipulation problem to have no approximation methods, or show that most instances of the manipulation problem are indeed hard.

In this paper we have shown that in the network flow domain, we can gain budget-balance by giving up strategy proofness, and replacing it with our notion of strategy-resistance. Assuming we are willing to accept strategy-resistance as a sufficient guarantee that agents would truthfully declare their types, we have improved the results obtained by VCG for this problem.

We have chosen the self-interested network flow domain, because in this case we were able to find a mechanism that was tractable in its computational properties, and also had good results in the sense of being budget-balanced. This domain demonstrates that by using a very simple payment scheme we can create a significant gap between the amount of work the mechanism performs (in this case a simple poly-time algorithm) and the amount of work an agent is required to perform in order to find a beneficial manipulation (in this case solving an NP-hard problem). We believe further research can find domains in which the mechanism is required to perform harder work (e.g., solving an NP-hard problem by approximation), and manipulations are completely intractable. It may be possible to achieve budget-balance while retaining a stronger notion of strategy-resistance, even in this domain. Also, it may be possible to find other valuable tradeoffs in other domains. It remains an open problem to characterize the domains in which using computational complexity in this way is possible, and to find domains in which a stronger sense of strategy-resistance can be achieved.

References

1. Green, J., Laffont, J.J.: Characterization of satisfactory mechanisms for the revelation of preferences for public goods. Econometrica **45**(2) (1977) 427–38
2. Hurwicz, L.: On the existence of allocation systems whose manipulative Nash equilibria are pareto-optimal. In: 3rd World Congress of the Econometric Society (Unpublished). (1975)
3. Conitzer, V., Sandholm, T.: Universal voting protocol tweaks to make manipulation hard. In: Proceedings of the Eighteenth International Joint Conference on Artificial Intelligence (IJCAI), Acapulco, Mexico (2003) 781–788
4. Bartholdi, J.J.: The computational difficulty of manipulating an election. Social Choice and Welfare **6**(3) (1989) 227–241
5. Conitzer, V., Sandholm, T.: Computing shapley values, manipulating value division schemes, and checking core membership in multi-issue domains. In: Proceedings of the 19th National Conference on Artificial Intelligence (AAAI), San Jose, California, USA (2004) 219–225
6. Shapley, L.S.: A value for n-person games. Contributions to the Theory of Games (1953) 31–40
7. Sandholm, T., Lesser, V.R.: Coalitions among computationally bounded agents. Artificial Intelligence **94**(1-2) (1997) 99–137
8. Sanghvi, S., Parkes, D.C.: Hard-to-manipulate combinatorial auctions. Technical report, Harvard University (2004)
9. Lavi, R., Mu'alem, A., Nisan, N.: Towards a characterization of truthful combinatorial auctions (extended abstract). In: Proceedings of the 44th Annual IEEE Symposium on Foundations of Computer Science (FOCS). (2003)

An Analysis of the Shapley Value and Its Uncertainty for the Voting Game

Shaheen S. Fatima[1], Michael Wooldridge[1], and Nicholas R. Jennings[2]

[1] Department of Computer Science,
University of Liverpool, Liverpool L69 7ZF, U.K.
{S.S.Fatima, M.J.Wooldridge}@csc.liv.ac.uk
[2] School of Electronics and Computer Science,
University of Southampton, Southampton SO17 1BJ, U.K.
nrj@ecs.soton.ac.uk

Abstract. The Shapley value provides a unique solution to coalition games and is used to evaluate a player's prospects of playing a game. Although it provides a unique solution, there is an element of uncertainty associated with this value. This uncertainty in the solution of a game provides an additional dimension for evaluating a player's prospects of playing the game. Thus, players want to know not only their Shapley value for a game, but also the associated uncertainty. Given this, our objective is to determine the Shapley value and its uncertainty and study the relationship between them for the voting game. But since the problem of determining the Shapley value for this game is #P-complete, we first present a new polynomial time randomized method for determining the approximate Shapley value. Using this method, we compute the Shapley value and correlate it with its uncertainty so as to allow agents to compare games on the basis of both their Shapley values and the associated uncertainties. Our study shows that, a player's uncertainty first increases with its Shapley value and then decreases. This implies that the uncertainty is at its minimum when the value is at its maximum, and that agents do not always have to compromise value in order to reduce uncertainty.

1 Introduction

Coalition formation is the process of joining together of two or more agents so as to achieve goals that individuals on their own cannot, or to achieve them more efficiently [9]. Often, in such situations, there is more than one possible coalition and a player's payoff depends on the coalition it joins. Given this, a key problem in this area is to ensure that none of the parties in a coalition has any incentive to break away from it and join another coalition (i.e., the coalitions are *stable*). However, in many cases there may be more than one solution (i.e., a stable coalition). In such cases, it becomes difficult to select a single solution from among the possible ones, especially if the parties are self-interested (i.e., they have different preferences over stable coalitions).

In this context, cooperative game theory deals with the problem of coalition formation and offers a number of solution concepts that possess desirable properties like *stability*, *fair division of joint gains*, and *uniqueness* [3,7]. Multiagent systems research has used and extended these game-theoretic solutions to facilitate automated coalition

H. La Poutré, N. Sadeh, and S. Janson (Eds.): AMEC and TADA 2005, LNAI 3937, pp. 85–98, 2006.

formation [9,14,12]. In this work, one of the most extensively studied solution concepts is the *Shapley value* [13]. The Shapley value provides a *unique* solution and is therefore used to evaluate a player's prospects of playing a game.

Although the Shapley value provides a unique solution, it has two key drawbacks. First, for the weighted voting game that we consider, the problem of determining the Shapley value is #P-complete [1]. Second, it provides the solution only with a limited degree of certainty [11]. Thus the uncertainty in the Shapley value provides an additional dimension for evaluating a player's prospects of playing a game and a measure of uncertainty would serve as a useful tool to investigate this aspect of a game. Characterizing a game by both its value and uncertainty is like characterising a weapon by its power and precision, or a financial stock by its expected return and risk [4].

The concept of uncertainty in the outcome of a game is not entirely new. For instance, Roth showed that the Shapley value of a game equals its utility, if and only if the underlying player preferences are neutral to both *ordinary*[1] and *strategic* risk [10,11]. Otherwise, the Shapley value is not the same as utility and is therefore insufficient for decision-making purposes. Kargin extended this concept further by introducing a measure for determining the strategic risk [4]. This measure is called the *uncertainty* of the Shapley value and it provides a yardstick for quantifying the strategic risk. Thus, in order for a player to make more informed decisions, it is important for it to not only know its Shapley value, but also the relation between this value and its uncertainty. However, to date, there has been no analysis of this relationship.

Given this, our objective is to analyse the relation between the Shapley value and its uncertainty for the *voting game* (since it is an important mechanism for multiple agents to reach consensus). However, uncertainty is defined in terms of the Shapley value (i.e., in order to find uncertainty, the Shapley value needs to be determined first). But, as we pointed out, the problem of determining the Shapley value has been shown to be #P-complete [1]. We therefore present a new *randomised* method (that has polynomial time complexity) for computing the *approximate* Shapley value. Using this method, we determine the Shapley value and correlate it with its uncertainty. Our study shows that each player's uncertainty first increases with its Shapley value and then decreases. This implies that the uncertainty is at its minimum when the value is at its maximum, and that agents do not always have to compromise value in order to reduce uncertainty.

To our knowledge, the only work that addresses the problem of uncertainty in the Shapley value is [10,11,4]. While [10,11] introduces the concept of strategic risk in the context of the Shapley value, [4] defines a measure (called uncertainty) for this risk. Our paper therefore makes a twofold contribution. First, we present a polynomial time method along the lines of *Monte Carlo simulation* (see Section 3 for details) for computing the Shapley value for the voting game. Second, using this method we compute the Shapley value and analyse its relation with uncertainty.

Section 2 defines the Shapley value and its uncertainty. Section 3 describes the weighted voting game. Section 4 to Section 7 determine the relation between the Shapley value and its uncertainty. Section 8 concludes.

---

[1] Ordinary risk involves the uncertainty that arises from the chance mechanism involved in lotteries. On the other hand, *strategic risk* involves the uncertainty that arises as a result of interaction in a game of strategic players (i.e., those players that are not dummy).

2   The Shapley Value and Its Uncertainty

We begin by introducing coalition games and then define the weighted voting game. Coalition games are of two types ([7]): those with *transferable payoff* and those with *non-transferable payoff*. A coalition game with transferable payoff, $\langle N, v \rangle$, consists of a finite set ($N = \{1, 2, \ldots, n\}$) of players and a function (v) that associates with every non-empty subset S of N (i.e., a *coalition*) a real number $v(S)$ (the worth of S).

For each coalition S, the number $v(S)$ is the total payoff that is available for division among the members of S (i.e., the set of joint actions that coalition S can take consists of all possible divisions of $v(S)$ among the members of S). Coalition games with non-transferable payoffs differ from ones with transferable payoffs in the following way. For the former, each coalition is associated with a *set* of payoff vectors that is not necessarily the set of all possible divisions of some fixed amount. In this paper, we focus on the Shapley value for a game with transferable payoffs.

Let S denote the set $N - \{i\}$ and $f_i : S \rightarrow 2^{N-\{i\}}$ be a random variable that takes its values in the set of all subsets of $N - \{i\}$, and has the probability distribution function (g) defined as:

$$g\{f_i(S) = S\} = \frac{|S|!(n - |S| - 1)!}{n!}$$

The random variable f_i is interpreted as the random choice of a coalition that player i joins. A player's Shapley value [13] is defined in terms of its *marginal contribution*. The marginal contribution of player i to coalition S with $i \notin S$ is a function $\Delta_i v$ that acts in the following way:

$$\Delta_i v(S) = v(S \cup \{i\}) - v(S)$$

Definition 1. *The Shapley value (φ_i) of the game $\langle N, v \rangle$ for player i is the expectation (E) of its marginal contribution to a coalition that is chosen randomly, i.e., $\varphi_i(N, v) = E\{\Delta_i v \circ f_i\}$*

The Shapley value is interpreted as follows. Suppose that all the players are arranged in some order, all orderings being equally likely. Then $\varphi_i(N, v)$ is the *expected marginal contribution*, over all orderings, of player i to the set of players who precede him. The *uncertainty* of the Shapley value, is defined as follows [4]:

Definition 2. *The uncertainty (β_i) for player i is the variance (Var) of its marginal contribution. Thus $\beta_i(N, v) = Var\{\Delta_i v \circ f_i\}$*

Thus, while a player's Shapley value is the expectation (i.e., the mean), its uncertainty is the variance (i.e., the square of the standard deviation) of its marginal contribution. In other words, the uncertainty is the expectation of the squared difference between the actual and expected marginal contributions.

The utility of a player that is not neutral to strategic risk depends on both its Shapley value and the associated uncertainty. Furthermore, such a player's utility function is subjective and different players may have different functions for the same game. But for a given game, the relation between the Shapley value and its uncertainty is not subjective to player preferences and is the same for all players. We therefore analyse this relation for the voting game described in Section 3.

3   The Weighted Voting Game

We adopt the definition of voting game given in [7]. There is a set of n players that may, for example, represent shareholders in a company or members in a parliament. The weighted voting game is a game $G = \langle N, v \rangle$ in which

$$v(S) = \begin{cases} 1 \text{ if } w(S) \geq q \\ 0 \text{ otherwise} \end{cases}$$

for some $q \in I\!R_+$ and $w_i \in I\!R_+^N$, where $w(S) = \sum_{i \in S} w_i$ for any coalition S. Thus w_i is the number of votes that player i has and q is the number of votes needed to win the game (i.e., the *quota*). For this game (denoted $\langle q; w_1, \ldots, w_n \rangle$), a player's marginal contribution is either zero or one.

The problem of determining the Shapley value for the weighted voting game is #P-complete [1]. A problem is #P-hard if solving that problem is as hard as counting satisfying assignments of propositional logic formulae [8, p442]. Since #P-completeness thus subsumes NP-completeness, this implies that computing the Shapley value for the weighted voting game will be intractable in general. To overcome this problem, two methods have been proposed: *Monte Carlo simulation* [5] and the method of *generating functions* [6]. The former method treats the number of *swings*[2] for each player as a random variable over a given distribution and defines the Shapley value in terms of these random variables. While this method gives the approximate Shapley value, the generating functions method is an exact procedure. Although it is an exact procedure, it requires very large arrays (i.e., it requires substantial storage space) and can only be applied to games with integer weights and quotas.

The method we present is similar to that of [5] in the sense that it is an approximation method. But the difference is that while [5] defines the Shapley value by treating a player's number of swings as a random variable, we treat the players' weights as random variables. Since the voting game is defined in terms of the players' weights and the number of swings are obtained from these weights, our method corresponds more closely to the definition of the voting game. Furthermore, it does not require large arrays and is therefore economical in terms of storage space. The proposed method has polynomial time complexity. We first consider a simple voting game in which all players have equal weight. We then extend our analysis to a game with two types of players: *large* and *small*, and finally generalise it to more than two player types.

4   All Players Have Equal Weight

Consider the game $\langle q; j, \ldots, j \rangle$ with m parties. Each party has j seats. If $q \leq j$, then there would be no need for players to form a coalition. On the other hand, if $q = mj$ ($m = |N|$ is the number of players), only the grand coalition is possible. Thus, the quota (q) satisfies the constraint: $(j + 1) \leq q \leq j(m - 1)$. A majority is decisive. The value of a coalition is one if the weight of the coalition is greater than or equal to q, otherwise it is zero.

---

[2] A swing for a player i is a pair of coalitions $(x, x \cup i)$ such that x is losing but $x \cup i$ is winning.

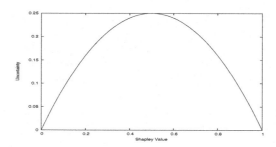

Fig. 1. Shapley value vs. uncertainty

Let φ denote the Shapley value for a player and β denote its uncertainty. Consider any one player. This player can join a coalition as the ith member where $1 \leq i \leq m$. However, the marginal contribution of the player is 1 only if it joins a coalition as the $\lceil q/j \rceil$th member. In all other cases, its marginal contribution is zero. Thus, the Shapley value for each player is $\varphi = 1/m$. We know from Definition 2, that a player's uncertainty is the variance of its marginal contribution. Hence, for each player, the uncertainty (denoted β) is:

$$\beta = (1 - \varphi)\varphi^2 + (1 - \varphi)^2 \varphi \tag{1}$$

Having expressed a player's uncertainty in terms of its Shapley value, we can now correlate them. To this end, Figure 1 shows how the uncertainty varies with the Shapley value. Since the Shapley value lies in the interval $[0, 1]$, Figure 1 plots uncertainty for this interval. As seen in the figure, uncertainty first increases as the Shapley value increases and then decreases. Uncertainty is maximum at $\varphi = 1/2$. The following sections analyse the voting game for the case where all parties do not have equal weight.

5 A Single Large Party

Consider a parliament in which there is one party with $j > 1$ seats, and m parties each with one seat. Thus, there are two types of players: *large* (with weight j) and *small* (with unit weight). The quota for this game is q, i.e., we have a game of the form $\langle q; j, 1, 1, \ldots, 1 \rangle$. The total number of players is $(m + 1)$. The value of a coalition is one if the weight of the coalition is greater than or equal to q, otherwise it is zero. Let φ_l denote the Shapley value for the large player and φ_s that for each small player. As we will show, the Shapley value of this game depends on whether or not q is greater than m. We therefore study the two possible cases: $q \leq m$ and $q > m$:

1. Consider $q \leq m$ first. The smallest possible value for q is $j + 1$. This is because, if $q \leq j$, then the large party can win the election on its own, without the need for a coalition. Thus, the quota for the game satisfies the relation $j + 1 \leq q \leq m + j - 1$. Also, the lower and upper limits for j are 2 and $(q - 1)$ respectively. The lower limit is 2 because the weight of the large party has to be greater than each small one. Furthermore, the weight of the large party cannot be greater than q, since in that case there would be no need for the large party to form a coalition. Recall that

for our voting game, a player's marginal contribution to a coalition has only two possible values: zero or one.

Consider the large party. This party can join a coalition as the ith member where i satisfies $1 \leq i \leq (m+1)$. However, the marginal contribution of the large party is one if it joins a coalition as the ith member where i satisfies the condition $(q-j+1) \leq i \leq q$. In all the remaining cases, its marginal contribution is zero. Thus, out of the total $(m+1)$ possible cases, its marginal contribution is one in j cases. Hence, the Shapley value of the large party is:

$$\varphi_l = j/(m+1) \tag{2}$$

Consider a small player. For a small player, the marginal contribution is one in two cases. First, if it joins a coalition (that already has the large party in it) as the $(q-j+1)$th member. Out of the $(m+1)!$ possible permutations, the number of permutations that satisfy this condition is $(q-j)(m-1)!$. Second, if it joins a coalition (consisting of $q-1$ small players) as the qth member. The number of permutations that satisfy this condition is $(m-q+1)(m-1)!$. Hence, the Shapley value of each small party is:

$$\varphi_s = (m-j+1)/m(m+1) \tag{3}$$

Using Definition 2, we get the uncertainty for the large party as:

$$\beta_l = (1-\varphi_l)\varphi_l{}^2 + \varphi_l(1-\varphi_l)^2 \tag{4}$$

For each small party, the uncertainty is:

$$\beta_s = (1-\varphi_s)\varphi_s{}^2 + \varphi_s(1-\varphi_s)^2 \tag{5}$$

2. Consider $q > m$. As before, the quota satisfies the relation $j+1 \leq q \leq m+j-1$. Also, $2 \leq j \leq (q-1)$. Consider the large party. As before, this party can join a coalition as the ith member where $1 \leq i \leq (m+1)$. However, its marginal contribution is one only if it joins as the ith member where $(q-j+1) \leq i \leq q$. Thus, out of all $(m+1)$ possible cases, its marginal contribution is one in j cases. Hence the Shapley value of the large party is:

$$\varphi_l = j/(m+1) \tag{6}$$

Consider a small player. Since $q > m$, a small player's marginal contribution is one in only one case: if it joins a coalition (that already has the large party in it) as the $(q-j+1)$th member. Out of the $(m+1)!$ possible permutations, the number of permutations that satisfy this condition is $(q-j)(m-1)!$. Hence the Shapley value of each small party is:

$$\varphi_s = (q-j)/m(m+1) \tag{7}$$

We get the uncertainty for the large party as:

$$\beta_l = (1-\varphi_l)\varphi_l{}^2 + \varphi_l(1-\varphi_l)^2 \tag{8}$$

For each small party, the uncertainty is:

$$\beta_s = (1-\varphi_s)\varphi_s{}^2 + \varphi_s(1-\varphi_s)^2 \tag{9}$$

Note that for each player, uncertainty (in Equations 4, 5, 8, and 9) has the same relation with Shapley value as that for Equation 1. Therefore, the plot in Figure 1 applies to Equations 4, 5, 8, and 9 as well. Thus, for the voting game with a single large player, each player's uncertainty first increases as its Shapley value increases. A player's uncertainty is at a maximum when its Shapley value is $1/2$. As the Shapley value increases further, uncertainty decreases.

6 Multiple Large and Multiple Small Parties

Consider a parliament in which there are m parties. The set of parties consists of km large parties and $(1 - k)m$ small parties where $0 \le k \le 1$. As before, each large party has j seats and each small one has one seat. The total seats in a coalition of size m is $mkj + (1 - k)m$. Thus, in a given population of players, the proportion of large players is k. Here, the quota (q) satisfies the constraint $(j + 1) \le q \le (kmj + (1 - k)m - 1)$. As before, the lower and upper limits for j are 2 and $(q - 1)$ respectively. Finally, the value of a coalition is one if it has q or more seats, otherwise it is zero.

A Randomised Method for the Shapley Value. In order to determine a player's Shapley value, we consider a sample from the above defined population of players. Let this sample be a large random coalition of size X. Let $\hat{k}$ denote the proportion of large players in this sample. Irrespective of how the population is distributed, the proportion of large players in a sample of size X is distributed approximately *normally*, with mean $\mu = k$ and variance $\nu = k(1 - k)/X$ (see [2] p435), i.e., we have:

$$\hat{k} \sim \mathcal{N}(k, \frac{k(1 - k)}{X}) \tag{10}$$

On the basis of Equation 10, we obtain the Shapley value as follows. Consider a large party. The marginal contribution of this party to the random sample is one if the weight of the sample is less than the quota (q) but is greater than or equal to $(q - j)$. Otherwise, its marginal contribution is zero. We know that the mean weight of the sample is $\hat{k}Xj + (1 - \hat{k})X$. Let a denote the proportion of large players that is required for the random sample to have mean weight $(q - j)$ (i.e., $a = (q - j - X)/(X(j - 1))$). Also, let b denote the proportion of large players that is required for the random sample to have mean weight $(q - \epsilon)$ (where ϵ is an infinitesimally small positive number) (i.e., $b = (q - X - \epsilon)/(X(j - 1))$). The expected marginal contribution of a large player to the random sample is the area under the curve defined by the normal distribution of Equation 10 between the limits a and b, i.e.,

$$\Delta_l^X = \frac{1}{\sqrt{(2\pi\nu)}} \int_a^b e^{-\frac{(x - \mu)^2}{2\nu}} dx \tag{11}$$

Therefore, a large player's Shapley value is:

$$\varphi_l = \frac{1}{m} \sum_{X=1}^m \Delta_l^X \tag{12}$$

and its uncertainty is:

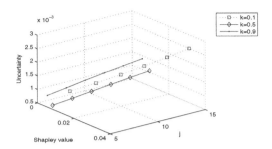

Fig. 2. A large player's Shapley value and uncertainty for a varying weight

$$\beta_l = \frac{1}{m} \sum_{X=1}^{m} (\Delta_l^X - \varphi_l)^2 \qquad (13)$$

Consider a small party. The marginal contribution of this party, when added to a sample, is one if the weight of the sample is less than the quota (q) but is greater than or equal to $(q - 1)$. Otherwise, its marginal contribution is zero. We know that the mean weight of the sample is $\hat{k}Xj + (1 - \hat{k})X$. Let c denote the proportion of large players that is required for the random sample to have mean weight $(q - 1)$ (i.e., $c = (q - 1 - X)/(X(j - 1))$). Also, let d denote the proportion of large players that is required for the random sample to have mean weight $q - \epsilon$ (i.e., $d = (q - X - \epsilon)/(X(j - 1))$). The marginal contribution of a small player is the area under the curve defined by the normal distribution of Equation 10 between the limits c and d, i.e.,

$$\Delta_s^X = \frac{1}{\sqrt{(2\pi\nu)}} \int_c^d e^{-\frac{(x-\mu)^2}{2\nu}} dx \qquad (14)$$

Therefore, for each small player, the Shapley value is:

$$\varphi_s = \frac{1}{m} \sum_{X=1}^{m} \Delta_s^X \qquad (15)$$

and the uncertainty is:

$$\beta_s = \frac{1}{m} \sum_{X=1}^{m} (\Delta_s^X - \varphi_s)^2 \qquad (16)$$

Theorem 1. *The time complexity of the above randomised method for determining the Shapley value is polynomial in the number of players. The inaccuracy of this method decreases with X and increases with ϵ.*

Proof. The time required to compute the marginal contribution of a player to a coalition of size i (for $1 \leq i \leq m$) is independent of the number of players (see Equations 11 and 14). A player can join the coalition as the ith member (for $1 \leq i \leq m$). The marginal contribution of a player is determined for each of these m possible cases. Therefore, the time taken to compute the Shapley value is $O(m)$.

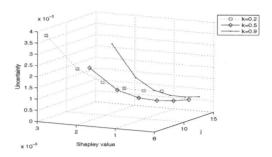

Fig. 3. A small player's Shapley value and uncertainty for a varying weight

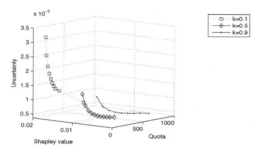

Fig. 4. A large player's Shapley value and uncertainty for a varying quota

The accuracy of the proposed method depends firstly on X. We know from [2], that the inaccuracy in Equation 10 decreases as X increases. Consequently, the inaccuracy of the proposed method decreases with X. The second source of inaccuracy is $\epsilon > 0$. It is obvious that the closer ϵ is to zero, the higher the accuracy. Thus, the inaccuracy of the proposed method increases with ϵ.   □

We now analyse the relation between the Shapley value and its uncertainty. From the above equations, we know that the Shapley value and its uncertainty depend on three parameters: the number of players (m), the weight associated with each large party (j), and the quota (q) for the game. Thus, we systematically vary these parameters in order to study the relation between a player's Shapley value and its uncertainty. These parameters are varied as follows. We varied k between 0.1 and 0.9. This is because we want multiple large and multiple small players, and for a large m, this range for k gives us that. For each k, we varied the parameters m, j, and q such that the following two constraints are satisfied:

C_1 No player can win an election on its own (i.e., $j < q$).
C_2 The maximum number of parties required to win an election is less than the total number of parties (i.e., $q < mkj + (1-k)m$).

Thus, for each k, we determined the Shapley value and its uncertainty for different values of j and q that satisfy constraints C_1 and C_2. This entire set of variations was repeated for different values of m.

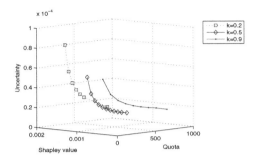

Fig. 5. A small player's Shapley value and uncertainty for a varying quota

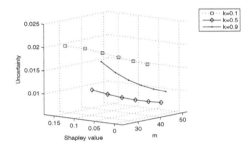

Fig. 6. A large player's Shapley value and uncertainty for a varying number of players

Although a player's Shapley value and its uncertainty vary with j, k, q, and m, the uncertainty was always found to increase with Shapley value. More specifically, for the constraints defined above, if the number of players is large (i.e., $m \geq 20$) and there are multiple large and multiple small players, we found the following relation. For each player, the uncertainty increases as its Shapley value increases (see Figures 2 to 7).

To begin, consider Figure 2. For $m = 200$ and $q = 200$, this is a plot of a large player's Shapley value and uncertainty for differing weights (i.e., different values for j). For each value of j, the figure shows the Shapley value and uncertainty for all k between 0.1 and 0.9. Likewise, Figures 3 is a plot for each small player.

For $m = 200$ and $j = 5$, Figure 4 is a plot for a large player's Shapley value and uncertainty for a varying quota. For each quota (i.e., q), the figure shows the Shapley value and uncertainty for all k between 0.1 and 0.9. Figure 5 is a plot for each small player.

Consider Figure 6. For $j = 5$ and $q = 25$, this is a plot of a large player's Shapley value and uncertainty for a varying number of players. For each m, the figure shows the Shapley value and uncertainty for k between 0.1 and 0.9. Likewise, Figures 7 is a plot for each small player.

Thus, for two player types and variations of j, k, q, and m that satisfy constraints C_1 and C_2, the uncertainty for each player (large or small) increases as its Shapley value increases. It is worth noting that in all the above figures, the number of players is at least 20, and there is more than one player of each type (i.e., $0.1 \leq k \leq 0.9$). For such games, the Shapley value of each player is less than 0.5. Thus, the relation between the

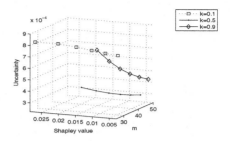

Fig. 7. A small player's Shapley value and uncertainty for a varying number of players

Shapley value and its uncertainty is the same as that for the left half of the curve of Figure 1 (i.e., for $\varphi < 0.5$).

7   More Than Two Player Types

Consider a voting game with more than two types of players. Let w_i denote the weight of player i. Thus, for m players and for quota q the game is of the form $\langle q; w_1, w_2, \ldots, w_m \rangle$. Consider a player population in which each individual player's weight has a *standard normal distribution*[3] $- \mathcal{N}(0, 1)$. Since this distribution allows negative weights, we transform this to $\mathcal{N}(4, 1)$ in order to get positive weights. We know from Definition 1, that the Shapley value for a player is the expectation (E) of its marginal contribution to a coalition that is chosen randomly. Thus, in order to determine the Shapley value for the above population of players (i.e., $\mathcal{N}(4, 1)$), we use the following rule from Sampling Theory (see [2] p417) that holds good for a normal distribution.

From a normal distribution (with mean μ and variance ν), if a sample of size m is drawn, then the sum of the weights of all m players in the sample has the distribution $\mathcal{N}(m\mu, m\nu)$. Thus, for the distribution ($\mathcal{N}(4, 1)$) we defined above, the sum of the weights of the players in a random sample of size m is given by the distribution $\mathcal{N}(4m, m)$. We use this rule to determine the Shapley value as follows.

A Randomised Method for the Shapley Value. For player i with weight w_i, let φ_i denote the Shapley value and β_i its uncertainty. Let X denote the size of a large random sample drawn from a population in which individual player weights have the distribution $\mathcal{N}(4, 1)$. The marginal contribution of player i to this random sample is one, if the total weight of the X players in the sample is greater than or equal to $q - w_i$ but less than q. Otherwise, its marginal contribution is zero. Thus, the expected marginal contribution of player i (denoted Δ_i^X) to the sample coalition is the area under the curve

---

[3] Note that in Section 6 when we dealt with two player types, there was no restriction on how the population was distributed. But for more than two player types, we assume that the population has a normal distribution. Thus, while the results of Section 6 are valid for two player types with any population distribution, the results of this section are valid for more than two player types that have a normal distribution.

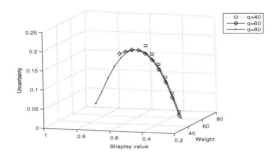

Fig. 8. Shapley value and uncertainty for a game of 20 players and a varying weight

defined by $\mathcal{N}(4X, X)$ in the interval $[q - w_i, q - \epsilon]$, i.e.,

$$\Delta_i^X = \frac{1}{\sqrt{(2\pi\nu)}} \int_{q-w_i}^{q-\epsilon} e^{-\frac{(x-4X)^2}{2X}} dx \qquad (17)$$

and its Shapley value is

$$\varphi_i = \frac{1}{n} \sum_{X=1}^{m} \Delta_i^X \qquad (18)$$

It is easy to verify that the time complexity of this method is $O(m)$. Also, the two sources of inaccuracy are X and ϵ. As in the case of the randomised method of Section 6, the inaccuracy decreases with X and increases with ϵ. The uncertainty associated with the Shapley value is:

$$\beta_i = \frac{1}{n} \sum_{X=1}^{m} (\varphi_i - \Delta_i^X)^2 \qquad (19)$$

For the case of more than two player types, we define the following constraints on q and w_i (for $1 \le i \le m$):

C_3 No player can win the game on its own (i.e., $(w_i < q)$ for $1 \le i \le m$).
C_4 The number of players required to win an election is less than m (i.e., the quota is less than $4m^2$).

We use the above equations and systematically vary parameters q, w_i (for $1 \le i \le m$), and m, such that constraints C_3 and C_4 are always satisfied, and determine the relation between the Shapley value and its uncertainty. These results are plotted in Figures 8 to 10. Consider Figure 8. For each quota, an individual player's weight is varied between 1 and $q - 1$. As seen in the figure, uncertainty first increases with Shapley value and then decreases. Figure 9 is a plot for $m = 50$ and Figure 10 that for $m = 100$. In all these figures, a player's uncertainty first increases with its Shapley value and then decreases. Thus, the relation between the Shapley value and its uncertainty is the same as that in Figure 1.

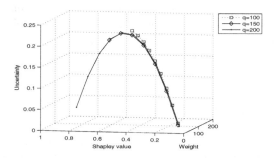

Fig. 9. Shapley value and uncertainty for a game of 50 players and a varying weight

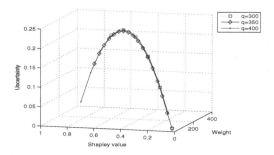

Fig. 10. Shapley value and uncertainty for a game of 100 players and a varying weight

To sum up, our study provides a basis for agents to compare games on the basis of both their Shapley values and the associated uncertainties. We showed that a player's uncertainty first increases with its Shapley value and then decreases. This implies that the uncertainty is at its minimum when the value is at its maximum, and that agents do not always have to compromise value in order to reduce uncertainty. This is because, if the Shapley value lies in the range $[0.5..1]$, then an increase in value is associated with a decrease in uncertainty.

8   Conclusions and Future Work

Although the Shapley value provides a unique solution that gives an indication of an agent's power relative to that of others, it also has an element of uncertainty associated with it. Given this, the uncertainty is an additional dimension that an agent should take into account for evaluating its prospects of playing a game. Against this background, this paper has analysed the relation between the Shapley value and its uncertainty for the weighted voting game. Since the problem of determining the Shapley value is #P-complete, we first presented a randomised method with polynomial time complexity. Using this method, we computed the Shapley value and correlated it with its uncertainty. Our study shows that a player's uncertainty first increases with its Shapley value and then decreases. Although our present work provides an analysis for the case where different players have different weights, the distribution of weights was assumed to be normal. In future, we will generalise our results, by extending this analysis to other types of distribution functions. Also, we will carry out the same analysis for other commonly occurring games like the production-economy and the market-economy.

References

1. X. Deng and C. H. Papadimitriou. On the complexity of cooperative solution concepts. *Mathematics of Operations Research*, 19(2):257–266, 1994.
2. A. Francis. *Advanced Level Statistics*. Stanley Thornes Publishers, 1979.
3. J. C. Harsanyi. *Rational behavior and bargaining equilibrium in games and social situations*. Cambridge University Press, 1977.
4. V. Kargin. Uncertainty of the Shapley value. *International Game Theory Review, (To appear)*, 2004.
5. I. Mann and L. S. Shapley. The bargaining problem. Technical report, The RAND Corporation, Santa Monica, 1960.
6. I. Mann and L. S. Shapley. The bargaining problem. Technical report, The RAND Corporation, Santa Monica, 1962.
7. M. J. Osborne and A. Rubinstein. *A Course in Game Theory*. The MIT Press, 1994.
8. C. H. Papadimitriou. *Computational Complexity*. Addison Wesley Longman, 1994.
9. J. S. Rosenschein and G. Zlotkin. *Rules of Encounter*. MIT Press, 1994.
10. A. E. Roth. The Shapley value as a von Neumann-Morgenstern utility. *Econometrica*, 45(3):657–664, 1977.
11. A. E. Roth. The expected utility of playing a game. In A. E. Roth, editor, *The Shapley value*, pages 51–70. University of Cambridge Press, Cambridge, 1988.
12. T. Sandholm and V. Lesser. Coalitions among computationally bounded agents. *Artificial Intelligence Journal*, 94(1):99–137, 1997.
13. L. S. Shapley. A value for n-person games. In A. E. Roth, editor, *The Shapley value*, pages 31–40. University of Cambridge Press, Cambridge, 1988.
14. O. Shehory and S. Kraus. Methods for task allocation via agent coalition formation. *Artificial Intelligence Journal*, 101(2):165–200, 1998.

An Analysis of the 2004 Supply Chain Management Trading Agent Competition

Christopher Kiekintveld, Yevgeniy Vorobeychik, and Michael P. Wellman

University of Michigan
Artificial Intelligence Laboratory
Ann Arbor, MI 48109-2110 USA
ckiekint@umich.edu

Abstract. We present and analyze results from the 2004 Trading Agent Competition supply chain management scenario. We identify behavioral differences between the agents that contributed to their performance in the competition. In the market for components, strategic early procurement remained an important factor despite rule changes from the previous year. We present a new experimental analysis of the impact of the rule changes on incentives for early procurement. In the finals, a novel strategy designed to block other agent's access to suppliers at the start of the game was pivotal. Some agents did not respond effectively to this strategy and were badly hurt by their inability to get crucial components. Among the top three agents, average selling prices in the market for finished goods were the decisive difference. Our analysis shows that supply and demand were key factors in determining overall market prices, and that some agents were more adept than others at exploiting advantageous market conditions.

1 Introduction

The Trading Agent Competition (TAC) provides an international forum for researching the design and analysis of automated trading agents. A new scenario in supply chain management (TAC/SCM) debuted in 2003 [1]. We will not describe the scenario here, but direct the reader to the game specification for details [2]. Studying the outcomes of these competitions is a valuable exercise that helps us to better understand the strengths and weaknesses of current approaches. Here we present and analyze results from the final round of the 2004 tournament. Our primary objective is to determine the important behavioral factors that distinguished the agents and contributed to their relative performance.

We start by presenting the main results from the 2004 finals. In Section 3 we consider procurement strategies. We discuss the role of strategic early procurement, and present new experimental analysis of the effect of the rule changes on early procurement. A novel blocking strategy was used in the final round, and we discuss the problems this cause for some of the agents. In Section 4 we consider the PC sales market. Agents had widely varying average selling prices (ASPs) for PCs, and this was a deciding factor between the top three agents. Further analysis identifies four factors strongly correlated with market ASPs, and reveals that the agents differed in their ability to target profitable markets. We conclude with a summary of the strengths and weaknesses of each agent.

H. La Poutré, N. Sadeh, and S. Janson (Eds.): AMEC and TADA 2005, LNAI 3937, pp. 99–112, 2006.

Table 1. Average scores and breakdowns from the TAC-04/SCM final round (in millions of dollars). Margin is the raw difference between revenue and supply costs.

Agent	Score	Revenue	Supplies	Margin	Storage	Penalty	Interest
FreeAgent	10.28	99.06	-80.94	18.12	-7.14	0	-0.61
Mr.UMBC	8.65	94.14	-76.49	17.65	-8.39	0	-0.61
UMTac-04	6.52	83.59	-67.21	16.37	-8.97	0	-0.88
Botticelli	0.44	25.83	-23.74	2.09	-0.39	-1.16	0
Deep Maize	-5.12	56.24	-48.32	7.92	-9.59	-2.49	-0.95
SouthamptonSCM	-10.41	71.37	-69.25	2.12	-11.34	0	-1.20

2   2004 Final Round Results

The 2004 competition started with qualifying and seeding rounds lasting two weeks each; these rounds were used primarily for development and testing. The top 24 agents participated in a three day tournament at AAMAS-04. A quarterfinal round eliminated 12 agents and a semi-final round eliminated 6 more. The surviving 6 agents played 14 games in the final round. Here we focus on analyzing the results of the final round, as it represents direct competition between the strongest agents. In Table 1 we see that the top three agents were very close, with scores in a narrow range of $4M. These agents had much higher raw margins than the bottom three agents, and generally higher transaction volume. Among the top three, small differences in storage costs and raw margins determined the ordering. SouthamptonSCM had supply volume comparable to the top finishers, but high storage costs and low revenue indicate possible sales problems. Botticelli and Deep Maize both transacted substantially less volume than the top finishers.

3   Agent Procurement in Supplier Markets

3.1   A History of Early Procurement

Understanding the market for PC components TAC-04/SCM is aided by discussion of results from the first competition. During the early rounds of the 2003 competition agent designers noticed that there were strong incentives to procure large quantities of components on the very first day of the simulation, day 0.[1] By the end of the seeding rounds most agents were making very large component purchases at the start of the game, before any information about customer demand was available. In games with low demand this could lead to large losses for all agents, as in one semi-final heat where all agents purchased aggressively and finished with negative average profits. In the other semi-final heat and the final round, Deep Maize surprised the field with a novel *preemptive* strategy that blocked the other agents from making large day-0 purchases.[2]

---

[1] Available supplier capacity was at a maximum, and prices were at a minimum.

[2] Essentially, the agent requested most of the supplier capacity for the entire game and the suppliers reserved it until the next day. Any requests considered after this request generated useless offers. The agent accepted a partial quantity from this request.

Post-tournament analysis showed that aggressive early procurement was a rational strategy despite the potential for negative profits, but that the presence of a preemptive agent could potentially improve profits for the entire field by knocking the agents out of the undesirable equilibrium [3].

While these strategic interactions were interesting, the extreme emphasis on early procurement detracted from other research problems, including factory scheduling [4], optimizing customer bids [5], and dynamically managing inventory in response to new information. The random order in which suppliers considered requests also introduced a "lottery effect," where these random outcomes had a strong effect on the overall outcome of the game [6]. Several changes were made to the specification for the 2004 competition; these were intended to reduce the incentives for day-0 procurement. The changes included modifications to the supplier pricing policy, segmentation of the customer markets, and the addition of storage costs.

3.2   Early Procurement in TAC-04/SCM

During the TAC-04/SCM qualifying round day-0 procurement remained very high, despite the rule changes. In response, the GameMaster increased storage costs fivefold for the remaining rounds. Even this did not dampen the day-0 purchasing; the number of components ordered based on day-0 requests actually *increased* by 14% from 2003 to 2004 (in games with no blocking strategies). This sequence of events raises questions about the impact of the rule changes (especially storage costs) on agent behavior. Do higher storage costs actually reduce incentives for early procurement, as suggested by intuitive arguments? Was the high level of early procurement observed in TAC-04/SCM a rational response to the new rules? Could any level of storage costs have reduced day-0 procurement to an acceptable level?

We address these questions with a systematic exploration of the relationship between storage costs and day-0 procurement. Conceptually, each setting of storage costs induces a different game between the agents. Game theory suggests that stable profiles (e.g. Nash equilibria) are likely to be played when rational, self-interested agents compete in games. In general, we model the strategic interactions between a mechanism designer and participants as a two-stage game. The designer moves first by setting the mechanism parameter θ (e.g. storage costs), and all the participants observe θ and move simultaneously thereafter (e.g. selecting a day-0 procurement quantity). We refer to game between the participants in the second stage as the game Γ_θ *induced* by θ:

$$\Gamma_\theta = [I, \{S_i\}, \{u_i(s, \theta)\}].$$

Here I is the set of participants, S_i the set of strategies for each participant, and $u_i(\cdot)$ the utility function for each participant. Suppose the goal of the designer is to optimize some welfare function $W(\cdot)$. Let $\{s^*(\theta)\}$ be the set of Nash equilibria of Γ_θ. Here we define $W(s^*(\theta), \theta) = \inf\{W(s, \theta) : s \in \{s^*(\theta)\}\}$. Alternatively, if one has a probability distribution over the Nash equilibria given θ, it may be natural to take the expectation of W instead: $W(s^*(\theta), \theta) = E_{s \in s^*}[W(s, \theta)].$[3] If there are no Nash equilibria of Γ_θ (a

---

[3] For example, such a distribution could be derived from analysis of evolutionary dynamics, as in [7].

possibility for infinite games), let $\bar{s}^*$ be the set of strategy profiles with the lowest benefit to deviation for any agent and define $W(s^*(\theta), \theta) = \inf\{W(s, \theta) : s \in \{\bar{s}^*(\theta)\}\}$. The designer's optimization problem is then

$$\max_{\theta \in \Theta} W(s^*(\theta), \theta).$$

To analyze the effect of storage costs in the TAC/SCM game we consider the correspondence between storage costs and equilibrium outcomes. The aggregate quantity of day-0 procurement in these stable profiles yields an estimate of the behavior we would expect to see in actual games. In the TAC/SCM domain, the designer's problem is to minimize aggregate day-0 procurement. In the notation above, the designer maximizes $W(s^*(\theta), \theta)$, defined by $\mathbf{I}\{\sup\{\phi(s^*(\theta))\} \leq \alpha\}$, where the aggregation function $\phi(s) = \sum_{i=1}^{6} s_i$, s_i is each agent's day-0 procurement choice, and α is a desired cap on aggregate day-0 procurement.

The full strategy space in TAC/SCM is very complex, but for the purposes of this analysis we define a restricted space that allows agent to select only day-0 purchase quantity multiplier. We implemented this strategy space by parameterizing our tournament agent, **Deep Maize**, with a multiplier on its day-0 requests.[4] Players select a multiplier from the set $\{0, 0.3, 0.6, \ldots, 1.5\}$. This strategy space defines the induced game Γ_θ. The payoffs for this game are not directly known, but we can obtain estimates by simulating games on the TAC server. We must do this for each setting of storage costs we wish to investigate, and collecting the samples is very time-consuming. Fortunately, the questions we would like to answer are high-level and we can gather evidence about them using approximate methods. Instead of requiring exact equilibrium solutions, we aim to find regions of the profile space that are likely to be stable using the notion of ϵ-Nash equilibrium, where agents cannot gain more than a small benefit ϵ by deviating to a different strategy. We also use two different techniques to approximate sets of stable profiles without sampling the full profile space.

The first method approximates payoff functions of the game using supervised learning. We tried three different learning techniques from those introduced in [8]: quadratic regression (QR), locally weighted average (LWA), and locally weighted linear regression (LWLR). For quadratic regression, it is possible to directly compute equilibria of the learned game analytically. For the other methods, we applied replicator dynamics [9] to a discrete approximation of the learned game. The second method uses directed search to find stable profiles. Given a partial game matrix we can compute a bound on the epsilon for each profile that we have sample data for; this bound is the maximum benefit for deviating to any profile in the data set. The current set of profiles with the best ϵ-bounds is the set of *candidate equilibria*. We employed a "best-first" search that always samples unexplored deviations from a candidate equilibria. The idea is to confirm or refute the stability of promising individual profiles without requiring the full game matrix to be sampled. A limitation of this approach is that it cannot rule out the existence of additional equilibria in the set of profiles that have not been sampled.

We gathered data for storage costs in the set $\{0, 50, 100, 150, 200\}$. An initial data set was generated by sampling 10 randomly generated profiles for each storage cost

---

[4] **Deep Maize** requested a total of 11800 components for each combination of supplier and product, spread out over different due dates.

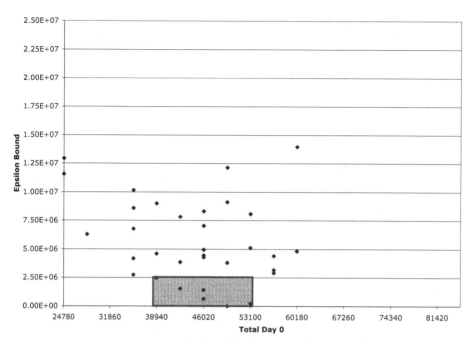

Fig. 1. Profile data for storage costs of 100% annually. The plot shows the ϵ-bound for explored profiles against the aggregate level of day-0 purchasing (per supplier/component) for all strategies in the profile. The dark box represents the region for which there are known profiles with ϵ-bounds less than $2.5M.

setting (playing 5–10 games for each profile). We then performed 12–32 iterations of the best-first search procedure for each setting of storage cost. We ran a total of 2670 games over 6 months, exploring approximately 10% of the total profile space for these discrete parameter and strategy settings.

Figure 1 shows a plot of the data for annual storage costs of 100% (the mean storage cost setting from the 2004 tournament). Each point represents the ϵ-bound for a sampled profile, plotted against the aggregate day-0 procurement in the profile. To calibrate, a total procurement of 35400 (total multiplier 3.0) corresponds to an expected commitment of approximately 1/3 of the total supplier capacity for the entire game. Note that many different profiles have the same aggregate procurement. The dark box shows the region with the most stable (lowest-ϵ) profiles. This region yields a predicted range for the total day-0 procurement induced by this storage cost setting.

Figure 2 shows results for a range of settings of the storage cost parameter. The SearchMin and SearchMax lines correspond to the endpoints of the region defined like the gray region in Figure 1. The other three lines indicate approximate equilibria found by the three learning methods, trained on the initial 10 randomly-generated profiles for each storage cost setting. It is encouraging that the results obtained using very different methods (learning and directed search) have the same qualitative structure. This experimental evidence supports the initial intuition that day-0 procurement should decrease with higher storage costs; all of the methods show this relationship. There is

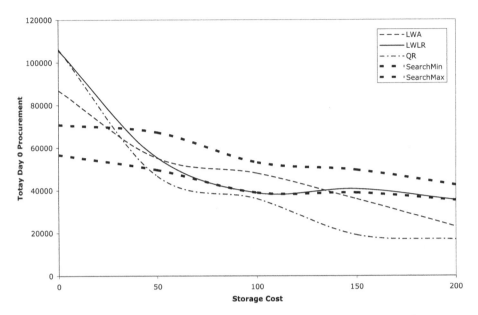

Fig. 2. Several different estimates for the correspondence between storage costs and aggregate day-0 purchases in equilibrium. Estimates from three learning methods are shown, along with an interval estimate from the best-first search algorithm. SearchMin is the minimum day-0 level for a profile with ϵ-bound less than 2.5M, and SearchMax is the corresponding maximum.

also evidence that high levels of day-0 procurement were a rational response by agents to the new specification. The minimum prediction of any method for the storage cost setting used in the final round was approximately 38000, and the maximum was considerably higher at approximately 60000. The observed levels during the tournament were somewhat above even the high estimate given by our methods, but it seems clear that undesirably high levels of early purchasing are rational.

We also considered whether any setting of storage costs could have resulted in a desirable outcome for day-0 purchasing. To test this, we attempted to find a setting that would yield equilibrium outcomes with aggregate procurement less than 23600 (still higher than we would want in practice). Linear extrapolation of the SearchMax line predicts that this should occur for a storage cost setting of 320%. However, further simulations resulted in an estimated outcome range of 31860-38940 for this profile, only slightly lower than the estimates for storage costs of 200%. There appears to be very little benefit to additional increases of storage costs beyond 200%. Furthermore, agent profits were almost always negative for storage costs of 320%, so additional increases would be undesirable even if day-0 procurement could eventually be reduced to acceptable levels.

Our analysis suggests that the changes to the game rules did have the desired effect to some extent, but that this effect was not as large as anticipated. In games as complex as TAC/SCM it is very difficult to asses the effects of potential rule changes. In principle, the techniques used here provide ways of gathering additional data to assess the impact of design decisions in games with important strategic interactions.

Table 2. A breakdown of the percentages of CPU and non-CPU components ordered in response to requests sent on days 0, 1, and 2+, with respect to the total quantity ordered by each agent

Agent	CPU 0	CPU 1	CPU 2+	Other 0	Other 1	Other 2+
FreeAgent	0.61	0.05	0.34	0	0.05	0.95
Mr.UMBC	0.57	0.16	0.27	0.29	0.47	0.24
UMTac-04	0.85	0.15	0.00	0.39	0.60	0.01
Botticelli	0	0	1	0	0	1
Deep Maize	0.90	0.01	0.09	0.46	0.02	0.52
SouthamptonSCM	0.81	0	0.19	0.54	0.38	0.07

3.3   A Blocking Strategy in TAC-04/SCM

The overall levels of day-0 procurement observed in TAC-04/SCM were similar to those observed in 2003, so it is perhaps not surprising that a blocking strategy again proved pivotal in the final round. However, the specific preemptive tactic employed by **Deep Maize** in 2003 was no longer useful due to changes in the supplier's pricing formula. The **Deep Maize** preemptive strategy relied on accepting partial fulfillment offers at low prices to purchase some cheap components on day 0, while still blocking some of the opponent's requests. In the 2004 rules these partial offers have very high prices, so a blocking agent must either pay high prices or try to purchase components later, despite a bad reputation with suppliers.

Blocking and purchasing later is a somewhat risky strategy, but **FreeAgent** used this tactic in the final round. [5] The strategy had a novel twist that mitigated some of the risks: **FreeAgent** only blocked requests for non-CPU components and purchased large quantities of CPU components on day 0 along with the other agents. This is significant because CPUs cost much more than any of the other components (on average, the CPU represents half of the total cost of components for a PC). The strategy locked in relatively low prices for the components with the highest base prices, but risked paying relatively higher prices for the cheaper components in order to disrupt the other agents' procurement strategies. Table 2 illustrates the effect of this blocking strategy on the distribution of purchases over the game for each agent. Most of the agents, including **FreeAgent**, procured the majority of their CPU components on day 0 to take advantage of the low prices. **FreeAgent** used its requests for "other" (non-CPU) components on day 0 to block opponents' requests. Consequently, it ordered no components of these types on day 0, and the quantities purchased by the other agents were reduced.

One of the crucial disparities between the agents was how they reacted to the new market environment created by **FreeAgent**'s blocking strategy. **Mr.UMBC**, **UMTac-04**, and **SouthamptonSCM** had backup strategies that procured large quantities of components again on the next simulation day. Since most of the supplier capacity was uncommitted at this point, the agents secured reasonably low prices for these backup

---

[5] **Mr.UMBC** also submitted large blocking requests for some types non-CPU components. However, these RFQs were relatively low in the priority ordering assigned by the agent and likely did not come into play.

Table 3. Average total quantities ordered and prices paid for components

Agent	Ordered	CPU Price	Other Price
FreeAgent	40199	0.60	0.88
Mr.UMBC	42557	0.61	0.71
UMTac-04	40738	0.56	0.61
Botticelli	11598	0.74	0.70
Deep Maize	26902	0.58	0.65
SouthamptonSCM	39350	0.58	0.71

Table 4. Inventory management statistics. CPU/Other is the ratio of CPUs ordered to the number of other components ordered. The ratio needed to produce PCs is 0.33 (1 CPU:3 Other).

Agent	CPU/Other	Unsold CPU	Unsold Other	Daily Inv.	Ave. Delivery Day
FreeAgent	0.34	3516	5956	30677	95
Mr.UMBC	0.31	713	15769	48877	85
UMTac-04	0.33	1832	2588	41975	94
Botticelli	0.33	475	1497	1317	160
Deep Maize	0.40	12153	10200	31026	88
SouthamptonSCM	0.33	13651	43922	67147	69

orders and were in much the same situation as if they had ordered all of their components on day 0 as originally planned. Botticelli made large day-0 requests like the rest of the agents, but chose not to accept any of the offers and waited until much later in the game to purchase supplies and start production. FreeAgent and Deep Maize did not come back with large requests immediately, but purchased additional components in smaller chunks throughout the rest of the game.

Additional details about overall procurement and pricing are in Table 3. Four of the agents (including the top three) purchased approximately the same number of components overall; Botticelli and Deep Maize purchased significantly fewer components. Prices paid for CPUs are comparable for all agents except Botticelli, which did not procure any cheap CPUs on day 0. The prices paid for non-CPU components show more disparity. UMTac-04 paid the lowest prices due to a large day-1 purchase. FreeAgent paid *very* high prices for non-CPU components. This stands in contrast to the much lower prices paid by Deep Maize, despite the similar approach these agents took in purchasing additional inventory over the duration of the game. FreeAgent seems to have disregarded the prices paid for these components, in part to compensate for its strategic maneuver on day 0.

3.4   Inventory Management

Agents' procurement strategies had important implications for inventory management. The two lowest-scoring agents in particular were crippled by difficulties in managing inventory that are at least partially attributable to FreeAgent's blocking tactic. There are a number of striking numbers in table 4, which lists inventory management statistics. The first is Botticelli's very late average delivery date for components. This agent effectively sat out most of the game after declining early component purchases. Equally

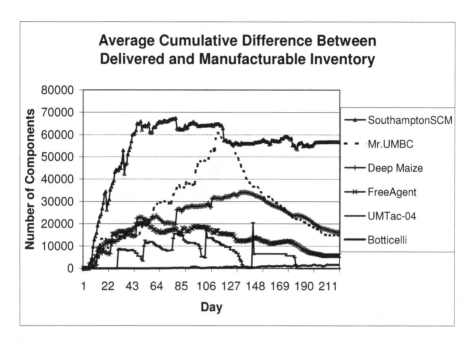

Fig. 3. The average cumulative difference between components delivered and components that could potentially be assembled into finished PCs for each agent. High differences indicate that the agent is missing one or more complementary components (e.g. the agent has no memory components). The ordering in the legend is the same as the visual ordering in the plot.

striking are the very large unsold inventories held by Deep Maize and Southampton-SCM at the end of the game. Mr.UMBC also had a substantial unsold inventory, but this inventory was almost exclusively composed of much cheaper non-CPU components.

Figure 3 gives a more detailed breakdown of inventory management over the course of the game. The plot shows the difference between the number of components delivered and the number that could possibly be assembled for sale, emphasizing management of the complementarities between components. The bulk of the unsold inventories could not have been sold due to not having the right combinations of components. The unsold inventory problem was not very severe for Mr.UMBC since it was composed of cheaper components; this may actually have been a deliberate hedge against production down time.

Deep Maize and SouthamptonSCM both purchased large quantities of some components, but had difficulties obtaining enough complementary components to allow full production. SouthamptonSCM had large differences in the orders it placed early on, and did not compensate for these disparities later in the game. The imbalances for Deep Maize were not quite as large as those for SouthamptonSCM, and it was able to mitigate them to some extent by procuring additional components throughout the game. However, the agent was very selective about the prices paid for these additional components (note the low price paid for non-CPUs from Table 3). That FreeAgent was very successful with a similar strategy that paid much higher prices for these

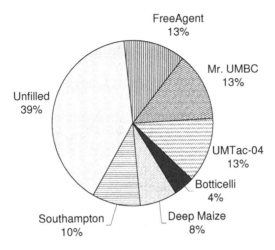

Fig. 4. Market share in the SCM finals

components suggests that Deep Maize was probably too selective about prices for certain key components.

A final point about inventory management is that FreeAgent had a substantially lower average daily inventory than the next two agents, despite comparable overall quantities purchased. This appears to be the result of ordering non-CPU inventory over many days, which allowed the agent to divide quantities into more requests and distribute them move evenly over time. This gave FreeAgent some advantage in storage costs over these two agents, and helped to offset the higher prices paid by the agent for non-CPU components.

4   Agent Sales Behavior

4.1   Basic Sales Data

We now attend to activity in the PC sales market, starting with overall market share in Figure 4 (raw sales numbers are listed in Table 5). Market shares mostly parallel the total quantities of components ordered, as given in Table 3. The major exception is SouthamptonSCM, which purchased similar quantities to the top three agents but took a much smaller share of the customer market. This reflects the large amount of unsold inventory for this agent noted in the previous section. We also note that almost 40% of the total customer demand was unmet. Some of this is unavoidable since agents must build inventory at the start of the game before they can sell PCs. However, there does seem to be significant opportunity for agents to expand market share by filling unmet demand.

More detailed information on sales activity is given in Table 5. The top three agents sold very nearly the same number of PCs, and won an almost identical fraction of their bids. However, they had strikingly different average selling prices (ASPs). This difference in ASPs is one of the major reasons that the three agents finished in the order

Table 5. Customer sales statistics for each agent

Agent	PCs sold	PCs bid on	Percent Won	ASP
FreeAgent	54660	166293	0.33	0.90
Mr.UMBC	56748	172517	0.33	0.83
UMTac-04	56341	167746	0.34	0.74
Botticelli	17290	28581	0.60	0.81
Deep Maize	33166	124485	0.27	0.92
SouthamptonSCM	41798	93936	0.44	0.85

they did. That the three agents bid on almost identical fractions of the market and win similar fractions of bids suggests that this difference in ASPs is due to targeting different types of markets. Deep Maize had the highest ASP of any agent and the lowest winning percentage, suggesting that this agent made systematically higher offers to customers. Conversely, Botticelli won a very high fraction of its bids with a relatively low ASP, suggesting systematically lower bids. SouthamptonSCM won a high fraction of bids with mid-range ASPs, but bid on a much smaller fraction of the market than the other three agents with similar component purchases.

4.2   Market Behavior

To better understand why the agents had different ASPs, we consider features that differentiate markets along the dimension of ASP. For this analysis we consider a "market" to be the set of customer requests for a PC type on a simulation day. We identify four factors that are strongly correlated with overall market ASPs. Figure 5 shows these relationships as scatter plots, with superimposed lines representing binned averages. Except for simulation day, all of these factors are measures of supply and demand motivated by basic economic principles. The simulation day is important primarily due to start- and end-game effects.

Plot 5(a) shows the relationship between prices and simulation day. Prices start very high early in the game as agents build inventory and decrease over time. At the end of the game prices can fall very low as agents try to recover some value for excess inventory. The second factor, shown in 5(b), is market demand (i.e., total quantity requested). Prices increase as demand increases, with any demand level less than 100 occasionally subject to very low ASPs. Plot 5(c) is a measure of bid density calculated this by summing the number of bids for each individual PC and dividing by the total number of PCs requested. ASPs fall approximately linearly as bid density increases. ASPs also fall approximately linearly as manufacturer PC inventory increases, as seen in 5(d).

We ran linear regressions to test the strength of these relationships with ASPs (all of the plots suggest a linear relationship, so this is a reasonably approximation). The individual R^2 values were 0.29 for simulation day, 0.13 for market demand, 0.42 for bid density, and 0.44 for PC inventory. A multiple regression using all four factors yields an R^2 value of 0.65, with all coefficients significantly different from 0. We could certainly improve this model by considering additional factors (e.g. reserve prices, lead times, smoothed market demand). However, a simple linear fit to these four variables is

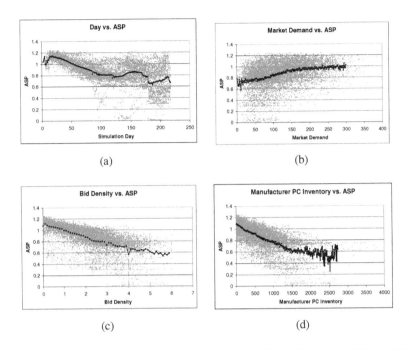

(a)   (b)

(c)   (d)

Fig. 5. Plots showing the relationships between four variables and market ASPs in SCM-04. 10000 randomly selected points are shown for each variable (out of approximately 45000 total). The dark lines on each plot are the average ASPs at each value for discrete variables or within small bins for continuous variables.

sufficient to explain 65% of the variance in ASPs. This surprisingly powerful result that speaks to the power of the basic forces of supply and demand in the SCM markets.

We take this analysis a step further by considering the features of the markets that individual agents bid and sold PCs in. Table 6 gives average values for each of these four factors for each of the PCs sold and PCs bid on by each agent. The two agents with the highest ASPs were **Deep Maize** and **FreeAgent**. These agents sold PCs earlier in the game, in markets with the lowest PC inventory, highest demand, and low bid densities; all of these are associated with high market ASPs. **UMTac-04** had the lowest ASP by a wide margin. This agent sold later than most agents in markets with low demand and high PC inventory levels; all of these are associated with low market ASPs. The other agents have mid-range ASPs, and seem to have a mix of factors working for and against them. For instance, **SouthamptonSCM** sells exceptionally early, but in lower demand markets with relatively high inventory levels.

5   Conclusions: Agent Performance

We have presented and analyzed data on many aspects of the TAC-04/SCM final round, which has revealed interesting details about the different strategies employed by the agents. We can now offer a reasonably compelling explanation for why the agents fin-

Table 6. Average values of four factors correlated with market ASPs given for the PCs each agent won and bid on. Day is the simulation day, Demand is market demand, Bids is the bid density (defined in text), and PC inv is average manufacturer PC inventory.

Agent	Sold, Day	Bid, Day	Sold, Demand	Bid, Demand
FreeAgent	122	130	160	147
Mr.UMBC	124	129	150	148
UMTac-04	135	126	143	140
Botticelli	163	164	153	146
Deep Maize	122	123	168	158
SouthamptonSCM	105	112	143	136

Agent	Sold, Bids	Bid, Bids	Sold, PC Inv	Bid, PC Inv
FreeAgent	2.89	3.39	588	832
Mr.UMBC	2.58	3.26	761	813
UMTac-04	2.90	3.48	933	925
Botticelli	3.75	3.99	730	822
Deep Maize	2.40	3.35	551	675
SouthamptonSCM	3.38	3.71	836	939

ished in the order they did. The following is a brief synopsis of the important points about each agent, starting from the lowest-scoring agent and working up.

SouthamptonSCM bought far more components than it sold, leaving it with large amounts of unsold inventory and high storage costs. The agent had reasonably high ASPs and winning percentages in the customer market, but bid on a very low fraction of customer orders. The underlying problem was that the agent was not successful at getting all of the complementary components needed for production of finished products.

Deep Maize had very high ASPs in the customer market. However, it also had inventory management problems with complementary components. The agent was often left with insufficient non-CPU inventory to manufacture and sell aggressively, and had large numbers of unsold CPU components. The agent paid low average prices for non-CPU components, so it may have been too selective about prices for these components.

Botticelli did not make any supply purchases at the start of the game, and did not enter the market substantially until very late in the game. By this time there was too little time remaining in the game and the customer market was too competitive to allow for large profits.

UMTac-04 compared favorably to FreeAgent on virtually every metric we considered except average daily inventory and customer market ASP. This agent had the lowest ASP of any agent. It sold later in the game in markets with relatively low demand, high PC inventory; all of these factors correlate with low market prices.

Mr UMBC had a better ASP than UMTac-04, but lower than FreeAgent. It sold in lower demand and higher inventory markets than FreeAgent. This agent also had a sizable amount of non-CPU inventory unsold at the end of the game and higher daily inventories than FreeAgent.

FreeAgent made some interesting strategic choices for the final round. It opted to block other agents only on non-CPU inventory, while acquiring CPUs at low prices on day 0. It then purchased additional components at very high prices during the rest of the game. It was able to compensate to some extent for these high prices through more evenly spaced deliveries of components and lower resulting storage costs. The major strength of this agent compared to the others was an ability to consistently sell high volumes of PCs throughout game at high prices by targeting profitable markets.

Acknowledgments

We thank SICS and the rest of the TAC/SCM organizers and participants for another interesting opportunity to analyze trading agent strategy. This work was supported in part by NSF grant IIS-0205435 and the DARPA REAL strategic reasoning program.

References

1. Arunachalam, R., Sadeh, N.M.: The supply chain trading agent competition. Electronic Commerce Research and Applications **4** (2005) 63–81
2. Arunachalam, R., Sadeh, N., Eriksson, J., Finne, N., Janson, S.: The supply chain management game for the trading agent competition 2004. Technical Report CMU-CS-04-107, Carnegie Mellon University (2004)
3. Wellman, M.P., Estelle, J., Singh, S., Vorobeychik, Y., Kiekintveld, C., Soni, V.: Strategic interactions in a supply chain game. Computational Intelligence **21** (2005) 1–26
4. Benisch, M., Greenwald, A., Naroditskiy, V., Tschantz, M.: A stochastic programming approach to scheduling in TAC SCM. In: Fifth ACM Conference on Electronic Commerce. (2004)
5. Pardoe, D., Stone, P.: TacTex-03: A supply chain management agent. SIGecom Exchanges **4**(3) (2004) 19–28
6. Ketter, W., Kryzhnyaya, E., Damer, S., McMillan, C.: Analysis and design of supply-driven strategies in TAC SCM. In: AAMAS-04 Workshop on Trading Agent Design and Analysis. (2004)
7. Walsh, W.E., Das, R., Tesauro, G., Kephard, J.O.: Analyzing complex strategic interactions in multi-agent systems. In: AAAI-02 Workshop on Game Theoretic and Decision Theoretic Agents. (2002)
8. Vorobeychik, Y., Wellman, M.P., Singh, S.: Learning payoff functions in infinite games. In: Ninth International Joint Conference on Artificial Intelligence. (2005) 977–982
9. Friedman, D.: Evolutionary games in economics. Econometrica **59**(3) (1991) 637–666

Identifying and Forecasting Economic Regimes in TAC SCM

Wolfgang Ketter, John Collins, Maria Gini, Alok Gupta⋆, and Paul Schrater

Department of Computer Science and Engineering
⋆Department of Information and Decision Sciences
University of Minnesota, Minneapolis, MN 55455, USA
{ketter, jcollins, gini, schrater}@cs.umn.edu,
agupta@csom.umn.edu

Abstract. We present methods for an autonomous agent to identify dominant market conditions, such as over-supply or scarcity, and to forecast market changes. We show that market conditions can be characterized by distinguishable statistical patterns that can be learned from historic data and used, together with real-time observable information, to identify the current market regime and to forecast market changes. We use a Gaussian Mixture Model to represent the probabilities of market prices and, by clustering these probabilities, we identify different economic regimes. We show that the regimes so identified have properties that correlate with market factors that are not directly observable. We then present methods to predict regime changes. We validate our methods by presenting experimental results obtained with data from the Trading Agent Competition for Supply Chain Management.

1 Introduction

In the Trading Agent Competition for Supply-Chain Management [1] (TAC SCM), six autonomous agents attempt to maximize profit by selling personal computers they assemble from parts, which they must buy from suppliers. The agent with the highest bank balance at the end of the game wins. Availability of parts and demand for computers varies randomly through the game and across three market segments (low, medium, and high computer prices). The market segments are affected not only by the random variations in supply and demand, but also by the actions of other agents. The small number of agents and their ability to adapt and to change strategy during the game makes the game highly dynamic and uncertain.

During the competition, an agent has to make many operational and strategic decisions, ranging from how many parts to buy, to when to get the parts delivered, how to schedule its factory production, what types of computers to build, when to sell them, and at what price.

The problem we address in this paper is how an agent can detect and exploit market conditions, such as oversupply or scarcity of products. We show that market conditions can be characterized by distinguishable statistical patterns, that we call *regimes*, we show how such patterns can be learned off-line from historical data, how they can be identified on-line during the game, and how future regimes and times of regime transitions can be forecast during the game.

H. La Poutré, N. Sadeh, and S. Janson (Eds.): AMEC and TADA 2005, LNAI 3937, pp. 113–125, 2006.

The long term objective of our work is to show how knowledge of current and anticipated market conditions enables an agent to make better decisions. While this type of prediction about the economic environment is commonly used at the macro economic level, such predictions are rarely done for a micro economic environment.

2 Economic Regime Identification

To give an intuition of how prices for the same type of computer change during the game, we show in Figure 1 the probability of receiving an order for a given offer price for computers of type 1 during one of the games played in the finals of TAC SCM 2004. We can see how the slope of the curve and its position change over time. According to economic theory high prices and a steep slope correspond to a situation of scarcity, where price elasticity is small, while a less steep slope corresponds to a balanced market where the range of prices is larger.

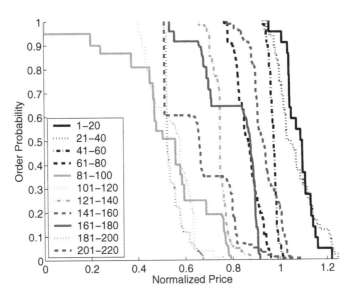

Fig. 1. Game 1189@tac4 (Final TAC SCM 04) – Probability of order for computer type 1 by offer price. The plot shows the curves every 20 days during the game.

Clearly market conditions change during the game, and this should affect the strategy of the agent. When there is scarcity, prices are higher, so the agent should price aggressively. In balanced situations, prices are lower and have more spread, so the agent has a range of options for maximizing expected profit. In over-supply situations prices are lower. The agent should primarily control costs, and therefore either do pricing based on costs, or wait for better market conditions.

Since supply and demand in TAC SCM change in each of the market segments (low, medium, and high computer prices) independently of the other segments, our considerations are to be applied to each individual market segment.

3   Off-Line Analysis of Data

The first step in our approach is to identify and characterize market regimes by analyzing off-line data from previous games. The agent will use these results along with real-time observable information to identify regimes during the game, forecast regime transitions, and adapt its procurement, production, and pricing strategy accordingly.

For our experiments, we used data from a set of 26 games played during the semifinals and finals of TAC SCM 2004. The number of games played was 30, but we left out the games where some computers were sold for $0. The mix of players changed from game to game, the total number of players was 12 in the semi-finals and 6 in the finals.

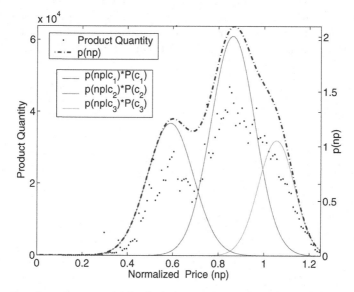

Fig. 2. The Gaussian mixture model for the low market segment. Data are from 26 games from finals and semi-finals of TAC SCM 2004.

Each computer type has a different nominal price, which is the sum of the nominal cost of each of the parts needed to build it. We normalize the prices across the different computer types in each market segment. We call np the normalized price.

We define regimes with the help of a Gaussian mixture model (GMM). We apply the EM-Algorithm [2] to determine the Gaussian components of the GMM, $N[\mu_i, \sigma_i](\text{np})$, and their prior probability, $P(c_i)$. The density of the normalized price can be written as:

$$p(\text{np}) = \sum_{i=1}^{N} p(\text{np}|c_i)\, P(c_i) \qquad (1)$$

where $p(\text{np}|c_i)$ is the i-th Gaussian from the GMM. An example of the Gaussians is shown in Figure 2. For our experiments we chose $N = 3$, because we found experimentally that this provides a good balance between quality of approximation and simplicity of processing.

Using Bayes' rule we determine the posterior probability:

$$P(c_i|\mathrm{np}) = \frac{p(\mathrm{np}|c_i)\,P(c_i)}{\sum_{i=1}^{N} p(\mathrm{np}|c_i)\,P(c_i)} \qquad \forall i = 1, \cdots, N \qquad (2)$$

We then define the N-dimensional vector, whose components are the posterior probabilities from the GMM,

$$\boldsymbol{\eta}(\mathrm{np}) = [P(c_1|\mathrm{np}), P(c_2|\mathrm{np}), \ldots, P(c_N|\mathrm{np})] \qquad (3)$$

and for each normalized price np_j we compute $\boldsymbol{\eta}(\mathrm{np}_j)$ which is $\boldsymbol{\eta}$ evaluated at the np_j price. We cluster these collections of vectors using k-means. The center of each cluster corresponds to regime R_k for $k = 1, \cdots, M$, where M is the number of regimes.

Figure 3 shows the cluster centers, which correspond to regimes, for the low market segment. The figure shows only some of sample points for better visualization.

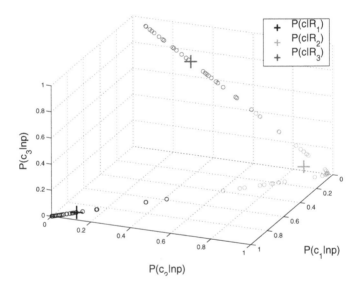

Fig. 3. K-means clustering applied to the posterior probability $P(c|\mathrm{np})$ in the low market segment

We distinguish three regimes, namely over-supply (R_1), balanced (R_2), and scarcity (R_3). Regime R_1 represents a situation where there is a glut in the market, i.e. an over-supply situation, which depresses prices. Regime R_2 represents a balanced market situation, where most of the demand is satisfied. In regime R_2 the agent has a range of options of price vs sales volume. Regime R_3 represents a situation where there is scarcity of products in the market, which increases prices. In this case the agent should price close to the customer reserve price – the maximum price a customer is willing to pay.

The number of regimes was selected a priori, after examining the data and looking at economic analyses of market situations. Both the computation of the GMM and k-means clustering were tried with different initial conditions, but consistently converged to the same results. Correlation analysis (see, later, Figure 8) shows that regimes can be characterized in terms of market quantities, such as prices and ratio of offer to demand.

We can rewrite $p(\mathrm{np}|c_i)$ in a form that shows the dependence of the normalized price np not on the Gaussian c_i of the GMM, but on the regime R_k:

$$P(\mathrm{np}|R_k) = \sum_{i=1}^{N} p(\mathrm{np}|c_i)\, P(c_i|R_k). \qquad (4)$$

The probability of regime R_k dependent on the normalized price np can be computed using Bayes rule as:

$$P(R_k|\mathrm{np}) = \frac{P(\mathrm{np}|R_k)\, P(R_k)}{\sum_{k=1}^{M} P(\mathrm{np}|R_k)\, P(R_k)} \quad \forall k = 1, \cdots, M. \qquad (5)$$

where M is the number of regimes, which in our case is 3. The prior probabilities $P(R_k)$ of the different regimes are determined by a counting process over multiple games.

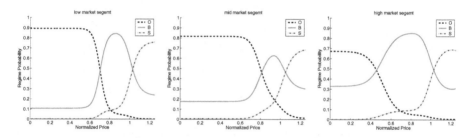

Fig. 4. Regime probabilities over normalized price for the low (left), medium (middle) and high (right) market segments. These are computed off-line from 26 games.

Figure 4 depicts the regime probabilities for the three market segments. Each regime is clearly dominant over a range of normalized prices. To make things more intuitive, we label regime R_1 as O for over-supply, regime R_2 as B for balanced, and regime R_3 as S for scarcity. The relative dominance and range of the different regimes varies among the market segments, but we can see, as expected, that oversupply corresponds to lower prices, a balanced situation to prices closer to the average, and scarcity to high prices. We assume this reflects different agent pricing and inventory-management strategies. The high market segment offers higher profit per computer, hence the balanced regime extends over a larger range of normalized prices. In the low market segment the profit per computer is low, hence the balanced regime extends over a much smaller range of normalized prices.

The intuition behind regimes is that prices communicate information about future expectations of the market. However, absolute prices do not mean much because the same price point can be achieved in a static mode (i.e., when prices don't deviate), or when prices are in ascent, or when prices are in descent. The variation of prices (the nature, variance, and the neighborhood) defines the regime. A regime captures a somewhat medium term mood in the market by looking at price and volume tradeoffs. A price point does not consider its neighborhood, an idea that regimes capture.

4 Online Identification of Current Regime

During the game, the agent can estimate every day the current regime by calculating the mean normalized price $\overline{np}_{day}$ for the day and by selecting the regime which has the highest probability, i.e. $\text{argmax}_{1 \leq k \leq M} P(R_k|\overline{np}_{day})$.

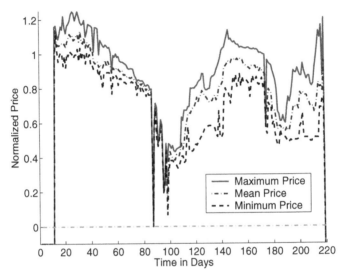

Fig. 5. Game 1189@tac4 (Final TAC SCM 04) – Minimum and maximum daily prices of computers sold, as reported during the game every day, and mean price. If nothing was sold in the market on a given day then the prices shown are below zero. The mean price is computed after the game using the game data, which include complete information on all the transactions.

Unfortunately, this is not simple, since the agent has only limited market information during the game. Every day the agent receives a report which includes the minimum and maximum prices of the computers sold the day before, but not the quantities sold. Using these reports, the agent can compute the mid-range of the normalized price of the computers sold the previous day. The mid-range is an estimate of the mean price, but not always a good one since the quantity of computers sold is not known. An example that shows how the mean differs from the mid-range value is shown in Figure 5.

The mid-range price can be used to identify the corresponding regime online, as shown in Figure 6 (left). The data are from game 1189@tac4, which was not in the training set of games used to develop the regime definitions. The middle and right parts of Figure 6 show respectively the probability of receiving an order in a balanced and in a scarcity situation for different prices. Scarcity typically occurs early in the game and

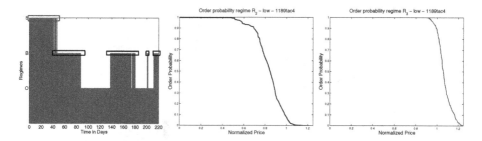

Fig. 6. Game 1189@tac4 (Final TAC SCM 04) – Regimes over time for the low market computed online every day (left), probability of receiving an order by normalized price for a balanced situation (R_2 indicated by B) (middle) and for a scarcity situation (R_3 indicated by S) (right).

at other times when supply is low. These probabilities are computed from past game data for each regime.

Eventual errors in regime identification can be corrected every 20 days when the agent receives a market report which includes the mean price of each of the computer types sold since the last market report. At that point, if needed, the agent can correct its current regime identification.

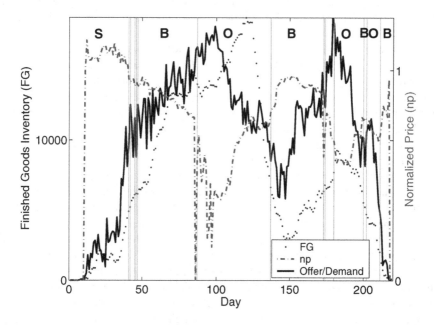

Fig. 7. Game 1189@tac4 (Final TAC SCM 04) – Relationships between regimes and normalized prices in the low market. On the left axis, we show the available finished goods inventory of all agents and the ratio of offer to demand (which ranges from 0 to 4.5), which is scaled to fit between the minimum and maximum values of the finished goods inventory. On the right axis we show the normalized prices. The dominant regimes are labeled along the top.

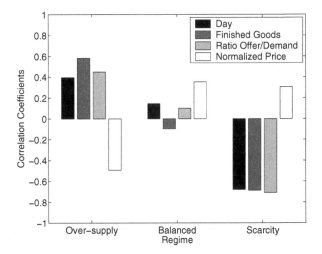

Fig. 8. Game 1189@tac4 (Final TAC SCM 04) – Correlation coefficients between regimes and day in the game, the ratio of offer to demand, normalized price (np), and quantity of finished goods inventory in the low market segment

Figure 7 shows the quantity of the finished goods inventory (FG), the ratio of offer to demand, which represents the proportion of the market demand that is satisfied, and the normalized price (np) over time[1].

The regimes identified by our approach are superimposed, where S (or R_3) represents scarcity, B (or R_2) balanced, and O (or R_1) over-supply. These factors clearly correlate with market regimes, but they are not directly visible to the agent during the game. For example, the figure shows that when the offer to demand ratio is high (i.e. over-supply) prices are low and vice versa. We can observe that the ratio of offer to demand changes significantly during the game. For instance, on day 141 the ratio of offer to demand is approximatively 1.4 and prices are high. On day 179 the ratio of offer to demand is much higher, approximatively 4.5, and prices are lower. We can also observe that prices tend to lag changes in ratio of offer to demand.

A correlation analysis of the market parameters is shown in Figure 8. The p-values for the correlation analysis are all less than 0.01. Regime R_1 (over-supply) correlates strongly and positively with time, ratio of offer to demand, and quantity of finished goods inventory, and negatively with normalized price. On the other hand, in Regime R_3 (scarcity) we observe a strong negative correlation with the selected market parameters.

Figure 9 shows the relative probabilities of each regime over the course of a game. The graph shows that different regimes are dominant at different points in the game, and that there are brief intervals during which two regimes are almost equally likely. An agent could use this information to decide which strategy, or mixture of strategies, to follow.

---

[1] The quantity of the finished goods inventory is affected by other factors, such as storage cost, which have changed in the TAC SCM 2005 games. In 2005 games agents tend to build to order and keep most of their inventory in the form of parts, not finished products.

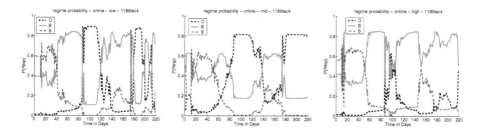

Fig. 9. Game 1189@tac4 (Final TAC SCM 04) – Regime probabilities over time computed online every day for the low (left), medium (middle) and high (right) market segment

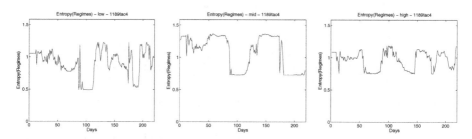

Fig. 10. Game 1189@tac4 (Final TAC SCM 04) – Daily entropy values of the three regimes for the low (left), medium (middle), and high (right) market segment

A measure of the confidence in the regime identification is the entropy of the set S of probabilities of the regimes given the normalized mid-range price from the daily price reports $\overline{np}_{day}$, where

$$S = \{P(R_1|\overline{np}_{day}), \cdots, P(R_M|\overline{np}_{day})\}$$

and

$$\text{Entropy}(S) \equiv \sum_{k=1}^{M} -P(R_k|\overline{np}_{day}) \log_2 P(R_k|\overline{np}_{day}). \tag{6}$$

An entropy value close to zero corresponds to a high confidence in the current regime and an entropy value close to its maximum, i.e. for M regimes $\log_2 M$, indicates that the current market situation is a mixture of M almost equally likely regimes. Examples for the three market segments in game 1189@tac4 are shown in Figure 10.

5   Regime Prediction

The behavior of an agent should depend on the current market regime as well as expectation of future regimes. This requires a way for the agent to predict future regimes and when regime switches will occur.

We model regime prediction as a Markov process. We construct a Markov transition matrix, $\mathbf{T}_{\text{predict}}(r_{t+1}|r_t)$ off-line by a counting process over past games. This matrix represents the posterior probability of transitioning to a regime given the current regime. To compute the Markov transition matrix, for each of the past games we compute the mean normalized price every day, we then estimate the regime probabilities dependent on that price, and we select the regime which has the maximum probability as the regime for the given day.

The prediction of regime probabilities is based on two distinct operations: a correction (recursive Bayesian update) of the posterior probabilities for the regimes based on the history of measurements of np obtained since the time of the last regime change, t_0, until the previous day, $t - 1$, $P(r_{t-1}|\{\overline{np}_{t_0}, \ldots, \overline{np}_{t-1}\})$, and a subsequent prediction of regime posterior probabilities for the current day, t, $P(r_t|\{\overline{np}_{t_0}, \ldots, \overline{np}_{t-1}\})$. Equation 7 describes a recursive computation for predicting the posterior distribution of regimes at time $t + n$ days into the future, where $k = n + 1$.

$$P(r_{t+k}|\{\overline{np}_{t_0}, \ldots, \overline{np}_{t-1}\}) =$$

$$\sum_{r_{t+k-1}} \cdots \sum_{r_{t-1}} P(r_{t-1}|\{\overline{np}_{t_0}, \ldots, \overline{np}_{t-1}\}) \cdot \prod_{j=1}^{k} \mathbf{T_{predict}}(r_{t+j}|r_{t+j-1}) \quad (7)$$

We measure the accuracy of regime prediction using two separate values:

1. a count of how many times the regime predicted is the correct one,
2. a count of how many times the predicted day of the regime switch is correct. We assume the prediction is correct when the regime switch prediction is -2/+2 days from the correct day of change.

As ground truth we measure regime switches and their time off-line using data from the game. We tested our approach on all 16 final games in the 2005 TAC SCM tournament. Starting with day 1 until day 199, we forecast every day the regimes for the next 20 days and we forecast when a regime transition would occur. Experimental results are in Table 1.

The reason for limiting the prediction to 20 days is that every 20 days the agent receives a report which includes the mean price of each of the computer types sold since the last market report, and so it can correct, if needed, its current regime identification.

Table 1. Percent of correct predictions of future regime (using Markov model) and predictions of time of regime change (using Semi-Markov model). We assume the prediction of the time of change is correct if it is within -2/+2 days. For the number of regime changes we show the average and standard deviation. Results shown are computed every day for the next 20 days from day 1 to day 199 (for a total of 3184 trials).

	low market	medium market	high market
	avg/stdev	avg/stdev	avg/stdev
# regime changes	9.75/9.85	7.88/4.97	3.69/1.72
correct regime	73.87%	85.30%	97.83%
correct time	74.43%	74.18%	93.12%

We hypothesized that the time a regime switch occurs is not exponential (Markov), i.e. the future depends not only on the present state, but also on the length of time the process has spent in that state. This requires modeling the regime transition as a semi-Markov process [3].

To model this we modify the Markov transition matrix, $\mathbf{T}_{\text{predict}}$, to be a weighted sum of two matrices, the steady state matrix $\mathbf{T}_{\text{steady}}$ and the change matrix $\mathbf{T}_{\text{change}}$. $\mathbf{T}_{\text{steady}}$ is the $M \times M$ identity matrix, where M is the number of regimes. $\mathbf{T}_{\text{change}}$ is the Markov transition matrix, which is computed off-line as described earlier.

$$\mathbf{T}_{\text{predict}}(r_{t+1}|r_t) = (1 - \omega(.))\mathbf{T}_{\text{steady}} + \omega(.)\mathbf{T}_{\text{change}}(r_{t+1}|r_t) \tag{8}$$

where $\omega(.)$ represents the probability of a regime change, and r_t represents the current regime. To compute the value of $\omega(.)$, we need to introduce a few variables. We define Δt as the time since the last regime transition at t_0: $\Delta t = t - t_0$. We model the time τ_i spent in regime R_i before the transition to regime R_j occurs as a random variable with distribution F_{ij}. τ_i is estimated from historical data. We hypothesized that the probability density of τ_i is dependent on the current regime, R_i, i.e. $p(\tau_i|R_i)$. We computed the frequency of all values of τ_i in ascending order and fitted different distributions. The Gamma distribution, $g(t; \alpha, \lambda)$ is a reasonable fit to the data.

The probability of a regime transition $\omega(r, \Delta t)$ from the current regime, r, with respect to the time Δt that has elapsed since the last regime transition, t_0, is given by:

$$\omega(r = R_i, \Delta t) = \int_0^{\Delta t} p(\Delta t|r = R_i) \, \mathrm{d}\Delta t \tag{9}$$

where $p(\Delta t|r = R_i) = g(\Delta t; \alpha_i, \lambda_i)$. Equation 10 describes a recursive computation for predicting the posterior distribution of regimes at time $t + n$ days into the future, where $k = n + 1$, for the semi-Markov process.

$$\mathbf{P}(r_{t+k}|\{\overline{\mathrm{np}}_{t_0}, \ldots, \overline{\mathrm{np}}_{t-1}\}) = \tag{10}$$

$$\sum_{r_{t+k-1}} \cdots \sum_{r_{t-1}} \mathbf{P}(r_{t-1}|\{\overline{\mathrm{np}}_{t_0}, \ldots, \overline{\mathrm{np}}_{t-1}\}) \cdot \prod_{j=1}^{k} \mathbf{T}_{\text{predict}}(r_{t+j}|r_{t+j-1}, \Delta t + j - 1)$$

The second measure of success, correctness of prediction of the time of regime change, which we obtained using the semi-Markov model, is shown in Table 1.

6   Related Work

Marketing research methods have been developed to understand the conditions for growth in performance and the role that marketing actions can play to improve sales. For instance, in [4], an analysis is presented on how in mature economic markets strategic windows of change alternate with long periods of stability.

Model selection is the task of choosing a model of optimal complexity for the given data. A good overview of concepts, theory and model selection methods is given in [5].

Much work has focused on models for rational decision-making in autonomous agents. Ng and Russel [6] show that an agent's decisions can be viewed as a set of linear constraints on the space of possible utility (reward) functions. However, the simple reward structure they used in their experiments will not scale to what is needed to predict prices in TAC SCM.

Carmel and Markovitch [7] describe a game-player that tries to analyze and learn the strategy of its opponent. They discuss the benefits of using a model of the opponent strategy, and give an algorithm called M* (a generalization of the standard minimax algorithm) that attempts to exploit the opponent strategy. M* assumes that the opponent's search depth and evaluation function are known, which is not the case in TAC SCM.

Chajewska, Koller, and Ormoneit [8] describe a method for predicting the future decisions of an agent based on its past decisions. They learn the agent's utility function by observing its behavior. Their approach is based on the assumption that the agent is a rational decision maker. According to decision theory, rational decision making amounts to the maximization of the expected utility [9]. In TAC SCM, we cannot apply these techniques because the behaviors of individual agents are not directly observable.

Sales strategies used in previous TAC SCM competitions have attempted to model the probability of receiving an order for a given offer price, either by estimating the probability by linear interpolation from the minimum and maximum daily prices [10], or by estimating the relationship between offer price and order probability with a linear cumulative density function (CDF) [11], or by using a reverse CDF and factors such as quantity and due date [12,13], or by letting other agents set the price and trying to follow [14].

All these methods fail to take into account market conditions that are not directly observable. They are essentially regression models, and do not represent qualitative differences in market conditions. Our method, in contrast, is able to detect and forecast a broader range of market conditions.

Regression based approaches (including non-parametric variations) assume that the functional form which defines the relationship between dependent and independent variables has the same structure. However, as shown in Figure 1, these functional relationships have a different structure for different regimes. Therefore, an approach that does not assume a functional relationship maybe the best way to identify a regime.

Wellman et al. [15] demonstrate a method for predicting future customer demand in the TAC SCM game environment, and use the predicted future demand to inform agent behavior. Their approach is specific to the TAC SCM situation, since it depends on knowing the formula by which customer demand is computed. Note that customer demand is only one of the factors for characterizing the multi-dimensional regime parameter space.

7   Conclusions and Future Work

We have presented an approach to characterizing and predicting economic market conditions in markets for durable goods. Our approach recognizes that different market situations have qualitative differences that can be used to guide the strategic and tactical behavior of an agent. Unlike regression-based methods that try to predict prices directly from demand and other observable factors, our approach recognizes that prices are also influenced by non-observable factors, such as the inventory positions of the other agents. Unlike price-following methods, our approach promises to enable an agent to anticipate and prepare for regime changes, for example by building up inventory in anticipation of better prices in the future or by selling in anticipation of an upcoming oversupply situation.

We have demonstrated the effectiveness of our approach by characterizing the market conditions in games played in the semi-finals and finals from TAC SCM 2004 and 2005.

Our next step is to complete the prediction of future regimes, to design and evaluate sales strategies that take advantage of regime prediction, and to integrate them into the decision making process of our agent. We believe that our proposed formulation will allow the agent to operate effectively on a daily basis as well as to engage in strategic pricing.

Acknowledgements

Partial funding for this work is acknowledged from NSF under grant IIS-0414466.

References

1. Sadeh, N., Arunachalam, R., Eriksson, J., Finne, N., Janson, S.: TAC-03: A supply-chain trading competition. AI Magazine 24(1) (2003) 9294
2. Dempster, A.P., Laird, N.M., Rubin, D.B.: Maximum likelihood from incomplete data via the EM algorithm. Journal of the Royal Statistical Society Series B, 39(1) (1977) 138
3. Levinson, S.E.: Continuously variable duration hidden markov models for automatic speech recognition. Comput. Speech Lang. 1(1) (1986) 2945
4. Pauwels, K., Hanssens, D.: Windows of Change inMatureMarkets. In: EuropeanMarketing Academy Conf., Braga, Portugal (2002)
5. Cherkassky, V.,Mulier, F.: Learning from data – Concepts, Theory, andMethods. JohnWiley & Sons, INC., New York (1998)
6. Ng, A., Russell, S.: Algorithms for inverse reinforcement learning. In: Proc. of the 17th Intl Conf. on Machine Learning, Palo Alto (2000) 663670
7. Carmel, D., Markovitch, S.: Learning models of opponents strategy in game playing. Technical report, Technion-Israel Institute of Technology (1993)
8. Chajewska, U., Koller, D., Ormoneit, D.: Learning an agents utility function by observing behavior. In: Proc. of the 18th Intl Conf. on Machine Learning, Lafayette (2001) 3542
9. von Neumann, J., Morgenstern, O.: Theory of Games and Economic Behavior. Princeton University Press, 2nd edition, Princeton, N.J. (1947)
10. Pardoe, D., Stone, P.: Bidding for Customer Orders in TAC SCM: A Learning Approach. In: Workshop on Trading Agent Design and Analysis at AAMAS, New York (2004) 5258
11. Benisch, M., Greenwald, A., Grypari, I., Lederman, R., Naroditskiy, V., Tschantz, M.: Botticelli: A supply chain management agent designed to optimize under uncertainty. ACM Trans. on Computational Logic 4(3) (2004) 2937
12. Ketter,W., Kryzhnyaya, E., Damer, S., McMillen, C., Agovic, A., Collins, J., Gini,M.: MinneTAC sales strategies for supply chain TAC. In: Proc. of the Third Intl Conf. on Autonomous Agents and Multi-Agent Systems, New York (2004) 13721373
13. Ketter,W., Kryzhnyaya, E., Damer, S.,McMillen, C., Agovic, A., Collins, J., Gini,M.: Analysis and design of supply-driven strategies in TAC-SCM. In: Workshop: Trading Agent Design and Analysis at the Third Intl Conf. on Autonomous Agents and Multi-Agent Systems, New York (2004) 4451
14. Dahlgren, E., Wurman, P.: PackaTAC: A conservative trading agent. SIGecom Exchanges 4(3) (2004) 3340
15. Wellman, M.P., Estelle, J., Singh, S., Vorobeychik, Y., Kiekintveld, C., Soni, V.: Strategic interactions in a supply chain game. Computational Intelligence 21(1) (2005) 126

Socrates: A Production-Driven SCM Agent

Carlos R. Jaimez González and Maria Fasli

University of Essex, Department of Computer Science
Wivenhoe Park, Colchester CO4 3SQ, UK
{crjaim, mfasli}@essex.ac.uk

Abstract. The Trading Agent Competition (TAC) is an open-invitation forum designed to encourage research into electronic markets and trading agents. In this paper we present the Socrates trading agent and the strategies that were developed for and used in the TAC Supply Chain Management game as part of the 2004 competition. The resulting behaviour and performance in the TAC competition as well as in a series of controlled experiments are discussed.

1 Introduction

In today's highly interconnected and networked world more and more businesses and organizations choose to do business online. This is a dynamic environment where manufacturers may negotiate with suppliers on the one hand, while at the same time compete for customer orders and have to arrange their production schedule and delivery so that orders are delivered on time. The ability to respond to changes as they happen and adapt to variations in customer demand and the restrictions as imposed by procurement, is of paramount importance. This is the kind of environment that agent technology is best suited for: dynamic, constrained and real-time. However, to be able to build agents that offer solutions to problems such as supply chain management, we need to have a very good understanding of the domain itself and the problems that arise in it. In particular, firstly we need to gain a better understanding of the problems that arise in supply chain negotiation situations. Secondly, we need to explore strategies for coping in dynamic and competitive environments, and finally develop agent-based systems for an automated supply chain process. Trial and error in a real environment carries very high risks. To demonstrate the potential of applying agent technology in complex domains like supply chain management, realistic testbeds are required that allow researchers and practitioners to test out and evaluate ideas and techniques. The TAC Supply Chain Management (SCM) game was designed to capture many of the dynamics of such an environment and provides an ideal forum for researchers to test, evaluate and learn.

This paper presents the Socrates trading agent and the strategies that were used in the TAC Supply Chain Management game in the 2004 competition. As a good strategy for obtaining components was essential for a good overall performance in the game, we decided to concentrate on this aspect of the agent. Socrates is a production-driven agent that attempts to keep factory utilisation to the maximum for as long as possible during the game. We present the problems that arise in dealing with the suppliers and the strategies that were developed to tackle them. The rest of the paper is organized as follows. The following section presents the TAC SCM game and a section describing related

H. La Poutré, N. Sadeh, and S. Janson (Eds.): AMEC and TADA 2005, LNAI 3937, pp. 126–139, 2006.

work follows. Next, the Socrates trading agent and the strategies that were developed to deal in particular with the supplier problem are described. Following this, we present the results of the competition as well as those of a series of controlled experiments. The paper closes with the conclusions and pointers to future work.

2 The SCM Game

In the TAC SCM game six agents compete against each other in a 220-day game which lasts 55 minutes in real time [1]. Each agent is a manufacturer which assembles PCs from CPUs, motherboards, memories, and hard disks. CPUs and motherboards are available in two different product families, Pintel and IMD. A Pintel CPU only works with a Pintel motherboard while an IMD CPU can be incorporated only in an IMD motherboard. CPUs are available in two speeds, 2.0 and 5.0 GHz, memories in sizes, 1 and 2 GB, and disks in sizes 300 and 500 GB. The ten different components can be combined into sixteen different PC models. The agents need to procure these components from eight different suppliers. On the other side, the agents need to secure customer orders each day. Once an agent has received an order it needs to assemble the required number and model of PCs in its factory and subsequently ship the finished products. All agents start the game with no money in their bank accounts, no components or assembled PCs in their inventory, and no pending customer orders while they enjoy unlimited credit from the bank. Each model of PC requires a different number of cycles to be produced and an agent has a limited assembly capacity every day which is 2000 cycles. The TAC server simulates the suppliers, customers, and the bank and provides production, and warehousing services to the individual agents. The agent who makes the most profit at the end is declared the winner.

During the game each agent negotiates contracts with the suppliers by first sending RFQ requests for a specific type of component. Suppliers, which are utility maximisers, reply with offers to these RFQs. In particular, in response to an agent's RFQ, they may send a complete offer which matches the agent's request in terms of delivery date and quantity, or partial offers that may not match the quantity or delivery date requested. If the supplier cannot satisfy an order, no offer is sent. For every offer sent, the agent needs to determine whether to accept it and place an order, or reject it. However, if both partial and complete offers have been sent, the agent can only accept one of them.

The customers request PCs models for a specific due date indicating their reservation price by sending RFQs to all agents. The agent may reply with an offer bid, and the customer awards the order to the lowest bid. The winning agent must deliver the PCs ordered by the due date, otherwise it incurs a penalty. An agent is responsible for its production and every day needs to send a schedule indicating how many PCs and of which model will be manufactured the next day based on its assembly capacity. Obviously, for manufacturing to take place the agent needs to have the necessary components in its inventory. Components that arrive the same day can only be used in production the day after. Each day the agent also needs to prepare a delivery schedule for the next day.

The TAC SCM game features two main interrelated problems:

The supplier problem. One of the main problems in the TAC SCM game is to plan a good strategy for ordering components from the suppliers. There are many factors to take into account such as the quantity of components to be ordered, the date by which they are required, the periodicity in which they are requested, the supplier who provides them, the prices offered, the storage cost to be paid for them once they have been received as well as the possible delivery delays that may occur among other things. In essence, in dealing with the suppliers the agent acts as a reverse auctioneer in multi-attribute auctions. Issues like sole sourcing and multiple sourcing are important in this respect as well as the ability of an agent to switch from one supplier to another if needed.

The customer problem. The success of an agent does not only depend on the supplier strategy adopted, but also on dealing with the customers and selling manufactured products. An agent competes with all other agents in the game to secure customer orders. The components acquired will have been bought at different prices throughout the game so a particular PC may cost a different price say on day 80, than on day 145. On top of that, the agents have to take into consideration the cost that they have to pay while the raw components and the finished products lie in storage. This side of the SCM game resembles competing against other bidders in an auction. Although some information on aggregate price statistics is revealed during the game, this is rather limited. For a more detailed description see [3].

3 Related Work

The TAC SCM game has been running since 2003 with minor modifications every year to improve its efficacy. One of the major problems in the game is obtaining components to start production. In particular, the way that the suppliers worked in 2003, i.e. the big discount rates given for orders early in the game, gives all agents the incentive to request large quantities of components in the beginning. This problem has been coined the "0-day effect". Most of the agents in the 2003 competition had a day-0 procurement strategy, i.e. they ordered large quantities in the beginning of the game. This was also helped by the fact that there was no storage cost for keeping massive numbers of components in the inventory.

RedAgent [11], the winner of TAC SCM'03, based its functionality on a multi-agent design, in which it used simple heuristic agents for procuring components from the suppliers. The main idea was to use internal markets to provide price estimates for the extra components that it needed to purchase. TacTex [12] used the day-0 strategy and sent extra RFQs during the game based on a prediction of the future inventory according to the current usage of components. HarTAC [7] procured components with the day-0 strategy and tried to maintain a reasonable quantity of all components in stock at all the times by ordering small quantities of components through the game; Botticelli [4] and PSUTAC [13] only relied on the day-0 strategy without sending extra RFQs during the game. DeepMaize [8] used a preemptive strategy to block agents that used day-0 strategy. The preemptive strategy worked by submitting a big RFQ to each supplier for each type of component. This RFQ had the effect of preempting subsequent RFQs because the supplier would have committed its production capacity for the rest of the game. There were few other agents using conservative strategies, such as PackaTac [6], who played a low-risk strategy maintaining a low level inventory of components. It decided to use this strategy to counteract the day-0 strategies that emerged during the competition. NaRC [5] constructed RFQs and accepted offers from suppliers based on projections for future prices and demand.

For the 2004 competition and in order to provide a disincentive for ordering and holding large numbers of components in the inventory, a storage cost was introduced and the pricing formula for the components was altered slightly. However, as it turned out this did not have a major effect on the agents' strategies regarding their RFQs to the suppliers during the first few days of the game.

4   Socrates

Socrates is an autonomous trading agent built in Java. It is production-driven, that is to say, we concentrated on strategies to deal with the suppliers, as despite the modifications made to the game, obtaining the components was essential to enable one to compete and acquire orders on the customers' side.

The development of Socrates for TAC SCM 2004 was based on the Agentware framework as provided by SICS, which includes a set of classes that provide the main functionality to establish communication with the TAC SCM server and receive all the events to be able to participate in the competition. The internal functionality of Socrates, which determines the way in which it keeps and processes information, is based on *Value Object* classes. A Value Object is a design pattern for representing objects as containers of information [9, 2]. Value Objects are used to represent transient objects to keep track of information during a TAC game. Hence, every RFQ, supplier offer, order, PC model, is represented as a Value Object. Socrates builds a number of different lists for these Value Objects in order to simplify their maintenance. Comparator classes, which are Java classes that implement the Comparable interface, are then used to sort the lists. The *Comparator* classes are defined by specifying the property or properties of the Value Object class to be used for sorting the list. Once the lists are sorted, it is easier to manipulate them. Socrates uses a *FileManager* class which is responsible for reading the configuration files at the beginning of every TAC game. There are two configuration files, the default *aw.conf* and our own configuration file *soc.conf*. The latter one is used to specify the initial parameters to be used by the agent during the game. The information contained in the files is then passed on to Socrates. The FileManager is also responsible for storing information during the game in log files, which are then used for subsequent analysis.

4.1   Preliminaries

As we are focusing on a production-driven strategy we need to estimate the number of PCs that can be manufactured to achieve near to 100% utilisation. To determine the components to be ordered we have to consider the duration of the game (220 days), and the number of PCs that can be manufactured daily based on the agent's assembly capacity (2000 cycles). The average number of manufacturing cycles for a PC is:

$AvgCycles = sum(Cycles_i)/16 = 5.5$ (i is the PC model)
The assembly capacity for an agent during the whole game is therefore:
$TotalAssemblyCycles = Days * DayCycles = 220 * 2000 = 440000$

The number of PCs that can be assembled by an agent during the game is:
$TotalPCs = 440000/5.5 = 80000$

This calculation assumes that the agent is making full use of its assembly capacity from day 0 to 219. But this is not realistic as the first components cannot arrive before day 3 and therefore the earliest that production can start is on day 4. Moreover, production on the last day is useless as the agent is unable to deliver the PCs manufactured that day. The number of effective cycles and total number of PCs then would be:

$EffectiveCycles = 215 * 2000 = 430000$
$TotalEffectivePCs = 430000/5.5 = 78181$

We also have to take into account the assembly capacity of the suppliers in order to determine how many components a day they can produce. The expected assembly capacity of a supplier is 500 components a day, and the real production capacity for every day for each supplier is calculated as follows:

$C_p(d) = max(0, C_p(d-1) + rnd(-0.05, 0.05)*C_{nominal} + 0.01*(C_{nominal} - C_p(d-1)))$

Where $C_{nominal}$ denotes the nominal or expected assembly capacity. We have determined experimentally that the average number of components that a supplier manufactures every day is 400 of each of the 2 types of components it can produce. Thus, the total number of components that can be produced during the whole game and the total number of PCs that can be manufactured can be calculated. CPUs are produced by two suppliers, Pintel and IMD, each of which provide two varieties of CPUs. If every supplier produces 400 CPUs of each variety daily, then 1600 CPUs are produced every day, which represents 1600 PCs. Considering that a supplier cannot produce any components on the first two days and that the production on the last two days is useless, we can approximate the total number of PCs that can be produced in a game:

$AllPCs = 1600 * 216 = 345600$

Assuming that all agents manufacture approximately the same number of PCs:

$345600 PCs/6\, agents = 57600\, PCs$

This number is only an approximation and can vary from game to game.

4.2 Supplier Strategies

We explored a number of strategies to deal with the suppliers in the TAC SCM 2004 competition as well as in a number of controlled experiments. The underlying strategy is based on what we call the Massive Simple Strategy (MSS) which simply sends 5 RFQs with big quantities to every supplier for every component they supply on day 0. The 5 RFQs are split taking into consideration the number of days that the components will last in the inventory, which can be computed by taking into consideration the assembly capacity of the agent and the average number of cycles needed for one PC to be manufactured. The 5 RFQs request a number of components enough to manufacture between 55000 and 65000 PCs during the entire game, which ensures a production between 150 and 180 days. For instance, the following RFQ bundle shows how Socrates splits the number of components to manufacture 56628 PCs: $\langle\langle$RFQ1,1452,10$\rangle$, $\langle$RFQ2,2178,25$\rangle$, $\langle$RFQ3,2904,49$\rangle$, $\langle$RFQ4,3630,81$\rangle$, $\langle$RFQ5,3993,121$\rangle\rangle$.

Once all these RFQs have been sent to the suppliers on day 0, the agent will receive offers for all or some of them on day 1. The basic version of the strategy considers accepting only complete or earliest complete offers whose delivery date is below a Cut-Off-Date, which is set to 180 considering that suppliers can delay the deliveries. This very simple strategy has a number of shortcomings:

1. It does not take into account that suppliers may not reply to all of the RFQs sent by the agents. If some of them are not matched by offers, the agent will end up with a number of unusable components in the inventory.
2. The same situation as above occurs if the agent receives offers with a delivery date above the Cut-Off-Date, which will not be accepted.
3. Suppliers can make offers with a delivery date below the Cut-Off-Date, but with a significant deviation from the requested date. This would cause the agent to wait for deliveries, which may lead to poor factory utilisation for a significant number of days due to lack of essential components.
4. If the components are received on time, the agent may exhaust them quite early in the game and then it remains idle.
5. The suppliers' delays may lead to gaps in the production.

To tackle the first two shortcomings, the agent detects on day 1 those RFQs that did not receive any offers from the suppliers, and also those that were not accepted by the agent because the offered delivery date was above the Cut-Off-Date. In both cases, this generates new RFQs which are re-sent to the suppliers. This process is carried out every day from day 1 onwards until the agent has received and accepted offers for all its RFQs.

Although this improvement helps, it does not solve the problem of lacking components of one or more types during a period in the game. If the agent has no memories, for instance, it cannot manufacture any PCs. This is because, although the supplier can supply the agent with the requested quantity this may be some time after all the other components essential for the production of specific types of PCs have been received. To tackle this, Socrates does not to accept earliest complete offers whose delivery date is greater than the requested date plus a fixed number of days, which was experimentally determined and set to a value between 30-40, and accepts partial offers instead (if any). The agent keeps track of the quantity of missing components of each type:

$$MissingComp[compId] = MissingComp[compId] + QRequested\text{-}QAccepted$$

Where every element in the array *MissingComp[]* is a type of component identified by *compId*; *MissingComp[compId]* is the existing quantity of missing components of type *compId* (generated due to previous partial offers accepted); *QRequested* is the quantity of components requested in the RFQ; and *QAccepted* is the quantity of components accepted in the partial offer. The missing quantities are then reordered in smaller quantities (400 components each). When suppliers send offers in response to these new RFQs, the agent accepts either partially complete or partial offers and keeps track of the number of missing components.

When components arrive on time, the agent will most likely have used its inventory for manufacturing PCs, and towards the end of the game it remains idle. To address this issue, another modification was introduced. To determine if the agent needs more components towards the end we have to ensure the agent has received all the components and calculate the number of PCs that can be manufactured with the current inventory. Considering the *LastDeliveryDate* (usually set to 121) that Socrates asks for components, the algorithm starts checking on day *LastDeliveryDate*+30 if all components have been received. If this is the case and there are enough days to manufacture more PCs, Socrates starts ordering more components in small quantities. The total quantity of components to be ordered depends on the number of remaining days in the game and the quantity of PCs that can be assembled.

4.3   Dealing with Gaps in the Production

Although the steps described so far deal with some of the problems in obtaining components and keeping the production steady, there are still gaps in the production schedule. To this end, a strategy that would detect the gaps in the factory utilisation for the whole game by analyzing all the *ActiveOrders* of components after the agent has accepted offers from suppliers for all the initial RFQs sent was deployed. The *ActiveOrders* provide information about when the components are supposed to be delivered and this will be known early in the game. The algorithm determines the gaps in the factory utilisation by looking at the delivery dates in the *ActiveOrders*:

1. Generate a virtual production of PCs with the current inventory (if any) utilising 100% of the assembly capacity, and determine the day in the game in which the production of PCs falls below 100%.
2. The day found in the previous step is used to look for *ActiveOrders* that should be delivered before that day or on that day. The agent has two alternatives: go to step 3 if there are *ActiveOrders*, or alternatively go to step 4.
3. The *ActiveOrders* found give the agent a virtual inventory of components that will be added up to the remaining inventory from step 1. The agent generates the virtual production of PCs with the new inventory (the remaining inventory from step 1 plus the virtual inventory) and determines the day in which the production stops due to lack of components. The agent continues with step 2.
4. This step is executed if there are no more *ActiveOrders*, that is the agent has no more components to manufacture for this day and probably for more days, because the next *ActiveOrders* (if any) will be delivered later in the game. This will lead to a gap of one or more days depending on when the next components arrive. The agent looks for the next *ActiveOrders* that give the 100% factory utilisation, keeps track of the days in which it cannot manufacture and goes to step 3. The number of days without production is used to generate new RFQs.
5. The algorithm attempts to fill in the detected gaps by sending RFQs only for those types of components necessary to have 100% factory utilisation during those periods in the game. The agent sends RFQs to cover production for 1 day, thus if there is a gap of 6 days in the production schedule 6 RFQs will be sent. The recursive algorithm described above is executed every TAC day until day 200 to determine if the gaps have

been covered by the RFQs sent. The agent will accept complete offers, earliest complete offers, or partial offers.

One problem with this strategy is that the virtual production can be unreliable as suppliers can delay the delivery of components. The gaps produced because of the initial RFQs can be covered, but new gaps can appear because of the delay of components.

4.4   Customers and Scheduling

Socrates' customer strategy is simple: it responds to customer RFQs which can be satisfied based on the current inventory of finished PCs. Three different ways of sorting the customer RFQs were considered and tested during the competition (a) quantity in RFQ; (b) reservation price; (c) expected profit. The method adopted was (b). Taking into account the reservation price in each RFQ, Socrates looks at the current inventory and decides which RFQs to bid for. The offered price depends on a number of factors including the current date, the quantity held in stock for the particular PC model and the average price as reported in the market report. These factors determine different levels of discounts during the game and are cumulative. However, Socrates also keeps track of how well its sales policy operates during the game by looking at the ratio of *OffersSent/OrdersReceived*. If the orders fall below certain thresholds and in combination with other conditions in the game, a price adjustment mechanism is triggered which overrides the discount price offered normally to improve Socrates' sales position. The delivery of finished PCs is arranged as soon as an order is confirmed by the customer, thus eliminating penalties. The major shortcoming of this aspect of Socrates is that future production is not taken into account.

The aim of the production schedule is to utilise the full assembly capacity of every TAC day. The agent assembles an almost equal number of PCs of each of the 16 models, provided that there are enough parts in the inventory to do so. If there is a lack of one or more components, which precludes the manufacturing of some particular PC models, Socrates adjusts its production so that an equal number of the other PC models can be manufactured. The production schedule does not take into account customer demand which is a major shortcoming. One way to address this is to either look at the customer RFQs and the most wanted or unwanted models of PCs and manufacture less of those, or look at the inventory of current PCs and if the quantities held reach certain thresholds, the production of those PC models can be temporarily suspended.

5   Results

The following supplier strategies were developed on top of the MSS strategy:

- Multi-Attempt Massive Strategy (MAMS): Tackles problems 1 and 2 by re-sending those RFQs that did not receive offers or are above the Cut-Off-Date.
- Enhanced Multi-Attempt Massive Strategy with Last Ordering (EMAMS-LO): This strategy works as MAMS, but it also addresses problem (4) by ordering components towards the end.

• Multi-Attempt Massive Strategy with Prediction of Gaps (MAMS-PG): As MAMS, but this strategy addresses problem (5) by predicting gaps in the production given the current inventory and the active orders.

• Multi-Attempt Massive Strategy with Small Orders (MAMS-SO): This strategy operates as MAMS, but orders small quantities of components for a period of time determined at the beginning of the game in an attempt to avoid gaps in the production (although these are not predicted as in the previous variation).

5.1   TAC SCM 2004

The TAC SMC 2004 competition involved five rounds: (a) qualifying, (b) seeding, (c) quarter finals, (d) semi-finals, and (e) finals. In the qualifying round 31 teams participated and games were played 24 hours each weekday for two weeks. All agents that were active over 50% of the games were allowed to advance to the seeding round (30 teams). The seeding rounds took place over a two-week period similarly to the qualifying round. The success of an agent was measured by a weighted average of its scores in all games for which it was scheduled. Games played during the second week were worth twice as much as those played in the first week. The top 24 agents proceeded to the quarter finals for which they were divided in four groups according to their final position in the seeding round:

group A: positions 1, 2, 3, 22, 23, 24; group B: positions 4, 5, 6, 19, 20, 21.
group C: positions 7, 8, 9, 16, 17, 18; group D: positions 10, 11, 12, 13, 14, 15.

Every group played 8 games. The top three teams from each group progressed to the semi-finals in which the agents were divided into two groups: group 1: agents from groups A and D, and group 2: agents from groups B and C. The top three teams in each semifinal progressed to the finals, in which they played 16 games in total. The top scoring agent in the finals was declared the winner.

In the first week of the qualifying rounds the MSS strategy was used and Socrates ended up in position 20 - this was due to the problems discussed in section 4.2. In the second week of the qualifying rounds the EMAMS-LO strategy was used. EMAMS-LO was quite effective in keeping the factory utilisation up towards the end of the game, if Socrates had already received the other components on time. One disadvantage of this strategy is that in some games it is not worth ordering components towards the end as the difference between the cost of the components purchased and the price of the PCs sold gives the agent no profit. Socrates was placed 16th at the end of the 2nd week.

In the seeding round Socrates (76 games) the strategy used was MAMS-PG which attempts to predict gaps in the production after accepting all the initial offers from the suppliers. Factory utilisation improved from 75% in the qualifying rounds to 81% in the seeding rounds, and the average score improved as well. Socrates was placed in the 13th position at the end of the seeding rounds.

Socrates qualified for the quarter finals and was placed in the most competitive group, D, in which all agents seemed to have similar average scores and used similar strategies. Socrates strategy in the quarter finals was EMAMS. The performance of EMAMS was

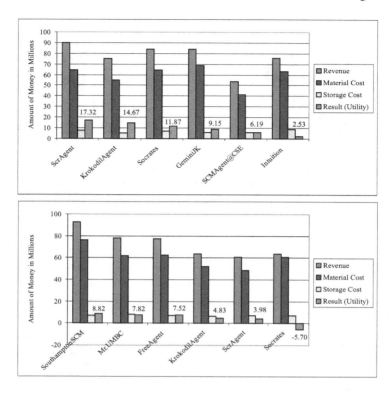

Fig. 1. Top: Average score of Socrates using EMAMS in quarter finals. Bottom: Average score of Socrates using MAMS-SO in semi-finals.

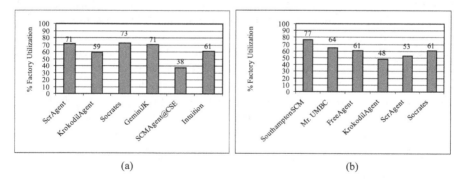

(a)   (b)

Fig. 2. Factory utilisation of Socrates with: (a) EMAMS in quarter finals; and (b) MAMS-SO in semi-finals

good in most of the games. The results from this round for group D are summarized in Fig. 1(a), 2(a) and 3(a).

Based on the quarter final results Socrates qualified for the semi-finals. The semifinal round which involved 16 games was a highly competitive environment with agents with very similar strategies procuring components on day 0. In this round, Socrates played with the MAMS-SO strategy. The strategy was not able to succeed in this

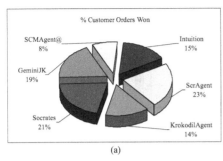

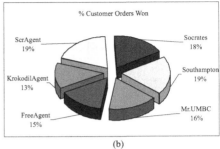

(a)   (b)

Fig. 3. Average percentage of customer orders won by each of the agents in (a) the quarter finals, (b) the semi-finals

		Number of C-S Agents					
		0	1	2	3	4	5
Number of M-S Agents	0	6	5	4	3	2	1
	1	5	4	3	2	1	
	2	4	3	2	1		
	3	3	2	1			
	4	2	1		Number of	
	5	1			Socrates Agents	

(a)

		Number of C-S Agents					
		0	1	2	3	4	5
Number of M-S Agents	0	73	77	82	86	86	86
	1	74	79	84	86	86	
	2	74	81	84	86		
	3	76	81	86			
	4	78	82		Average of	
	5	80			Factory Utilization	
					for Socrates Agents	

(b)

Fig. 4. (a) Number of agents per game; (b) Factory utilisation of Socrates agents in respective game

environment as SouthamptonTAC was using a strategy (initially used the day before by another agent) which consisted of purchasing large quantities of memories by sending RFQs on day 0 to all the suppliers of this type of component. The agents whose RFQs were processed after the RFQs of SouthamptonTAC suffered from the lack of this type of component for long periods since all of the suppliers' production capacity was committed. As a result and since an agent is not allowed to change its strategy during a round, Socrates did not qualify for the next round. This also had an impact on the other agents. The overall results are shown in Fig. 1(b), 2(b) 3(b). The top scoring agent of TAC SCM 2004 was FreeAgent, followed by Mr.UMBC and UMTac-04.

5.2   Controlled Experiments

To evaluate the performance of our agent, in terms of factory utilisation, we ran a set of controlled experiments (in a similar way to [10]) in which we included 3 types of agents according to the way in which they order components:

• Conservative-Strategy Agents (C-S Agents) which order in small quantities.
• Massive-Strategy Agents (M-S Agents) which order large quantities in the beginning of the game to guarantee production the rest of the game.

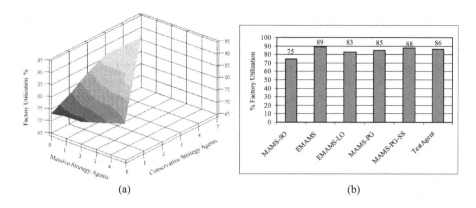

Fig. 5. (a) Average factory utilisation for Socrates agents playing against M-S and C-S agents. (b) Factory utilisation in experiments using the MAMS-PG-SS strategy.

● Socrates Agents. These use the Multi-Attempt Massive Strategy with Prediction of Gaps which orders big quantities at the beginning and fills the gaps throughout the game to maintain 100% factory utilisation (section 3).

Fig. 4(a) shows the 21 different scenarios used in the experiments, in which we have all the possible combinations of C-S, M-S and Socrates agents for a TAC 6-player game. The first line of the table indicates the number of C-S agents, the first column the number of M-S agents, while the main part of the table indicates the number of Socrates agents in the game. We ran 50 games for each scenario to test the performance of the agents in the different environments.

Fig. 4(b) shows the average of factory utilisation for Socrates agents in each scenario. For example for a game with 2 C-S agents and 1 M-S agent there are 3 Socrates agents, which achieve in average a factory utilisation of 84%. When there is more than 1 Socrates agent in a game we take the average of factory utilisation. Fig. 4(b) indicates that in non-competitive environments the factory utilisation for Socrates agents is better than that in competitive environments. We define a non-competitive environment as the environment in which the number of C-S agents is less than the sum of M-S agents and Socrates agents:

(# of C-S agents) <(# of M-S agents) + (Socrates agents)

Those environments in which the sum of M-S agents and Socrates agents is greater than the number of C-S agents are referred to as "competitive". Fig. 5(a) graphically illustrates the results from Fig. 4(a) in which as one can observe the more Socrates agents playing in a game (including M-S agents), the more competitive the environment is. The z axis in Fig 5(a) shows the average percentage of factory utilisation for Socrates agents, which demonstrates that they behave much better in non-competitive environments than they do in competitive ones.

One of the main weaknesses of the supplier strategies that were considered and tested during TAC SCM is their inability to adapt dynamically to conditions in the game that affect the procurement of components. One possibility was to allow the agent to switch between suppliers and components when one supplier fails to supply them. This new strategy, Multi-Attempt Massive Strategy with Prediction of Gaps with Supplier Switching (MAMS-PG-SS), combines the prediction of gaps with a strategy that looks for substitutable components. It determines the set of components that can be substituted for every component that the agent can order. For instance, if Socrates cannot obtain memory 1GB from supplier Queenmax, then it looks for substitutable components in the following order: memory 1 GB (MEC), memory 2 GB (Queenmax) and finally memory 2 (MEC). This list indicates the order in which the agent will try to satisfy the number of components needed. The agent keeps track of the number of attempts to every supplier and if it reaches a threshold value the agent switches supplier or in the appropriate case supplier and type of component. This process is carried out until the agent satisfies the quantity needed of every component. The strategy works as expected when a supplier cannot provide the specific component, and the agent has to look for a replacement. Since it works by substituting the supplier or the type of component, the number of PCs of each model assembled in a TAC day will be different. In some cases, the agent will be left with a number of unused components in its inventory. This occurs when the agent has ordered a greater number of CPUs than the number of motherboards of one specific type (Pintel or IMD) in its attempt to find substitutable components and manufacture alternative PC models. We run a series of 100 games to compare this strategy against all the previous ones developed, while introducing a SouthamptonTAC-like behaviour (TestAgent) to observe the results. However, as we haven't had the chance to test this strategy against other real agents and all our strategies operate in a similar way, the results as shown in Fig. 5(b) are not conclusive.

6   Conclusions

This paper presented the Socrates trading agent and the strategies employed in the TAC SCM 2004 competition. Socrates is a production-driven agent which attempts to keep factory utilisation to the maximum throughout the game. As such it is plagued by a number of problems as has been described, more so as customer demand is not taken into consideration when making orders to the suppliers or scheduling production. We hope to address some of these problems for the TAC SCM 2006 competition. In particular, we are working on a strategy that concentrates equally on the customers' side as well as on the supplier side. We would like to explore the idea of using variable scoring functions to deal with the supplier side. We are also considering the scheduling problem under a new light, using a daily schedule as well as a dynamic global production schedule that takes into account the current inventory of components and the component *ActiveOrders* in deciding which customer orders can be satisfied.

References

1. TAC SCM specification. Available at http://www.sics.se/tac/.
2. Sun Java Center J2EE Patterns.   http://java.sun.com/developer/technicalArticles/J2EE/patterns/, March 2001.

3. R. Arunachalam and N. Sadeh. The 2003 supply chain management trading agent competition. In *Proceedings of the Trading Agent Analysis and Design Workshop (TADA)*, 2004.

4. M. Benisch, A. Greenwald, I. Grypari, R. Lederman, V. Naroditskiy, , and M. Tschantz. Botticelli: A supply chain management agent designed to optimize under uncertainty. *SIGecom Exchanges*, 4:29–37, 2004.

5. S. Buffett and N. Scott. An algorithm for procurement in supply chain management. In *Proceedings of the Trading Agent Analysis and Design Workshop*, 2004.

6. E. Dahlgren and P. Wurman. Packatac: A conservative trading agent. *SIGecom Exchanges*, 4:38–45, 2004.

7. R. Dong, T. Tai, W. Yeung, and D. Parkes. Hartac - the harvard tac scm03 agent. In *Proceedings of the Trading Agent Analysis and Design Workshop (TADA)*, 2004.

8. J. Estelle, Y. Vorobeychik, M. Wellman, S. Singh, C. Kiekintveld, , and V. Soni. Strategic procurement in tac/scm: An empirical game-theoretic analysis. In *Proceedings of the Trading Agent Analysis and Design Workshop (TADA)*, 2004.

9. Helm R. Johnson R. Vlissides J. Gamma, E. *Design Patterns: Elements of Reusable Object-Oriented Software*. Addison-Wesley, 1995.

10. M. He and R.N. Jennings. SouthamptonTAC: An adaptive autonomous trading agent. *ACM Transactions on Internet Technology*, 3:218–235, 2003.

11. P. Keller, F. Duguay, and D. Precup. RedAgent - Winner of TAC SCM 2003. *SIGecom Exchanges*, 4:1–8, 2004.

12. D. Pardoe and P. Stone. Tactex-03: A supply chain management agent. *SIGecom Exchanges*, 4:9–18, 2004.

13. S. Sun, V. Avasarala, T. Mullen, and J. Yen. Psutac: A trading agent designed from heuristics to knowledge. In *Proceedings of the Trading Agent Analysis and Design Workshop (TADA)*, 2004.

Designing and Evaluating an Adaptive Trading Agent
for Supply Chain Management

Minghua He, Alex Rogers, Esther David, and Nicholas R. Jennings

School of Electronics and Computer Science, University of Southampton,
Southampton, SO17 1BJ, United Kingdom
{mh, acr, ed, nrj}@ecs.soton.ac.uk

Abstract. This paper describes the design and evaluation of SouthamptonSCM, a finalist in the 2004 International Trading Agent Supply Chain Management Competition (TAC SCM). In particular, we focus on the way in which our agent sets its prices according to the prevailing market situation and its own inventory level (because this adaptivity and flexibility are the key components of its success). Specifically, we analyse our pricing model's performance both in the actual competition and in controlled experiments. Through this evaluation, we show that SouthamptonSCM performs well across a broad range of environments.

1 Introduction

Internet technologies have contributed significantly to e-commerce by increasing the mutual visibility of consumers and suppliers, and by raising the possibility that some of their trading processes may be automated. However, despite these advances, most procurement activities within supply chains are still based on static long-term contracts and relationships. Now, in many cases, such contracts are detrimental because they fail to handle the dynamic nature of these environments, where new suppliers and consumers may enter the market at anytime and where trading partners may fail to fulfill their commitments. To rectify this, we believe agent-based solutions are needed. To date, however, the use of agents within e-commerce has generally focused on simple auctions [4]. Whereas, the supply chain domain typically requires handling a more complex setting in the presence of much greater degrees of uncertainty and dynamism [6].

To this end, the International Trading Agents Competition for Supply Chain Management (http://www.sics.se/tac) (TAC SCM [1]) represents an ideal environment in which to test the autonomous agents that we develop. Such multi-agent research competitions present well-defined problems in which alternative solutions can be tested, compared and evaluated. In the TAC SCM scenario, agents are competing as computer manufacturers in a virtual business world to handle three basic subtasks: acquiring components, managing manufacturing process, and selling assembled computers to customers.

Against this background, we present our work in developing an adaptive agent that was a finalist in the 2004 TAC SCM competition (6 out of 29 participants reached the finals). The key contribution of this work is the techniques that we develop to enable the

H. La Poutré, N. Sadeh, and S. Janson (Eds.): AMEC and TADA 2005, LNAI 3937, pp. 140–156, 2006.

agent to adapt its price setting to the prevailing market situation, its own internal state (inventory level) and the time that has elapsed. At their core, these techniques employ fuzzy reasoning in order to allow the agent to adapt its prices daily so that it can fully exploit its production capacity, while still maximising its revenue by selling at appropriate prices. Previously, fuzzy techniques have been successfully applied to solve the problems of automated auction [3,5], TAC classic (SouthamptonTAC [3]) and negotiation [7]. We believe fuzzy logic provides an effective tool to cope with the uncertainty inherent in a complex decision making problem (e.g. the supply chain context) and to make trade-offs between the variants of attributes (e.g. price and quantity). Also, fuzzy rules are the most visible and interpretable manifestation of this approach and have been successfully used in a variety of areas [10].

The remainder of the paper is organized as follows. Section 2 outlines the TAC SCM. Section 3 presents our agent. Section 4 evaluates the performance of the agent. Finally, Section 5 concludes.

2   The TAC SCM Game

In this game, six agents (competition entrants) compete with one another to procure raw components and fulfil customer orders for assembled PCs. Each PC is assembled from four components: CPU, motherboard, memory and hard disk (e.g. a PC with a 2GHz IMD processor with 1GB memory and a 300GB hard drive). Each agent is able to produce any of the 16 distinct computer types (different PC types require a different number of production cycles) and is limited to a capacity of 2000 cycles daily.

The agents operate simultaneously in separate markets to buy components from a number of suppliers and to sell PCs to customers. Both of these markets operate as follows: (i) the buyer issues Request For Quotes (RFQs) to the sellers; (ii) the sellers respond to the RFQs with offers detailing the price, quantity or delivery date; and (iii) the buyer sends orders to accept offers.

Consequently, on each of the 220 simulation days of the game, agents receive from the customers a new set of RFQs and, in response to previously sent offers, they receive orders for assembled computers. Likewise, component suppliers that were previously sent RFQs respond with offers. Thus, in each day of the game (lasting 15 seconds), the agent must decide on the following: (i) which new supplier RFQs to issue and which supplier offers to accept; (ii) which customer RFQs to respond to, and what price to offer; and (iii) how to schedule the production and delivery of PCs given the availability of components, the limited capacity of the factory and the delivery deadlines of pending orders.

An agent spends money on buying the components, paying for the storage of both components and PCs, paying penalties if it defaults on a promised delivery date and paying overdraft penalties if it is in debt to the bank. The agent earns money by selling PCs and receives interest from the bank if its balance is positive. Success of an agent is measured in terms of its profit (*i.e.*, its bank balance at the end of the game).

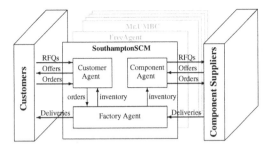

Fig. 1. Overview of the SouthamptonSCM agent

3   SouthamptonSCM

SouthamptonSCM can be decomposed into three sub-agents (see Figure 1).[1] The *component agent* decides which RFQs and which orders to send to which suppliers. The *customer agent* receives RFQs from the customers and decides what offers to respond with. It also communicates with the factory agent to obtain the updated inventory levels and to send the relevant customer PC orders. The *factory agent* receives the supplies delivered from the suppliers, decides based on the available resources (computer components and factory cycles) in what order the customer orders should be produced, and determines the schedules for delivering the finished PCs to the customers. We now deal, in turn, with each of these sub-agents.

3.1   The Component Agent

The price offered by a supplier in response to an RFQ is based entirely on its available production capacity and the quantity agents ask for (*i.e.*, price increases as capacity decreases or quantity required increases). On Day 0, all the suppliers have their full capacity available, thus the prices they offer are at their lowest value. Therefore, intuitively, it makes sense to order a large number of components on Day 0 (indeed this was a widely used tactic in the 2003 competition [9]). However, due to a rule change, the components now attract a storage cost. Thus the more the agent stores and the longer it stores it, the higher the storage cost. This means the key challenge of the component agent is to attain an appropriate balance between availability and timeliness. This is hard because if the agent buys more units early (at lower prices) it has to pay for storage and some components may be unused at the end of the game. However if the agent just buys what it needs when it is needed, it may end up without the necessary components at the necessary time (since there is often a delay between the actual delivery date and the one the suppliers promise). Given this, our agent makes a trade-off between placing a big order on Day 0 and buying gradually during the rest of the game.

In more detail, experience from practise games showed that despite the storage cost, having a reasonably big order on Day 0 is still profitable because of the low prices that

---

[1] Here we use the notion of sub-agents (instead of modules) because each of them can autonomously communicate with the suppliers and customers to get the RFQs, can send offers and obtain orders, and can decide how to respond to this information.

can be obtained. Specifically, we found it most effective when this number just covers the quantity the agent needs in low demand games. Thus on Day 0, SouthamptonSCM orders a large number of components (2000, 2000, 2500, 3500, 5000) from each supplier with corresponding delivery dates of Day 10, 25, 40, 70 and 110. These dates were chosen in order to give the agent a steady stream of components for the early to middle part of the game. The agent accepts the corresponding offer if the delivery date is not too far from the date it asks for. However, if the demand turns out to be greater than what the agent ordered, it can still buy components (at higher prices) during the rest of the game. In particular, after the Day 0 order, the agent keeps asking for small quantities of components from the suppliers and placing orders for them if the offer price is low. At about Day 140, the agent starts to order components for the rest of the game. It does this based on the average daily demand for computers (as a predictor of how many components are needed) and buys gradually if the offer prices from the suppliers are low.

3.2   The Customer Agent

The customer agent is the key component in SouthamptonSCM's strategy (because we believe that offering the appropriate price at the right time is vital for success). If the price is too low, the agent will receive a low profit and if it is too high it will fail to win any orders (because customers always choose the lowest offer price among those they receive). Here, the key challenges are to determine which customer RFQs to bid for and at what price. To achieve this, we use inventory driven methods to choose RFQs and soft computing techniques to calculate the price (see below).

Choosing RFQs and setting prices.   The customer agent uses an inventory driven strategy when selecting customer RFQs. That is, it only offers customers PCs according to what is presently available in its inventory. By doing this, the agent avoids getting penalties for committing to more than it can produce (the quantity of PCs it can produce is constrained by the availability of components and factory cycles).

In more detail, Table 1 shows the strategy we use. Given a customer RFQ $(i, q, p_{res}, c_{penalty}, d_{due})$, where $i \in \{1, \cdots, 16\}$ is the type of PC the customer wants, $q > 0$ the quantity, $p_{res} > 0$ the reservation price (maximum it will pay), $c_{penalty} > 0$ the fine if the computers are not delivered on time, and d_{due} the desired delivery date. On each day, the customer agent receives a bundle of such RFQs and sorts them in the order of decreasing $(p_{res} - c_{penalty}/q)$. The intuition here is that the agent will first serve customers with high reserve prices and low penalties. This is because the higher the p_{res}, the more profit will be made (compared to selling the same product to a customer with a low p_{res}). At the same time, the agent also wants to avoid getting high penalty orders because of the inherent uncertainties that exist in the game.

The next consideration relates to the agent's production capacity. Specifically, as there is only limited production capacity per day, the agent needs to calculate the number of cycles that can be offered to respond to the customer RFQs of that day.[2] Thus, it

---

[2] Note here the agent does not offer the exact number of cycles that are available ($C[d_{due} - 2]$) on day $(d_{due} - 2)$, but rather it includes a risk factor ($\lambda \times C[d_{due} - 2]$) which enables it to offer more than it actually has in order to maximise the production utilisation. Here $\lambda > 1$.

Table 1. Pricing strategy on day d

- list RFQs in decreasing order of $(p_{res} - c_{penalty}/q)$
- update the production capacity $C[k]$ of each day k
- $offeredCycles = 0$ and $reservedCycles[k] = 0$
- calculate the reference price for each kind of PC p_{ref}^i
- for each RFQ in the list
  - $p_{offer} = max\{p_{ref}^i \times (1 + f(d_{due})), p_{base}^i\}$
  - if PC inventory $\geq q$ then
    - offer q PCs at p_{offer}
    - decrease PC inventory by q
  - else if component inventory $\geq q$ and
    $reservedCycles[d_{due} - 2] + q \times o^i \leq C[d_{due} - 2] \times \lambda$ then
    - offer q PCs at p_{offer}
    - increase $offeredCycles$ by $q \times o^i$
    - decrease $reservedCycles[d_{due} - 2]$ by $q \times o^i$
    - decrease component inventory accordingly
  - else do not offer PCs to this customer

---

updates the available production cycles for each day based on the customer orders that have just been received. Specifically, for each RFQ, the agent first checks whether it can be supplied from its stock of finished PCs (see Section 3.3). If it can, the corresponding PC inventory is decreased. Otherwise, the agent checks whether it holds enough components in its inventory and whether it has a sufficiently high remaining production capacity $C[d_{due} - 2]$ on day $(d_{due} - 2)$, which is the latest the PCs can be produced.[3] If it does, the agent decreases its component inventory and $reservedCycles$ for day $(d_{due} - 2)$ accordingly and increases the number of cycles offered ($q \times o^i$, where o^i is the cycles needed for PC type i) on that day.

Now the agent needs to consider what price can be offered to the RFQ. Based on the demand in the market, the inventory level, and how far we are into the game, the agent first computes a *reference price* (p_{ref}^i) that corresponds to a reasonable current market price. Thus for PC type i:

$$p_{ref}^i = p_{low}^i + (p_{high}^i - p_{low}^i)r, \tag{1}$$

where p_{low}^i, p_{high}^i are the lowest and highest transaction prices of PC type i on the previous day, and $r \in [0.4, 1.2]$ is an *adjustment factor* that determines how far away the reference price is from the lowest price. This adjustment factor is set through the fuzzy reasoning mechanism and is adapted according to the quantity of orders received and the number of orders expected (see Section 3.2 for more details). However, given an RFQ, the offer price is not the reference price of PC type i. Rather, p_{offer} is the maximum of the cost for PC type i (p_{base}^i is the money spent buying the constituent components)

---

[3] Note that for an RFQ with the due date d, the agent checks whether it can be produced on the latest possible day $(d - 2)$ because this has previously been shown to be effective in this scenario [2].

and the reference price modified by a factor related to the requested delivery date. This ensures the agent sells the PC at least for its cost. The use of d_{due} means that the sooner the due date, the higher the offered price is compared to the reference price (because the agent has little time to produce the computers with a bigger risk of being penalised for being late).

In more detail, the fuzzy reasoning inference mechanism employed to set the adjustment factor in Equation (1) is based on the standard Sugeno controller [8]. Our agent uses two rule bases: one for the end stage of the game (about last 40 days) and one for other days in the game. Both rule bases incorporate some 20 rules[4] which vary the price according to the market demand, its inventory level and time into the game (see Appendix for details of the rule bases). We show two representative rules below:

$\mathcal{R}_j$: if D is $high$ and I is $high$ and ND is far then r_j is big
$\mathcal{R}_q$: if D is $high$ and E is $close$ then r_q is $very\text{-}small$

where the customer demand (D) is expressed in the fuzzy linguistic terms $high$, $medium$, and low, the inventory level (I) in the terms $high$, $medium$, and low, next delivery date of a big amount of components (ND) in the terms far, $medium$, and $close$ and days to the end of the game (E) in the terms: far, $medium$, and $close$. r_j is the output of the individual rule j (i.e., the adjustment factor discussed above). Thus, rule $\mathcal{R}_j$ captures the fact that if the type of PC is in high demand in the market, the agent has a high inventory for this kind of PC and there is a long time until the next delivery for a high volume of components, then r_j should be big (thus resulting in a higher bid price). The second rule $\mathcal{R}_q$ captures the fact that if there is high demand for a particular type of PC and there is a little time until the end of the game, then r_q should be very small (thus ensuring a low offer price and hence reducing the risk of being left with inventory at the end of the game). The firing level $\alpha_j \in [0, 1]$ of rule $\mathcal{R}_j$ is computed in the standard way by using the Min operator on the membership values of the corresponding fuzzy sets. According to the Sugeno controller definition, the crisp control action (i.e., the output of the fuzzy rule base fed into Equation (1)) is:

$$r = \frac{\sum_{j=1}^{n} \alpha_j r_j}{\sum_{j=1}^{n} \alpha_j} \qquad (2)$$

Adaptation of offer prices. Given the uncertainty in TAC SCM, we believe it is essential for the agents to be responsive to the prevailing situation during the course of bidding for customer orders. The idea is that the agent can only use 2000 production cycles every day, so, to maximise throughput, the number of cycles necessary to produce the received customer orders should also be 2000. Thus if the received orders require

---

[4] In generating the rules, we followed the steps below: (1) determine what to reason about in this SCM game – the offer price; (2) choose the factors that should be used in the rules – inventory level, demand, and time into the game (there may be some other factors, but these are the most relevant ones); (3) structure the fuzzy rules – based on the relationship of the factors to the reasoning value and experiences in the field; (4) decide how to adapt the parameters in the rules – SouthamptonSCM adapts the price based on the quantity of the received customer orders and the expected number of orders. (5) refine the rules and parameters.

Table 2. Adaptation of the offer prices

- update $receivedTotalCycles$;
- calculate $receivedCycles$;
- $expectedCycles = min\{2000, offeredCycles \times \mu\}$;
- if $receivedCycles < \overline{expectedCycles}$ then $r = r - \delta$;
- else if $receivedCycles > \overline{expectedCycles}$ then $r = r + \delta$.

---

more than this figure, it means that the agent has set its offer price too low. In contrast, if the number is too small, it means the agent is not winning enough customer orders (which implies that its offer price is too high). However, we cannot just base our decision on 2000 cycles because some of that day's production cycles might be reserved by the orders of previous days (because more than 2000 cycles were needed previously). In this case, the number of expected cycles for the day's order is only part of the offered cycles of the previous day (because all agents compete for customer orders and only the lowest price can be accepted). With this information, the agent can adapt its offer prices in order to try and keep the factory working at high capacity, but still be responsive to the prices other agents offer (based on the highest and lowest transaction prices of the previous day). Specifically, the adaptation rule is if the orders the agent receives need more cycles than it expected, it will increase its price, otherwise it will decrease it.

Table 2 shows how the price adaptation works. Here, $receivedTotalCycles$ represents the total number of cycles needed to produce the PCs for the orders just received; $receivedCycles$ represents the cycles needed for the orders that the agent offers from the component inventory rather than the finished PCs (finished PCs do not count since they do not require more cycles to produce them); $offeredCycles$ is the actual total number of cycles offered on the previous day (as per Table 1) and $expectedCycles$ is $offeredCycles$ multiplied by the expected acceptance rate ($\mu = 0.75$), *i.e.*, how many cycles are expected to win customer orders among all the cycles offered. Now if $receivedCycles$ is much less than the expected number of cycles, the agent will decrease the adjustment factor (thus the price is decreased, see Equation (1)) by δ (here $\delta = 0.02$), otherwise it will increase the adjustment factor (thus the price is increased). However sometimes if the expected number of cycles is only slightly smaller than the actual number of received cycles, we do not decrease the offer prices (since this is a close enough approximation in a noisy environment). To realise this, we view $\overline{expectedCycles}$ as a fuzzy number [11].

3.3   The Factory Agent

One of the main challenges for the factory agent is scheduling what to produce and when to produce it (*i.e.*, how to allocate supply resources and factory time). The strategy we use includes: manufacturing PCs according to customer orders and satisfying orders with an earlier delivery date (see Table 3 for more detail). Now, since the computers stored in the factory will be charged storage cost, each order will be delivered as soon as it is filled. The agent builds the PCs according to the customers' orders it has obtained (which has the advantage of ensuring that the factory always produces the

Table 3. Production scheduling for day d

- list the orders with due date $d + 2$ in list 1;
- list late orders (but still valid $d - 3 \leq d_{due} \leq d + 1$) in the decreasing order of the due date into list 2;
- list the future orders (due date $\geq d + 3$) in the increasing order of the due date into list 3;
- append list 2 to list 1 and list 3 to list 2;
- for each order in the combined list
  - if computers in the inventory can fill the order then deliver computers;
  - else if components are available and factory capacity is not full then produce more PCs to fill the order;
- if there is extra factory capacity left and enough components, then check whether additional PCs should be produced.

---

needed computers on time). However, if there are still factory assembling cycles left and the numbers of finished PCs are below a certain threshold then the agent produces additional PCs of each kind uniformly (if there are enough components) to maximise the factory utilisation. In particular, this strategy benefits the agent when there is a low demand in the market (because there are actually spare cycles) and it works well in the final stages of the game. For example, on Day 217, the agent can bid on customer orders that come in on that day, meaning it gets the orders on Day 218 and delivers the computers on the last day of the game. If it just used the *build-to-order* strategy, the agent would not be able to bid for the customer orders on Day 217 because after it wins the order, there would be no time for it to buy the needed components and produce the PCs.

4 Evaluation

Our evaluation is composed of three components: (i) the results from the 2004 competition; (ii) our post-hoc analysis of some of the games in the actual competition; and (iii) a systematic range of controlled experiments.

4.1 TAC SCM Results

TAC SCM consists of a preliminary round (mainly used for practice and fine tuning), a seeding round, quarter-finals, semi-finals, and final. The seeding round determined groupings for the quarter-finals. The top 24 agents were organised into 4 "heats" for the quarter-finals based on the positions in the seeding round and the first 3 teams for the quarter-finals of heat 1 and 3 entered into semi-final 1 and, similarly, the first 3 teams from heat 2 and 4 were entered into semi-final 2. Finally, the first 3 teams in both semi-finals entered into the final round. In the seeding round, SouthamptonSCM obtained the third highest score among all the participants and entered heat 1 for the quarter-final. In the quarter-final, we had the second highest score and we were first in our semi-final. In the final, our agent finished in 6th position. In the final, our agent was adversely affected by the fact that several agents sent RFQs on Day 0 for huge quantities of components.

Then, if the corresponding offers were expensive they declined to buy them or if they were cheap they took up the offers. However, in the meantime, since the suppliers have limited capacity they scheduled other Day 0 orders for much later in the game. Thus when this happened our Day 0 bidding was severely effected (sometimes up to Day 70) and we received severely delayed delivery dates for our orders. In such cases, we were simply unable to obtain the components we needed through our Day-0 procurement policy and so we made very few sales.

4.2   Competition Game Analysis

To complement and better understand the competition result and to evaluate the effectiveness of our pricing model we conducted a post hoc analysis. However it is hard to see how the pricing works from only the game results since the competition entrants contain a variety of interrelated strategies (for the different facets of their operation). Thus we decided to compare for the RFQs that the agents responded to, how the price varies among different agents.[5] To do this, we analysed competition games and we were especially interested in those cases where there were strong agents. Here we take a randomly chosen representative game in the semi-final (game 1136) and analyse it in more detail.[6]

In this game, we compare our agent with FreeAgent and Mr.UMBC which were the first and second placed agents in the final. Thus, in each such competition, we extracted from the game data, details of the RFQs that were received by the competing agents, the offers that they sent to the customers in response and the orders that resulted.[7] This data enabled us to compare the orders that the agents were winning with the prices that they offered. Specifically, Figure 2 shows for each simulation day, the daily price (per production cycle, see Figure 2 (a)) offered by each agent and the cumulative order quantity that each agent won (expressed as factory production cycles averaged over all products see Figure 2 (b)). Since the ultimate profitability of the agents depends on both these factors, we also calculate the average cumulative revenue (i.e. the number of PC orders multiplied by their prices, see Figure 2 (c)).

Throughout the game, SouthamptonSCM adaptively adjusts the price offered to the customer to ensure that the factory maintains as close to full production as possible (the factory utilisation for our agent, FreeAgent and Mr.UMBC are 76%, 58%, and 61%). Generally, having a high factory utilisation means the agent can produce more PCs and thus win more customer orders. For example, in this game, the number of orders for these three agents are 5405, 4011, and 4300. In this example, all three agents have sufficient components to allow them to compete for the same orders. However, our

---

[5] We aim to compare the pricing model and the revenue made by responding to the customer RFQs. Thus the price paid for the components and any late penalties need not be considered here.

[6] We did not choose a game from the final because of the skewing introduced by the Day 0 bidding strategies used by some of the agents. Also it is impossible to compare the pricing of multiple games in one figure, thus we only show one representative game. However, the following discussion also applies to the other games we analysed.

[7] For clarity, we omit from this plot the other three agents, and just show data for Southampton-SCM, FreeAgent and Mr.UMBC. The plots of the other agents show they were less effective.

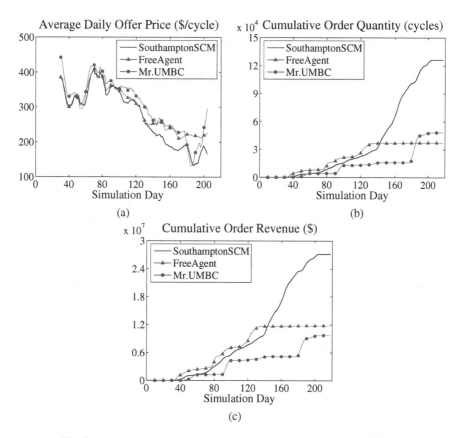

Fig. 2. Comparison of offer prices, quantity and revenue in game 1136

pricing model is particularly successful. The prices offered by SouthamptonSCM are just low enough that the offers of the competing agents are undercut, but high enough that the resulting orders generate as much revenue as possible.

After analysing more semi-final games, we found that the prices SouthamptonSCM offers follow the same broad trend compared with the other two. And, in particular, the trend is when the customer demand is high, the prices are high, and vice versa. This can be seen from Figure 2 (a), where the demand for the first half of the game is high, and the demand decreases gradually till Day 160 and increases again. Accordingly, the prices are high before Day 110 and then start to decrease gradually. At the end of the game, although the demand is increasing, the agents do not increase their prices because they want to offload their stock. Moreover, in most of the games we considered, the prices SouthamptonSCM offered just undercut the other two. This is also reflected by the quantity of orders our agent won which was again usually the highest.

4.3   Controlled Experiments

To evaluate the performance of our agent in a more systematic fashion than is possible in the competition, we decided to run a series of controlled experiments. As mentioned before, we attribute the success of our agent to the adaptive control of the offering price and this is what we are most interested in here. Thus, we decided to analyse how the pricing works compared with other methods. To do this, we devised two competitor agents that adopt identical strategies to SouthamptonSCM except for the method they use to offer prices. The alternative methods[8] we consider are consistent with the broad classes of behaviour that were adopted by several of the agents in the competition:

- **High-Price agent (HP-agent).** This agent bids aggressively at high offer prices to obtain a higher profit margin in selling the PCs. It will take the risk of stocking a large number of PCs and components in the factory and paying storage cost for them. But when its PCs are sold they fetch high prices and mean it can very quickly build up profits. In more detail, the prices that HP-agent offer are the *maximum* of the cost of the computer plus a fixed profit margin (here it is 300) and the computers' reserve price minus 1. Thus, when the reserve price is high enough, it sells at reserve price minus 1. Otherwise, it sells at the price of the cost of components plus a fixed margin.
- **High-Volume agent (HV-agent).** This agent bids cautiously and only seeks to attain a reasonable profit margin for each order, but it tries to maximise the volume of orders. This means that the agent wants to sell its PCs quickly and it does not want to take the risk of stocking components or PCs (especially in games with low customer demand). Specifically, it offers the computers at the cost of the computer plus a small margin. Here the margin is set to 300 in the first 180 days of the game and this is then decreased to 0 linearly till the end of the game. This policy is adopted because the agent hopes that it can sell all the computers by the end of the game.

Besides these two kinds of agents, the other competing participants are the dummy agents provided by the organisers. These use a build-to-order method and offer prices which are chosen uniformly from $80 - 100\%$ of the reserve prices. Generally, the dummy agent can be viewed as being high-volume because it often offers a low price (but it differs from our HV-agent in that it uses the build-to-order method). Given this background, three groups of experiments were conducted to examine the performance of each kind of agent in various situations. In experiment A, there is one SouthamptonSCM, one HP-agent, one HV-agent and three dummy agents. In experiment B, we increase the number of HP-agents to 2 and decrease the number of dummy agents to 2. In experiment C the number of HP-agents is 3 and the number of dummies is 1. The average revenue of each kind of agent in each of the experiments are then plotted.[9]

---

[8] Although neither alternative we chose employs market history information (*i.e.* the highest and lowest transaction prices of the previous day), they represent the two common attitudes for setting bidding prices: "High-Price" and "High-Volume".

[9] Note that the dummy agents in the game represent default players. We aim to evaluate the performance of the other three types of agents instead of dummy agents. In order to obtain valid results that represent realistic games, we varied the number of dummy agents and in some games, there is only one dummy agent (e.g. experiment C). We believe this environment is able to represent realistic games since even in real games there are some players who use build-to-order like strategies.

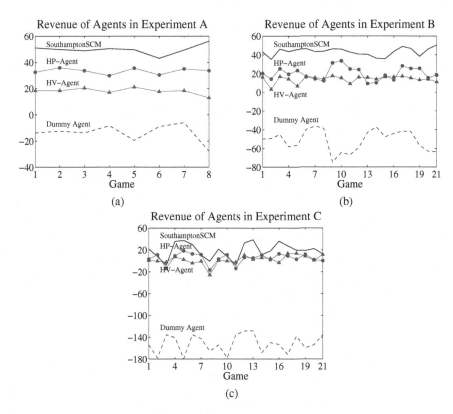

Fig. 3. Revenue of each kind of agent

We now start to analyse the performance of the different agents as shown in Figure 3.[10] In experiment A, it can be seen that SouthamtptonSCM performs significantly better than the other two agents and that the HP-agent is better than the HVs. In experiment B, SouthamptonSCM is significantly better than both HP-agents and HV-agents and the HP-agents are better than the RAs. In experiment C, SouthamptonSCM is significantly better than the other two, however we cannot differentiate statistically which agent is better between HP and HV agents. Now, in all cases, we can attribute this success of SouthamptonSCM solely to the adaptivity aspect of its pricing (because this is the only difference between the agents). Moreover, we found that the average revenue SouthamptonSCM obtained is 49.7% higher than HP-agents in experiment A, 129.7% higher in experiment B, and 58% higher in experiment C. This means, relatively speaking, SouthamptonSCM does best in experiment B. It is interesting that there are more HP-agents in experiment B than in A (*i.e.*, our agent performs better in a more uncertain environment). This further shows that the adaptivity of prices are effective in this case. However, in experiment C, more agents use the Day-0 bidding strategy and this affects all the agents greatly (see the discussion below).

---

[10] Statistical significance is computed by a Student's t-test and this shows all results are significant ($p < 0.05$).

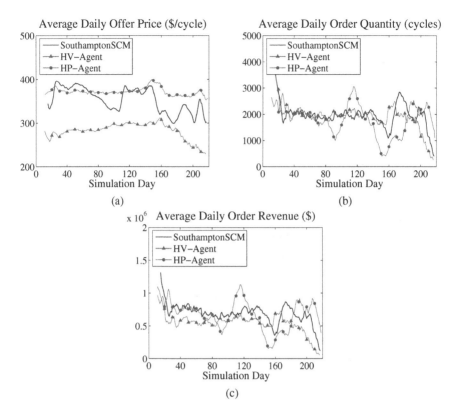

Fig. 4. Comparison of offer prices, quantity and revenue in the controlled experiment

To understand better about how the pricing of SouthamptonSCM works, we further observed for each simulation day, the daily price (Figure 4 (a)) offered by each agent and the average daily order quantity that each agent won (Figure 4 (b)). These values are averaged over all PC types. We then plot the average daily revenue (Figure 4 (c)). Here, again, we take a randomly chosen representative game to show how the pricing of these three kinds of agents operates. As expected, the prices that SouthamptonSCM offers are roughly between the other two (below that of HP-agents and above that of HV-agents). For an HV-agent, the offer prices are very low, thus, although it can sell a large quantity of PCs, it cannot make much profit. Specifically, we found that the HV-agent can almost always win orders (the ratio of the number of orders offered to the quantity of orders won is almost 1 : 1 and the factory utilisation is almost 100%). For the HP-agent, however, the prices are always high, meaning they build up a large stock of PCs and components in the factory. Thus only a small number of their orders make much profit although selling prices are high. Through adaptation, SouthamptonSCM can make its offer prices high enough (sometimes the average prices are even higher than HP-agents, see Figure 4 (a)), but, at the same time, guarantee a large number of orders (see Figure 4 (b)). This is demonstrated by the fact that its factory utilisation is almost 100%. Consequently, its revenue is higher than the other two (see Figure 4 (c)).

Besides these observations about the performance of each agent, the following general observations can be made. First, in all cases, the three kinds of agents perform much better than the Dummy agents. This means that our Day-0 procurement strategy can be viewed as being more effective than build-to-order procurement. This happens because when the Dummy agent starts to order the components after it wins the customer order, there will always be a delay between the delivery date the agent asks for and the real one. Thus the Dummy agents are often penalised for being late or missing the delivery deadline. Moreover, as shown in Figure 3, the more risky agents there are, the worse the Dummy agent behaves.

Second, as more agents use the same broad strategy of Day-0 procurement, it is more likely that there will be a bigger delay between the original delivery date and the actual one (because each agent sends RFQs with a big quantity of components and the production capability of the supplier is limited, see Section 3.1). Thus, this phenomena greatly increases the uncertainty in the game and the performance of all the agents are negatively affected, (*i.e.*, the performance of all the agents is getting worse from experiment A to B and B to C). This can be seen clearly in Figure 3 and explains why SouthamtptonSCM sometimes got the second or third position in a game. Through the analysis of the game data, we found that in those games, there is a significant delay in the component delivery and the factory stops working for about 20 days. This is also what happened in the final of the competition (as detailed in Section 4.1).

Third, as more agents use the high-price strategy, the performance of the HP-agents is more negatively affected. This happens because the HP-agents are mutually destructive. In this situation (*e.g.*, in experiment C), although HP-agents sell PCs at high prices, the quantity of PCs sold is not sufficient to make up the cost they have spent on the materials of the PCs they produce. In contrast, HV-agents sell many PCs at reasonably low prices and their revenue remains high. Thus, as we can see in Figure 3 (c), it is sometimes the case that the HV-agent is doing the best.

Fourth, the agent that can best adapt its offer price to the changing environment will thrive best in the game. This is because the random nature of the customer demand and the strategies of other participants make the environment highly unpredictable in terms of what is the appropriate price to set for the PCs. As can be seen from the above experiments, neither the agent that seeks a high price, nor the one that only pursues a fixed margin are effective in all cases. Thus adaptivity is a critical requirement for effective performance in dynamic games.

5   Conclusions

This paper provides a number of insights into building agents for supply chain applications. Specifically, it details the design, implementation and evaluation of SouthamptonSCM; an agent that successfully participated in the 2004 trading agent competition. The agent employs fuzzy techniques at its core. In particular, it uses fuzzy reasoning to determine how to set prices according to its inventory level, the market demand and the time into the game. Moreover, the parameters involved in the fuzzy rules can be adapted according to the quantity of the received customer orders and the expected number of orders so as to maximise the factory utilisation. To evaluate the efficiency of our pricing model, we analysed actual competition games and conducted controlled experiments where we compete our agents with various numbers of high-price and high-volume agents. The actual game analysis shows that our agent is able to obtain a high revenue by offering high prices that are, nevertheless, low enough to win customer orders. In the controlled experiments, we show that in all environments we considered, SouthamptonSCM is significantly better than the other two kinds of agents (with highest average performance and lowest variance). When taken together, these evaluations show that out pricing model is both efficient and robust.

We also believe several aspects of our agent design and strategy are applicable outside the confines of this competition. First of all, the general idea of the component agent is to periodically request large orders to cover the baseline quantities needed in low demand (steady state) markets and, at the same time, buy smaller amounts of supplies when the selling price is low during the rest of the production. This mixture of baseline and opportunistic purchasing behaviour is a common strategy in this domain and the technology we develop for achieving this can be readily transferred. Second, we believe our pricing model technology will also be useful in real SCM applications where just undercutting competitors' prices can significantly improve profitability. Specifically, to apply our model in other domains, the designers of the rule base would need to adapt the fuzzy rules to reflect the factors that are relevant to their domain. Now we believe that customer demand and inventory level are highly likely to be critical factors for almost all cases and thus these rules can remain unaltered. However, the time into the game is not so broadly applicable since there is not always a rigidly fixed deadline to real life supply chains (thus some changes may be needed here). Third, the strategy employed by the factory agent for managing resources in uncertain and dynamically changing environments is generally applicable. In this case, it incorporates little in the way of domain specific knowledge and so it can remain broadly as is.

Acknowledgments

The authors would like to thank the anonymous reviewers for helpful comments and Xudong Luo for his support during the course of the TAC/SCM competition. This research is partially funded by the DIF-DTC project (8.6) on Agent-Based Control and the ARGUS II DARP (Defence and Aerospace Research Partnership).

References

1. J. Collins, R. Arunachalam, et al. The supply chain management game for the 2005 trading agent competition. Technical Report CMU-ISRI-04-139, School of Computer Science, Carnegie Mellon University, December 2004.
2. E. Dahlgren and P.R. Wurman. PackaTAC: A conservative trading agent. *SIGecom Exchanges*, 4(3):33–40, 2004.
3. M. He and N. R. Jennings. Designing a successful trading agent: A fuzzy set approach. *IEEE Transactions on Fuzzy Systems*, 12(3):389–410, 2004.
4. M. He, N. R. Jennings, and H. F. Leung. On agent-mediated electronic commerce. *IEEE Transactions on Knowledge and Data Engineering*, 15(4):985–1003, 2003.

5. M. He, H. F. Leung, and N. R. Jennings. A fuzzy logic based bidding strategy for autonomous agents in continuous double auctions. *IEEE Transactions on Knowledge and Data Engineering*, 15(6):1345–1363, 2003.
6. K. Kumar. Technology for supporting supply-chain management. *Comms of the ACM*, 44(6):58–61, 2001.
7. X. Luo, N. R. Jennings, N. Shadbolt, H.F. Leung, and J.H.M. Lee. A fuzzy constraint based model for bilateral, multi-issue negotiation in semi-competitive environments. *Artificial Intelligence*, 148(1-2):53–102, 2003.
8. M. Sugeno. An introductory survey of fuzzy control. *Information Sciences*, 36:59–83, 1985.
9. M.P. Wellman, J. Estelle, S. Singh, et al. Strategic interactions in a supply chain game. *Computational Intelligence*, 21(1):1–26, 2005.
10. J. Yen. Fuzzy logic — a modern perspective. *IEEE Trans. Knowledge and Data Engineering*, 11(1):153–165, 1999.
11. H.-J. Zimmermann. *Fuzzy Set Theory and Its Applications*, chapter 11, pages 203–240. Kluwer Academic Publishers, 1996.

A   Rule Base for the First 180 Days

1. IF D is *high* and I is *high* and ND is *far* THEN r is *big*.
2. IF D is *high* and I is *medium* and ND is *far* THEN r is *big*.
3. IF D is *high* and I is *low* and ND is *far* THEN r is *very-big*.
4. IF D is *medium* and I is *high* and ND is *far* THEN r is *medium*.
5. IF D is *medium* and I is *medium* and ND is *far* THEN r is *medium*.
6. IF D is *mediium* and I is *low* and ND is *far* THEN r is *big*.
7. IF D is *low* and I is *high* and ND is *far* THEN r is *small*.
8. IF D is *low* and I is *medium* and ND is *far* THEN r is *small*.
9. IF D is *low* and I is *low* and ND is *far* THEN r is *medium*.
10. IF D is *high* and I is *high* and ND is *close* THEN r is *medium*.
11. IF D is *high* and I is *medium* and ND is *close* THEN r is *big*.
12. IF D is *high* and I is *low* and ND is *close* THEN r is *very-big*.
13. IF D is *medium* and I is *high* and ND is *close* THEN r is *small*.
14. IF D is *medium* and I is *medium* and ND is *close* THEN r is *medium*.
15. IF D is *mediium* and I is *low* and ND is *close* THEN r is *big*.
16. IF D is *low* and I is *high* and ND is *close* THEN r is *very-small*.
17. IF D is *low* and I is *medium* and ND is *close* THEN r is *small*.
18. IF D is *low* and I is *low* and ND is *close* THEN r is *medium*.
19. IF D is *high* and I is *high* and ND is *medium* THEN r is *big*.
20. IF D is *high* and I is *medium* and ND is *medium* THEN r is *big*.
21. IF D is *high* and I is *low* and ND is *medium* THEN r is *very-big*.
22. IF D is *medium* and I is *high* and ND is *medium* THEN r is *medium*.
23. IF D is *medium* and I is *medium* and ND is *medium* THEN r is *medium*.
24. IF D is *mediium* and I is *low* and ND is *medium* THEN r is *big*.
25. IF D is *low* and I is *high* and ND is *medium* THEN r is *small*.
26. IF D is *low* and I is *medium* and ND is *medium* THEN r is *small*.
27. IF D is *low* and I is *low* and ND is *medium* THEN r is *medium*.

B   Rule Base for the Last 40 Days of the Game

1. IF D is *high* and I is *high* and E is *far* THEN r is *big*.
2. IF D is *high* and I is *medium* and E is *far* THEN r is *big*.
3. IF D is *high* and I is *low* and E is *far* THEN r is *very-big*.
4. IF D is *medium* and I is *high* and E is *far* THEN r is *medium*.
5. IF D is *medium* and I is *medium* and E is *far* THEN r is *medium*.
6. IF D is *medium* and I is *low* and E is *far* THEN r is *big*.
7. IF D is *low* and I is *high* and E is *far* THEN r is *small*.
8. IF D is *low* and I is *medium* and E is *far* THEN r is *small*.
9. IF D is *low* and I is *low* and E is *far* THEN r is *medium*.
10. IF D is *high* and E is *close* THEN r is *very-small*.
11. IF D is *medium* and E is *close* THEN r is *small*.
12. IF D is *low* and E is *close* THEN r is *small*.
13. IF D is *high* and I is *high* and E is *medium* THEN r is *big*.
14. IF D is *high* and I is *medium* and E is *medium* THEN r is *big*.
15. IF D is *high* and I is *low* and E is *medium* THEN r is *very-big*.
16. IF D is *medium* and I is *high* and E is *medium* THEN r is *medium*.
17. IF D is *medium* and I is *medium* and E is *medium* THEN r is *medium*.
18. IF D is *medium* and I is *low* and E is *medium* THEN r is *big*.
19. IF D is *low* and I is *high* and E is *medium* THEN r is *small*.
20. IF D is *low* and I is *medium* and E is *medium* THEN r is *small*.
21. IF D is *low* and I is *low* and E is *medium* THEN r is *medium*.

Searching for Walverine 2005

Michael P. Wellman, Daniel M. Reeves, Kevin M. Lochner, and Rahul Suri

University of Michigan
Ann Arbor, MI 48109-2110 USA
{wellman, dreeves, klochner, rsuri}@umich.edu

Abstract. We systematically explore a range of variations of our TAC travel-shopping agent, **Walverine**. The space of strategies is defined by settings to behavioral parameter values. Our empirical game-theoretic analysis is facilitated by approximating games through hierarchical reduction methods. This approach generated a small set of candidates for the version to run in the TAC-05 tournament. We selected among these based on performance in preliminary rounds, ultimately identifying a successful strategy for **Walverine** 2005.

1 Introduction

There are many ways to play the TAC travel-shopping game. Our agent, **Walverine** [1], employs competitive analysis to predict hotel prices and formulate an optimal bidding problem. Other agents take different approaches to predicting hotel prices [2], bidding under uncertainty [3], and many other facets of TAC. Even within a particular approach to a particular subproblem, there is no end to possible variations one might consider, ranging from fine-tuning of policy parameters to qualitatively different strategies.

Like most TAC participants, we apply a mix of modeling and experimentation in developing our agent. Since our models of the TAC environment necessarily simplify the actual game, we rely on experimental offline trials to validate the ideas and set parameters. And since these offline experiments incorporate assumptions about other agents' behavior, we also depend on online experiments (e.g., during preliminary tournament rounds) to test our designs in the most realistic setting available. Also like most other participants (with the notable exception of **Whitebear** [4], discussed below), our combination of modeling and experimentation was essentially *ad hoc*, with only informal procedures for fixing a particular agent behavior based on the results.

For 2005 (following a preliminary effort for 2004), we decided to adopt a more systematic approach. The first element of our method is fairly standard: define a space of strategies to consider by *parametrizing* the baseline agent **Walverine**. We then explore the space through extensive simulation. A less conventional element of our method is that we use the simulation results to estimate an *empirical game*, and apply standard game-theoretic analysis to derive strategic equilibria. The particularly novel element we introduce in the current work is *hierarchical game reduction*, a general technique for approximating symmetric games by smaller games with fractional numbers of agents. In this instance, we show that 4-player and 2-player reductions of the TAC game are far more manageable than the full 8-player game, and argue that little fidelity is lost by the reduction proposed here.

H. La Poutré, N. Sadeh, and S. Janson (Eds.): AMEC and TADA 2005, LNAI 3937, pp. 157–170, 2006.
© Springer-Verlag Berlin Heidelberg 2006

In the next section we illustrate the parametrization of strategy space by describing some of Walverine's key parameters. Section 3 appeals to the TAC literature to demonstrate the importance of accounting for strategic interactions in evaluating agent designs. We describe the explosion of strategy profile space in Section 4, and introduce our hierarchical reduction operator. Results from our empirical game-theoretic analysis to date are summarized in Section 5.[1] The remaining sections describe our selection of a particular strategy for TAC-05, and report results.

2 Walverine Parameters

TAC travel-shopping is an 8-player symmetric game, with a complex strategy space and pivotal agent interactions. Strategies include all policies for bidding on flights, hotels, and entertainment over time, as a function of prior observations. To focus our search, we restrict attention to variations on our basic Walverine strategy [1], as originally developed for TAC-02 and refined incrementally for 2003 and 2004.

We illustrate some of the possible strategy variations by describing some of the parameters we have exposed to the calling interface. To invoke an instance of Walverine, the user specifies parameter values dictating which version of the agent's modules to run, and what arguments to provide to these modules.

2.1 Flight Purchase Timing

Flight prices follow a random walk with a bias that is determined by a hidden parameter that is chosen randomly at the start of the game. Specifically, at the start of each game, a hidden parameter x is chosen from the integers in $[-10, 30]$. Define $x(t) = 10 + (t/9{:}00)(x - 10)$. Every 10 seconds thereafter, given elapsed time t, flight prices are perturbed by a value chosen uniformly, with bounds $[lb, ub]$ determined by

$$[lb, ub] = \begin{cases} [x(t), 10] & \text{if } x(t) < 0, \\ [-10, 10] & \text{if } x(t) = 0, \\ [-10, x(t)] & \text{if } x(t) > 0. \end{cases} \tag{1}$$

Whereas flight price perturbations are designed to increase in expectation given no information about the hidden parameter, conditional on this parameter prices may be expected to increase, decrease, or stay constant.

Walverine maintains a distribution $\Pr(x)$ for each flight, initialized to be uniform on $[-10, 30]$, and updated using Bayes's rule given the observed perturbations Δ at each iteration: $\Pr(x|\Delta) = \alpha \Pr(x) \Pr(\Delta|x)$, where α is a normalization constant.

Given this distribution over the hidden x parameter, the expected perturbation for the next iteration, $E[\Delta'|x]$, is simply $(lb + ub)/2$, with bounds given by (1). Averaging over the distribution for x, we have $E[\Delta'] = \sum_x \Pr(x) E[\Delta'|x]$.

Given a set of flights that Walverine has calculated to be in the optimal package, it decides which to purchase now as a function of the expected perturbations, current

---

[1] Another paper presenting the hierarchical game-reduction idea and appealing to the TAC case study was presented at AAAI-05 [5]; some of the material in Sections 4 and 5 also appears in that work.

holdings, and marginal flight values. On a high level, the strategy is designed to defer purchase of flights that are not quickly increasing, allowing for flexibility in avoiding expensive hotels as hotel price information is revealed.

The flight purchase strategy can be described in the form of a decision tree as depicted in Figure 1. First, Walverine compares the expected perturbation $(E[\Delta'])$ with a threshold $T1$, deferring purchase if the prices are not expected to increase by $T1$ or more. If $T1$ is exceeded, Walverine next compares the expected perturbation with a second higher threshold, $T2$, and if the prices are expected to increase by more than $T2$ Walverine purchases all units for that flight that are in the optimal package.

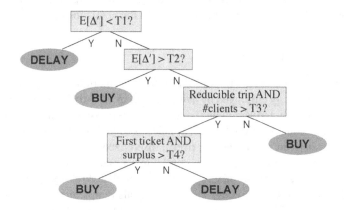

Fig. 1. Decision tree for deciding whether to delay flight purchases

If $T1 < E[\Delta'] < T2$, the Walverine flight delay strategy is designed to take into account the potential benefit of avoiding travel on high demand days. Walverine checks whether the flight constitutes one end of a *reducible* trip: one that spans more than a single day. If the trip is not reducible, Walverine buys all the flights. If reducible, Walverine considers its own demand (defined by the optimal package) for the day that would be avoided through shortening the trip, equivalent to the day of an inflight, and the day before an outflight. If our own demand for that day is $T3$ or fewer, Walverine purchases all the flights. Otherwise (reducible and demand greater than $T3$), Walverine delays the purchases, except possibly for one unit of the flight instance, which it will purchase if its marginal surplus exceeds another threshold, $T4$.

Though the strategy described above is based on sound calculations and tradeoff principles, it is difficult to justify particular settings of threshold parameters without making numerous assumptions and simplifications. Therefore we treat these as strategy parameters, to be explored empirically, along with the other Walverine parameters.

2.2 Bid Shading

The Walverine *optimal shading* algorithm [1] identifies, for each hotel auction, the bid value maximizing expected utility based on a model of other agents' marginal value distributions. Because this optimization is based on numerous simplifications and approximations, we include several parameters to control its use.

Through a *shading mode* parameter, bid shading can be turned off, in which case Walverine bids its marginal value. Another parameter defines a *shade percentage*, specifying a fixed fraction to bid below marginal value. There are two modes corresponding to the optimal shading algorithm, differing in how they model the other agents' value distributions. In the first, the distributions are derived from a simplified competitive analysis. For this mode, another parameter, *shade model threshold* turns off shading in case the model appears too unlikely given the price quote. Specifically, we calculate the probability that the 16th highest bid is greater than or equal to the quote according to the modeled value distributions, and if too low we refrain from using the model for shading. For the second optimal shading mode, instead of the competitive model we employ empirically derived distributions keyed on the hotel closing order.

2.3   Entertainment Trading

We choose among a discrete set of policies for trading entertainment. As a baseline, we implemented the strategy employed by livingagents in TAC-01 [6]. We also applied reinforcement learning to derive policies from scratch, expressed as functions of marginal valuations and various additional state variables. The policy employed by Walverine in TAC-02 was derived by Q-learning over a discretized state space. For TAC-03 we learned an alternative policy, this time employing a neural network to represent the value function. Our analysis of other agents indicated that Whitebear performs particularly well in entertainment trading. Therefore, we also implemented an entertainment module based on the Whitebear policy,[2] adapted for the Walverine architecture.

2.4   Other Parameters

Walverine predicts hotel prices based on competitive equilibrium analysis [2]. The result, however, does not account for uncertainty in the predictions. We developed a simple method to hedge on our price estimates, by assigning an *outlier probability* to the event that a hotel price will be much greater than predicted. We can hedge to a greater or lesser degree by modifying this outlier parameter.

Given a price distribution, one could optimize bids with respect to the distribution itself, or with respect to the *expected* prices induced by the distribution. Although the former approach is more accurate in principle, necessary compromises in implementation render it ambiguous in practice which produces superior results [2,3,7]. Thus, we include a parameter controlling which method to apply in Walverine.

Several agent designers have reported employing *priceline* predictions, accounting for the impact of one's own demand quantity on price. We implemented a version of the *completion algorithm* [8] that optimizes with respect to pricelines, and included it as a Walverine option. A further parameter selects how price predictions and optimizations account for outstanding hotel bids in determining current holdings. In one setting current bids for open hotel auctions are ignored, and in another the current hypothetical winnings are treated as actual holdings.

---

[2] Thanks to Ioannis Vetsikas for providing a version of the 2003 source code for Whitebear.

3   Strategic Interactions in TAC Travel

TAC agents interact in the markets for each kind of good, as competing buyers or potential trading partners. Based on published accounts, TAC participants design agents given specified game rules, and then test these designs in the actual tournaments as well as offline experiments. The testing process is crucial, given the lack of any compact analytical model of the domain. During testing, agent designers explore variations on their agent program, for example by tuning parameters or toggling specific agent features.

That strategic choices interact has been frequently noted in the TAC literature. A report on the first TAC tournament [9] observes that the strategy of bidding high prices for hotels performed reasonably in preliminary rounds, but poorly in the finals when more agents were high bidders (thus raising final prices to unprofitable levels). Stone et al. [10] evaluate their agent ATTac-2000 in controlled post-tournament experiments, measuring relative scores in a range of contexts, varying the number of other agents playing high- and low-bidding strategies. A report on the 2001 competition [11] concludes that the top scorer, livingagents, would perform quite poorly against copies of itself. The designers of SouthamptonTAC [12] observed the sensitivity of their agent's TAC-01 performance to the tendency of other agents to buy flights in advance, and redesigned their agent for TAC-02 to attempt to classify the competitive environment faced and adapt accordingly [13]. ATTac-2001 explicitly took into account the identity of other agents in training its price-prediction module [7]. To evaluate alternative learning mechanisms through post-competition analysis, Stone et al. recognized the effect of the policies on the outcomes being learned, and thus adopted a carefully phased experimental design in order to account for such effects.

One issue considered by several TAC teams is how to bid for hotels based on predicted prices and marginal utility. Greenwald and Boyan [3] have studied this in depth, performing pairwise comparisons of four strategies, in profiles with four copies of each agent.[3] Their results indicate that absolute performance of a strategy indeed depends on what the other agent plays. We examined the efficacy of bid shading in Walverine, varying the number of agents employing shading or not, and presented an equilibrium shading probability based on these results [14].

By far the most extensive experimental TAC analysis reported to date is that performed by Vetsikas and Selman [4]. In the process of designing Whitebear for TAC-02, they first identified candidate policies for separate elements of the agent's overall strategy. They then defined extreme (boundary) and intermediate values for these partial strategies, and performed systematic experiments according to a deliberately considered methodology. Specifically, for each run, they fix a particular number of agents playing intermediate strategies, varying the mixture of boundary cases across the possible range. In all, the Whitebear experiments comprised 4500 game instances, with varying *even* numbers of candidate strategies (i.e., profiles of the 4-player game). Their design was further informed by 2000 games in the preliminary tournament rounds. This systematic exploration was apparently helpful, as Whitebear was the top scorer in the 2002 tournament. This agent's predecessor version placed third in TAC-01, following a less

---

[3] In our terminology introduced below, their trials focused on the 2-player reduced version of the game.

comprehensive and structured experimentation process. Its successor placed third again in 2003, and regained its first-place standing in 2004. Since the rules were adjusted for TAC-04, this most recent outcome required a new regimen of experiments.

4 Hierarchical Game Reduction

4.1 Motivation

Suppose that we manage to narrow down the candidate Walverine variants to a reasonable number of strategies (say 40). Because the performance of a strategy for one agent depends on the strategies of the other seven, we wish to undertake a game-theoretic analysis of the situation. Determining the payoff for a particular strategy profile is expensive, however, as each game instance takes nine minutes to run, plus another minute or two to calculate scores, compile results, and set up the next simulation. Moreover, since the environment is stochastic, numerous samples (say 12) are required to produce a reliable estimate for even one profile. At roughly two hours per profile, exhaustively exploring profile space will require $2 \cdot 40^8$ or 13 trillion hours simply to estimate the payoff function representing the game under analysis. If the game is symmetric, we can exploit that fact to reduce the number of distinct profiles to $\binom{47}{8}$, which will require 628 million hours. That is quite a bit less, but still much more time than we have.

The idea of hierarchical game reduction is that although a strategy's payoff does depend on the play of other agents (otherwise we are not in a game situation at all), it may be relatively insensitive to the exact numbers of other agents playing particular strategies. For example, let $(s, k; s')$ denote a profile where k other agents play strategy s, and the rest play s'. In many natural games, the payoff for the respective strategies in this profile will vary smoothly with k, differing only incrementally for contexts with $k \pm 1$. If such is the case, we sacrifice relatively little fidelity by restricting attention to subsets of profiles, for instance those with only even numbers of any particular strategy. To do so essentially transforms the N-player game to an $N/2$-player game over the same strategy set, where the payoffs to a profile in the reduced game are simply those from the original game where each strategy in the reduced profile is played twice.

The potential savings from reduced games are considerable, as they contain combinatorially fewer profiles. The 4-player approximation to the TAC game (with 40 strategies) comprises 123,410 distinct profiles, compared with 314 million for the original 8-player game. In case exhaustive consideration of the 4-player game is still infeasible, we can approximate further by a corresponding 2-player game, which has only 840 profiles. Approximating by a 1-player game is tantamount to ignoring strategic effects, considering only the 40 profiles where the strategies are played against themselves. In general, an N-player symmetric game with S strategies includes $\binom{N+S-1}{N}$ distinct profiles. Figure 2 shows the exponential growth in both N and S.

4.2 Hierarchy of Reduced Games

We develop our hierarchical reduction concepts in the framework of *symmetric normal-form games*.

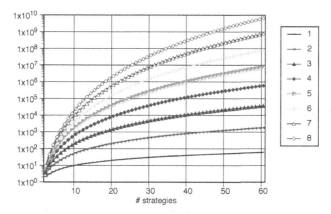

Fig. 2. Number of distinct profiles (log scale) of a symmetric game, for various numbers of players and strategies

Definition 1. $\Gamma = \langle N, \{S_i\}, \{u_i()\}\rangle$ *is an N-player normal-form game, with* strategy set S_i *the available strategies for player i, and the* payoff *function $u_i(s_1,\ldots,s_N)$ giving the utility accruing to player i when players choose the* strategy profile $(s_1,\ldots,s_N)$.

Definition 2. *A normal-form game is* symmetric *if the players have identical strategy spaces $(S_1 = \cdots = S_N = S)$ and $u_i(s_i,s_{-i}) = u_j(s_j,s_{-j})$, for $s_i = s_j$ and $s_{-i} = s_{-j}$ for all $i, j \in \{1,\ldots,N\}$. Thus we can write $u(t,s)$ for the payoff to any player playing strategy t when the remaining players play profile s. We denote a symmetric game by the tuple $\langle N, S, u()\rangle$.*

Our central concept is that of a *reduced* game.

Definition 3. *Let $\Gamma = \langle N, S, u()\rangle$ be an N-player symmetric game, with $N = pq$ for integers p and q. The p-player reduced version of Γ, written $\Gamma\!\downarrow_p$, is given by $\langle p, S, \hat{u}()\rangle$, where*

$$\hat{u}_i(s_1,\ldots,s_p) = u_{q\cdot i}(\underbrace{s_1,\ldots,}_{q}\underbrace{s_2,\ldots,}_{q}\ldots,\underbrace{s_p,\ldots}_{q}).$$

In other words, the payoff function in the reduced game is obtained by playing the specified profile in the original q times.

The idea of a reduced game is to coarsen the profile space by restricting the degrees of strategic freedom. Although the original set of strategies remains available, the number of agents playing any strategy must be a multiple of q. Every profile in the reduced game is one in the original game, of course, and any profile in the original game can be reached from a profile contained in the reduced game by changing at most $p(q-1)$ agent strategies.

The premise of our approach is that the reduced game will often serve as a good approximation of the full game it abstracts. We know that in the worst case it does not. In general, an equilibrium of the reduced game may be arbitrarily far from equilibrium with respect to the full game, and an equilibrium of the full game may not have any near neighbors in the reduced game that are close to equilibrium there. Elsewhere we provide evidence that the hierarchical reduction provides an effective approximation in several natural game classes [5]. Intuition suggests that it should apply for TAC, and the basic agreement between $TAC\downarrow_2$ and $TAC\downarrow_4$ seen in our results tends to support that assessment.

5 TAC Experiments

To apply reduced-game analysis to the TAC domain, we identified a restricted set of strategies, defined by setting parameters for **Walverine**. We considered a total of 40 distinct strategies, covering variant policies for bidding on flights, hotels, and entertainment. We collected data for a large number of games: over 47,000 as of the start of the TAC-05 finals, representing over one year of (almost continuous) simulation.[4] Each game instance provides a sample payoff vector for a profile over our restricted strategy set.

Table 1 shows how our dataset is apportioned among the 1-, 2-, and 4-player reduced games. We are able to exhaustively cover the 1-player game, of course. We could also have exhausted the 2-player profiles, but chose to skip some of the less promising ones (around one-quarter) in favor of devoting more samples elsewhere. The available number of samples could not cover the 4-player games, but as we see below, even 1.7% is sufficient to draw conclusions about the possible equilibria of the game. Spread over the 8-player game, however, 47,000 instances would be insufficient to explore much, and so we refrain from any sampling of the unreduced game.

Table 1. Profiles evaluated, reduced TAC games ($TAC\downarrow_p$)

p	Profiles			Samples/Profile	
	total	evaluated	%	min	mean
4	123,410	2114	1.7	12	22.3
2	840	586	71.5	15	31.7
1	40	40	100.0	25	86.5

In the spirit of hierarchical exploration, we sample more instances per profile as the game is further reduced, obtaining more reliable statistical estimates of the coarse backbone relative to its refinement. On introducing a new profile we generate a minimum required number of samples, and subsequently devote further samples to particular profiles based on their potential for influencing our game-theoretic analysis. The sampling policy employed was semi-manual and somewhat *ad hoc*, driven in an informal way by

---

[4] Our simulation testbed comprises two dedicated workstations to run the agents, another RAM-laden four-CPU machine to run the agents' optimization processes, a share of a fourth machine to run the TAC game server, and background processes on other machines to control the experiment generation and data gathering. We have continued to run the testbed since the tournament, accumulating over 56,000 games as of this writing. Results presented here correspond to a snapshot at the end of July 2005, right before the final tournament.

analyses of the sort described below on intermediate versions of the dataset. Developing a fully automated and principled sampling policy is the subject of future research.

5.1   Control Variates

Since we estimate the payoffs (expected scores) by Monte Carlo simulation, there are several off-the-shelf variance reduction techniques that can be applied. One is the method of *control variates* [15], which improves the estimate of the mean of a random function by exploiting correlation with observable random variables. In our case the function is the entire game server plus eight agents playing a particular strategy profile, evaluating to a vector of eight scores. Random factors in the game include hotel closing order, flight prices, entertainment ticket endowment, and, most critically, client preferences. The idea is to replace sampled scores with scores that have been "adjusted for luck". For example, an agent whose clients had anomolously low hotel premiums would have its score adjusted upward as a handicap. Or in a game with very cheap flight prices, all the scores would be adjusted downward to compensate. Such adjustments reduce variance at the cost of potentially introducing bias. Fortunately, the bias goes to zero as the number of samples increases [16].

For the analysis reported here, we adjust scores based on the following control variables (for a hypothetical agent A):

- ENT: Sum of A's clients' entertainment premiums ($8 \cdot 3 = 24$ values). $E[\text{ENT}] = 2400$.
- FLT: Sum of initial flight quotes (8 values; same for all agents). $E[\text{FLT}] = 2600$.
- WTD: Weighted total demand: Total demand vector (for each night, the number of the 64 clients who would be there that night if they got their preferred trips) dotted with the demand vector for A's clients. $E[\text{WTD}] = 540.16$.
- HTL: Sum of A's clients' hotel premiums (8 values). $E[\text{HTL}] = 800$.

The expectations are determined analytically based on specified game distributions.

Given the above, we adjust an agent's score by subtracting

$$\beta_{\text{ENT}}(\text{ENT} - E[\text{ENT}]) + \beta_{\text{FLT}}(\text{FLT} - E[\text{FLT}])$$
$$+ \beta_{\text{WTD}}(\text{WTD} - E[\text{WTD}])$$
$$+ \beta_{\text{HTL}}(\text{HTL} - E[\text{HTL}]),$$

where the βs are determined by performing a multiple regression from the control variables to score using a data set consisting of 2190 games. Using adjusted scores in lieu of raw scores reduces overall variance by 22 based on a sample of 9000 all-**Walverine** games.

We have also estimated the coefficients based on the 107 games in the TAC Travel 2004 semi-finals and finals and have proposed these as the basis for official score adjustments for the competition:

- $\beta_{\text{ENT}} = 0.349$
- $\beta_{\text{FLT}} = -1.721$
- $\beta_{\text{WTD}} = -2.305$
- $\beta_{\text{HTL}} = 0.916$

Note that we can see from these coefficients that it improves an agent's score somewhat to have clients with high entertainment premiums, it hurts performance to be in a game with high flight prices, it hurts to have clients that prefer long trips (particularly when other agents' clients do as well), and finally, having clients with high hotel premiums improves score. Applying the score adjustment formula to the 2004 finals yields a reduction in variance of 9%.

5.2   Results

A detailed presentation of an earlier snapshot of our experimental results, along with game-theoretic analysis, is provided elsewhere [5]. Here we present only a brief summary. A final account based on the ongoing simulations is forthcoming.

Analysis of the TAC$\downarrow_1$ "game" tells us which strategy performs best assuming it plays with copies of itself. We included a strategy (S34) designed to do well in this context: it shades all hotel bids by a fixed 50% rate. This indeed performs best, by about 250 points, since the result is very low hotel prices. However, the profile is quite unstable, as an agent who shades less can get much better hotel rooms, but still benefit from the low prices. Thus, this is not nearly an equilibrium in the less-reduced games.

With over 70% of profiles evaluated, we have a reasonably complete description of the two-player game, TAC$\downarrow_2$, among our 40 strategies. At this point in the experiment, we identified ten candidate strategy profiles that represent pure ϵ-Nash equilibria, for $\epsilon \leq 27$. Four of these were confirmed, meaning that all deviations had been evaluated. We also identified 41 symmetric mixed-strategy profiles in equilibrium. Less than 1/3 of the considered strategies participate with probability exceeding 0.15 in some equilibrium found.

Results for TAC$\downarrow_4$ must be considered relatively tentative. Based on the profiles evaluated, we can identify a few good candidate equilibrium mixtures over pairs of strategies. Further simulation in the next few months may confirm or refute these, or identify additional candidates. With a few exceptions, strategies and combinations evaluated as stable in TAC$\downarrow_2$ tend to produce similar results in TAC$\downarrow_4$.

Analysis of the reduced games does validate the importance of strategic interactions. As noted above, the best strategy in self-play, S34, is not nearly a best response in most other environments, though it does appear in a few mixed-strategy equilbria of TAC$\downarrow_2$. Strategy S34 achieves a payoff of 4302 in self-play. For comparison:

- The top scorer in the 2004 tournament, Whitebear, averaged 4122.
- The best payoff we found in TAC$\downarrow_2$ in a two-action mixed-strategy equilibrium candidate is 4220 (and this involves playing S34 with probability 0.4).
- The best corresponding equilibrium payoff we have found in TAC$\downarrow_4$ is 4031. No such equilibrium includes S34.

6   Walverine 2005

Given all this simulation and analysis, how can we determine the "best" strategy to play in TAC? We do have strong evidence for expecting that all but a fraction of the original 40 strategies will turn out to be unstable within this set. The supports of candidate equilibria tend to concentrate on a fraction of the strategies, suggesting we may limit consideration to this group. Thus, we employ the preceding analysis primarily to identify promising strategies, and then refine this set through further evaluation in preliminary rounds of the actual TAC tournament.

For the first stage—identifying promising strategies—the 1-player game is of little use. Even discounting strategy S34 (the best strategy in the 1-player game, specially crafted to do well with copies of itself) our experience suggests that strategic interaction is too fundamental to TAC for performance in the 1-player game to correlate more than loosely with performance in the unreduced game. The 4-player game accounts for strategic interaction at a fine granularity, being sensitive to deviations by as few as two of the eight agents. The 2-player game could well lead us astray in this respect. For example, that strategy S34 appears in mixed-strategy equilibria in the 2-player game is likely an artifact of the coarse granularity of that approximation to TAC.

Cooperative strategies like S34 might well survive when deviations comprise half the players in the game, but in the unreduced game we would expect them to be far less stable. Nonetheless, the correlation between the 2- and 4-player game is high. Furthermore, we have a much more complete description of the 2-player game, with more statistically meaningful estimates of payoffs. Finally, empirical payoff matrices for the 2-player game are far more amenable to our solution techniques, in particular, exhaustive enumeration of symmetric (mixed) equilibria by GAMBIT [17]. For all of these reasons, we focus on the 2-player game for choosing our final Walverine strategies, augmenting our selections with strategies that appear promising in $TAC\downarrow_4$.

Informally, our criteria for picking strong strategies include presence in many equilibria and how strongly the strategy is supported. We start with an exhaustive list of all symmetric equilibria in all cliques of $TAC\downarrow_2$, filtered to exclude any profiles that are refuted in the full game (considering all strategies, not just those in the cliques). There are 68 of these. We next operationalize our criteria for promising strategies with three metrics that we can use to rank strategies given an exhaustive list of equilibria in all cliques of the 2-player game:

- number of equilibria in which the strategy is supported
- maximum mixture probability with which the strategy appears
- sum of mixture probabilities across all equilibria

Based primarily on these metrics, we chose $\{4, 16, 17, 35\}$ as the most promising candidates, and added $\{3, 37, 39, 40\}$ based on their promise in $TAC\downarrow_4$. Figure 3 reveals strategies 37 and 40 to be the top two candidates after the seeding rounds. In the semifinals we played 37 and 40 and found that 37 outperformed 40, 4182 to 3945 ($p = .05$). Based on this, we played 37 as the Walverine strategy for the finals in TAC-05.

7   TAC 2005 Outcome

Officially, Walverine placed third, based on the 80 games of the 2005 finals. In part this reflected some poor luck, as a network glitch early that morning at Michigan caused our

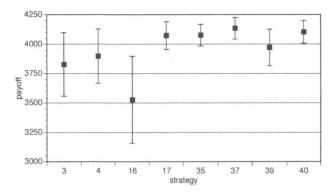

Fig. 3. Performance of eight **Walverine** variants in the TAC-05 seeding rounds (507 games)

agent to miss two games. Moreover, it was clear to all present that the first 22 games were tainted, due to a serious malfunction by **RoxyBot**.[5] Since games with erratic agent behavior add noise to the scores, the TAC operators published unofficial results with the errant **RoxyBot** games removed (Table 2). **Walverine**'s missed games occurred during those games, so removing them corrects both sources of our bad luck, and renders **Walverine** the top-scoring agent.

Table 2. Scores, adjusted scores, and 95% mean confidence intervals on control variate adjusted scores for the 58 games of the TAC Travel 2005 finals, after removing the first 22 tainted games. (**LearnAgents** experienced network problems for a few games, accounting for their high variance and lowering their score.)

Agent	Raw Score	Adjusted Score	95% C.I.
Walverine	4157	4132	± 138
RoxyBot	4067	4030	± 167
Mertacor	4063	3974	± 152
Whitebear	4002	3902	± 130
Dolphin	3993	3899	± 149
SICS02	3905	3843	± 141
LearnAgents	3785	3719	± 280
e-Agent	3367	3342	± 117

Figure 4 shows the adjusted scores with error bars. **Walverine** beat the runner up (**RoxyBot**) at the $p = 0.17$ significance level. Regardless of the ambiguity (statistical or otherwise) of **Walverine**'s placement in the competition, we consider its strong performance under real tournament conditions to be evidence (albeit limited) of the efficacy of our approach to strategy generation in complex games such as TAC.

---

[5] The misbehavior was due to a simple human error: instead of playing a copy of the agent on each of the two game servers per the tournament protocol, the **RoxyBot** team accidentally set both copies of the agent to play on the same server. **RoxyBot** not only failed to participate in the first server's games, but placed double bids in games on the other server.

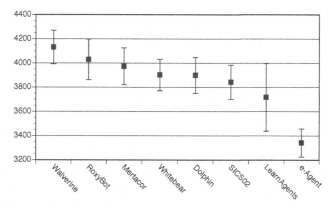

Fig. 4. Comparison of the eight agents in the TAC-05 finals, adjusted as in Table 2

8   Conclusion

Games as complex as TAC Travel generally present agent designers with a wealth of policy choices, not amenable to analytic optimization. The typical recourse is to experiment-guided search through a limited design space. We likewise follow such an approach, but attempt to introduce some systematic game-theoretic reasoning to the process. Our year-long search through the space of parametrized **Walverine** profiles helped us to sort through 40 candidate strategies. Empirical game-theoretic analysis justified pruning this set to a more manageable number we could test during the preliminary rounds. This testing in turn proved valuable, as the leading contenders based on tournament play appeared substantially better than some others surviving our testbed analysis. In the end, our selected **Walverine** strategy performed ably in the 2005 tournament, placing third officially and first after removing tainted games.

To further systematize the process, we require principled techniques for generating parameter settings, and automating the selection of profiles to sample. This is the subject of ongoing research, including continuing exploration of the space of strategies for the TAC travel-shopping game.

Acknowledgments

Shih-Fen Cheng, Kevin O'Malley, and Julian Schvartzman have also contributed to the 2005 version of **Walverine** and our simulation process. We thank the anonymous reviewers for constructive comments. This work was supported in part by the National Science Foundation under grants IIS-0205435 and IIS-0414710.

References

1. Cheng, S.F., Leung, E., Lochner, K.M., O'Malley, K., Reeves, D.M., Wellman, M.P.: Walverine: A Walrasian trading agent. Decision Support Systems **39** (2005) 169–184
2. Wellman, M.P., Reeves, D.M., Lochner, K.M., Vorobeychik, Y.: Price prediction in a trading agent competition. Journal of Artificial Intelligence Research **21** (2004) 19–36

3. Greenwald, A., Boyan, J.: Bidding under uncertainty: Theory and experiments. In: Twentieth Conference on Uncertainty in Artificial Intelligence, Banff (2004) 209–216

4. Vetsikas, I.A., Selman, B.: A principled study of the design tradeoffs for autonomous trading agents. In: Second International Joint Conference on Autonomous Agents and Multi-Agent Systems, Melbourne (2003) 473–480

5. Wellman, M.P., Reeves, D.M., Lochner, K.M., Cheng, S.F., Suri, R.: Approximate strategic reasoning through hierarchical reduction of large symmetric games. In: Twentieth National Conference on Artificial Intelligence, Pittsburgh (2005)

6. Fritschi, C., Dorer, K.: Agent-oriented software engineering for successful TAC participation. In: First International Joint Conference on Autonomous Agents and Multi-Agent Systems, Bologna (2002)

7. Stone, P., Schapire, R.E., Littman, M.L., Csirik, J.A., McAllester, D.: Decision-theoretic bidding based on learned density models in simultaneous, interacting auctions. Journal of Artificial Intelligence Research **19** (2003) 209–242

8. Boyan, J., Greenwald, A.: Bid determination in simultaneous auctions: An agent architecture. In: Third ACM Conference on Electronic Commerce, Tampa, FL (2001) 210–212

9. Greenwald, A., Stone, P.: The first international trading agent competition: Autonomous bidding agents. IEEE Internet Computing **5** (2001) 52–60

10. Stone, P., Littman, M.L., Singh, S., Kearns, M.: ATTac-2000: An adaptive autonomous bidding agent. Journal of Artificial Intelligence Research **15** (2001) 189–206

11. Wellman, M.P., Greenwald, A., Stone, P., Wurman, P.R.: The 2001 trading agent competition. Electronic Markets **13** (2003) 4–12

12. He, M., Jennings, N.R.: SouthamptonTAC: Designing a successful trading agent. In: Fifteenth European Conference on Artificial Intelligence, Lyon (2002) 8–12

13. He, M., Jennings, N.R.: SouthamptonTAC: An adaptive autonomous trading agent. ACM Transactions on Internet Technology **3** (2003) 218–235

14. Wellman, M.P., Cheng, S.F., Reeves, D.M., Lochner, K.M.: Trading agents competing: Performance, progress, and market effectiveness. IEEE Intelligent Systems **18** (2003) 48–53

15. Ross, S.M.: Simulation. Third edn. Academic Press (2002)

16. L'Ecuyer, P.: Efficiency improvement and variance reduction. In: Twenty-Sixth Winter Simulation Conference, Orlando, FL (1994) 122–132

17. McKelvey, R.D., McLennan, A., Turocy, T.: Gambit game theory analysis software and tools (1992) http://econweb.tamu.edu/gambit.

Trading Strategies for Markets: A Design Framework and Its Application

P. Vytelingum, R.K. Dash, M. He, A. Sykulski, and N.R. Jennings

School of Electronics and Computer Science, University of Southampton,
Southampton, SO17 1BJ, UK
pv03r@ecs.soton.ac.uk

Abstract. In this paper, we present a novel multi-layered framework for design-ing strategies for trading agents. The objective of this work is to provide a frame-work that will assist strategy designers with the different aspects involved in de-signing a strategy. At present, such strategies are typically designed in an ad-hoc and intuitive manner with little regard for discerning best practice or attaining re-usability in the design process. Given this, our aim is to put such developments on a more systematic engineering footing. After we describe our framework, we then go on to illustrate how it can be used to design strategies for a particular type of market mechanism (namely the Continuous Double Auction), and how it was used to design a novel strategy for the Travel Game of the International Trading Agent Competition.

1 Introduction

The last decade has seen a significant change in the nature of electronic commerce with the emergence of economic software agents [11]: rational players that are capable of autonomous and flexible actions to achieve their objectives [12] and that are endowed with sophisticated strategies for maximising utility and profit on behalf of their human owners. Today, electronic trading markets[1] allow access to a plenitude of information that enables such software agents to be more informed and respond more efficiently than humans could ever hope to. Now, such trading markets are governed by protocols that define the rules of interaction amongst the economic agents. In some cases, these protocols have a clearly optimal strategy. For example in the Vickrey auction, the best strategy is to reveal one's true valuation of the item and for English auctions it is to bid up to one's true valuation in small increments. However, in other settings, the analyses yielding these best strategies often make use of a range of restrictive assumptions; rang-ing from analysing the market in isolation (i.e. not taking into account dependencies on other related markets), to assumptions on the agent behaviour (such as perfect and com-plete information availability). Furthermore, several of the standard market mechanisms have been modified or certain complex mechanisms may have been implemented such that an analytical approach cannot yield a best strategy. For example, in eBay auctions[2]

---

[1] An electronic trading market is here defined as an online institution in which there is an ex-change of resources or services using a currency as the trading token. Such markets range from auctions, to supply chains, to barter systems.

[2] www.ebay.com

H. La Poutré, N. Sadeh, and S. Janson (Eds.): AMEC and TADA 2005, LNAI 3937, pp. 171–186, 2006.

(which are multiple English auctions modified with a deadline, proxy bidding and discrete bids) bidding until one's valuation is no longer always the optimal strategy and in Continuous Double Auctions (CDAs) (which are a symmetric auction mechanism with multiple buyers and sellers) there is no known optimal strategy [7].

Given this background, there has been considerable research endeavour to develop trading agents with heuristic strategies that are effective in particular marketplaces [18,22]. Though more of a black art than an engineering endeavour at present, we believe the design of successful strategies in such marketplaces can nevertheless be viewed as adhering to a fundamental and systematic structure. To this end, in this paper, we provide a general framework for designing strategies which is simple enough to be applicable in a broad range of marketplaces, but modular enough to be used in the design of complex strategic behaviour. We believe such a model is important for the designers of trading agents because it provides a principled approach towards the systematic engineering of such strategies which, in turn, can foster more reliable and robust strategies.

As there is no systematic software engineering framework currently available for designing strategies for trading agents, this paper advances the state of the art by providing the first steps towards such a model. Specifically, our framework is based upon three main principles:

1. An agent requires information about itself and its environment in order to make informed decisions.
2. An agent rarely has full information or sufficient computational resources to manage all the extracted information.
3. Given its limited computational resources and information, an agent needs to employ heuristics in order to formulate a successful strategy.

In order to operate in such situations, we advocate a multi-layered design framework. We believe this is appropriate because most strategies can be viewed as breaking down the task of bidding into a set of well defined sub-tasks (such as gathering relevant information, processing that information and using that processed information in a meaningful manner). This decomposition can be viewed as a series of (semi-) distinct steps that are handled by different layers. Furthermore, our aim is to ensure our model is sufficiently abstract to be used as the agent model in more general agent-oriented software engineering frameworks, such as Gaia [23] and Agent UML [1]. To this end, our framework is inspired by the distinction made in economics between information and the knowledge derived thereof [6], and is augmented by the Behavioural Layer (since the behaviour dictates which knowledge an agent seeks within an environment). Specifically, our framework consists of three layers: the *Information*, *Knowledge* and *Behavioural* layers (hence we term our framework the *IKB* model hereafter).

In more detail, the information layer records raw data from the market environment. This is then processed by the knowledge layer in order to provide the intelligent data which is used by the behavioural layer to condition the agent's strategy. To illustrate the use of our framework, we chose two example marketplaces that are popular for trading agents. Firstly, we consider the marketplaces with one auction protocol, the CDA, which is widely used in trading stocks. We place a number of the standard CDA strategies within it. Secondly, we consider a more complex scenario, the Travel Game of the International Trading Agent Competition (TAC) where an agent has to strategise in multiple simultaneous auctions of different formats. In both cases, we employed our IKB model successfully.

The remainder of this paper is structured as follows. We review related work in the field in Section 2. Section 3 outlines the IKB model, which is then applied to our trading market examples in Sections 4 and 5. Section 6 concludes.

2   Related Work

Much work has been carried out on abstracting the design of electronic markets [13,16]. However, this work tends to emphasise the methodologies for designing the markets themselves or on proposing new market infrastructures [2,19]. The systematic design of strategies for agents operating in these markets has, in general, been considered to a lesser extent. In this latter vein, however, Vetsikas *et al.* [20] proposed a methodology for deciding the strategy of bidding agents participating in simultaneous auctions. Their methodology decomposes the problem into sub-problems that are solved by *partial* or *intermediate* strategies and then they advocate the use of rigorous experimentation to evaluate those strategies to determine the best overall one across all the different auctions. However, their methodology is very much tailored to simultaneous auctions in general and the TAC in particular [22]. Thus, it cannot readily be generalised to other auction formats or other market mechanisms. Furthermore, other approaches, including [2,8], look at the strategic behaviour of agents. However, they avoid issues related to the information and knowledge management aspects of designing trading agents (focusing instead mainly on the strategic behaviour of the strategy).

3   The IKB Model

In this section, we detail the main components that the designer of a trading agent strategy should pay attention to. In so doing, we develop a framework for designing strategies in trading markets. In our model, we have a market $\mathcal{M}$ regulated by its predefined protocol. The collection of variables representing the dynamics of the system at time t_k (where k indexes changes in the market) is represented by the state variable $p_{\mathcal{M}}(t_k)$. Within this market, there is a set of trading agents, $\mathcal{I}$, that approach the market through a set of actions which are determined by their strategies. In order to formulate its best strategy, an agent *ideally* needs to know which state it is currently in (agent state), the market state and the actions it can take.

Definition 1. Agent's State. *An agent i's state, $p_i(t_k)$, at time t_k is a collection of variables describing its resources (computational and economic) and privately known preferences.*

Definition 2. Market State. *The market state, $p_{\mathcal{M}}(t_k)$, at time t_k is a collection of variables describing all the (public and private) attributes of the market.*

Definition 3. *Strategy. A strategy, S_i, for agent $i \in \mathcal{I}$, defines a mapping from the history of the agent state $H(p_i(t_{k-1}))$ and the market states $H(p_\mathcal{M}(t_{k-1}))$, and current agent state $p_i(t_k)$ and the market state $p_\mathcal{M}(t_k)$ to a set of atomic actions $SA_i = \{a_1^i, a_2^i, \ldots, a_r^i, \ldots\}, a_r^i \in \mathcal{A}_i$ where $\mathcal{A}_i$ is the set of all possible actions for agent i at time t_k.*

The actions chosen by strategy S_i then affect the external environment such that it causes a change in the market state. In fact, this strategy could interplay with strategies selected by other agents, $\mathcal{I} \setminus i$, as well as some external input(s), ext_n, (where n is the number of external signals not caused by participatory agents) so as to lead the market to the new state:

$$p_\mathcal{M}(t_{k+1}) = T(p_\mathcal{M}(t_k), H(p_\mathcal{M}(t_{k-1})), SA_1, \ldots, SA_\mathcal{I}, ext_1, \ldots, ext_n) \qquad (1)$$

where $T(.)$ is the state transfer function. From Definition 3, it is clear that in order for an agent to know which strategy is best, it should know the complete description and history of the states (all market information), a complete description of all actions available to it, its preferences over the states, a model of its opponents' state, behaviour and preferences, and the state transfer function.

In practice, however, an agent will typically not have all this information (for numerous reasons, such as limited sensory capabilities, privacy of opponent's information and limited knowledge of relevant external signals). Furthermore, an agent's limited computational resources imply that it might not be able to keep a history of all past interactions. Given this, there is a need for designing feasible strategies that use limited computational and sensory resources. To this end, we advocate the following design principle where an agent manages its limited capabilities through its Information Layer (IL), its Knowledge Layer (KL) and its behavioural Layer (BL) (as shown in figure 1).

In more detail, the Market State (MS) contains public information (i.e. information *available* to all agents in the market) and private/semi-private information (i.e. information *available* to one/some agents). We now provide a description of each of the layers that pertain to the agent:

- **Information Layer.** The IL contains data which the agent has extracted from the MS and private information about its own state. This extraction is a filtering process (which we represent as the Information Filter in figure 1) whose objectives are defined by the KL (e.g. filtering out only transaction prices).
- **Knowledge Layer.** The KL represents the gathered *knowledge* that is aggregated from the data in IL (e.g. bids submitted in the market). The BL queries the KL to obtain the knowledge it requires.
- **Behavioural Layer.** The BL determines the agent's strategic behaviour by deciding on how to use the information available to it in order to interact with the market through a set of actions (e.g. submitting a bid). It queries the KL for the relevant knowledge it requires (e.g the belief that a bid will be accepted in the market).

We next describe each of these layers in further detail, whilst explaining the process through which an agent uses a plethora of raw data to select appropriate actions.

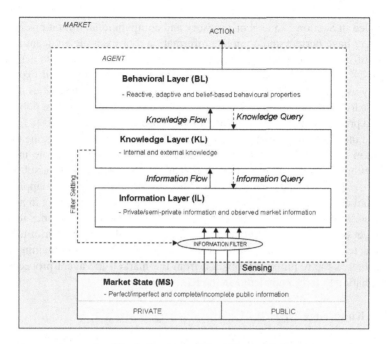

Fig. 1. Structure of the IKB Model

3.1   The Information Layer

This section deals with how an agent gathers information which is then passed on to the KL. The KL will select the data being stored in the IL by modifying the information filter (see figure 1) appropriately. This filter will screen the data from the MS with some noise (due to environmental noise or the agent's sensory limitations). As a result, the IL of an agent will contain a noisy, restricted view of all information which it can observe. Furthermore, the IL will also contain information about the agent's state, $p_i(t)$, as well as its action set $\mathcal{A}_i$.

We distinguish between information and knowledge in the following way:

Definition 4. *Information. Information is raw data that can be sensed by an agent.*

Definition 5. *Knowledge. Knowledge is the processed data that is computed by an agent from the information it has gathered.*

Now, information is typically categorised as follows [15]:

- Complete/Incomplete: An agent has complete information if it is aware of the complete structure of the market (that is, its action sets and the result of each action). Otherwise, it has incomplete information.
- Perfect/Imperfect: An agent has perfect information if it is certain of its state, the history of the market's and the agent's states ($H(p_\mathcal{M}(t_{k-1}))$ and $H(p_i(t_{k-1}))$) that have led it into this state. Otherwise, it has imperfect information.

As argued in Section 1, an agent's sensory and computational limitations imply that it will rarely have perfect and complete information. For example an agent might not be aware of its complete action set (i.e. an agent might believe that its action set at time t_k is $\mathcal{A}'_i \subset \mathcal{A}_i$) or it may be unsure of which state it is in (i.e. it expresses an uncertainty over $p_i(t_k)$). Thus, the agent will need to have certain heuristics in order to guide its search for information. This information can be gathered from public, semi-private and private sources. Public information is observable by all agents ($i \in \mathcal{I}$) in the market and includes things such as the market price in a stock exchange, the minimum increment in an eBay auction and the number of lots of flowers on sale in a Dutch flower auction. Semi-private information is that which is available to a subset of the agents ($i \in \mathcal{J} \subset \mathcal{I}$) and includes things such as the amount that a supplier might require from an agent and the code to signalling actions by a bidder ring in an auction [14]. Private information is only observable by a single agent and includes items such as its budget or the goods it is interested in. Thus, given the required information that the KL has requested, the agent will devote its limited resources to obtaining it. Then having gathered the required information from the market, the agent proceeds to use this information to infer knowledge in the KL.

3.2   The Knowledge Layer

The Knowledge Layer connects the Information and the Behavioural layers (see Section 3.3). It infers knowledge from the information sensed by the agent and passes it to the BL which acts upon it. In order to do so, the KL is requested by the BL as to which knowledge to acquire. This knowledge could be, for example, the current Sharpe ratio[3] of a stock or a forecast of market price based on a particular prediction model. Based on this and the current knowledge of the agent's state, the KL will decide upon the information it requires and set the information filter accordingly. The KL will then use the input from the IL to infer the appropriate knowledge which it will output to the BL.

Mirroring the IL, the KL can be segmented into knowledge about the agent's and the market's state. The former is what the agent knows about itself. This includes knowledge pertaining to its sub-goals (such as its risk attitude or the deadline by which a good is to be delivered) and knowledge about its state $p_i(t_k)$. The latter is what the agent knows about the market and would include items such as the degree of competitiveness in the market, the opponents' state and any available market indicators.

3.3   The Behavioural Layer

The Behavioural Layer represents the decision-making component of the strategy. In this context, such strategies are targeted towards finding the optimal action[4] in the market. However, as outlined earlier, more often than not, there is no known optimal action, as the market is too complex and the set of actions too large to determine such an optimal action analytically. Then, as there is no best strategy, a heuristic approach is taken. Thus, the BL instructs the KL as to what knowledge it needs to gather from the market

---

[3] The Sharpe ratio is a measure of a stock's excess return relative to its total variability [17].

[4] Here, "optimal" means the agent's most profitable action, given the current market conditions.

which, as described in Subsection 3.2, is computed from the market information. With the relevant knowledge of the market and its goals, the agent i forms a decision based on its strategy S_i and interacts with the market through actions SA_i. The goal of an agent's strategy is typically profit-maximisation, with the more sophisticated strategies considering both short-term and long-term risk. The formulation of the strategy usually depends on such goals and the market protocols.

Given this insight, we categorise the different behavioural properties of the strategy into different levels. In more detail, we distinguish those strategies in terms of the type of information (in Equation 1) that is used, *i.e.*, whether they use a history of market information or not, and, where they consider external information or not.

1. **No History** (ignores $H(p_\mathcal{M}(t_{k-1}))$ from Equation 1). Such reactive strategies make myopic decisions based only on current market conditions, $p_\mathcal{M}(t_k)$. The myopic nature of these strategies imply a lower workload on the KL since they require less information to sense and process. Reactive strategies usually exploit the more complex bidding behaviour of competing strategies and thus require less computational resources to strategise. One example of such a strategy is the *eSnipe* strategy[5] which is frequently used on Ebay to submit an offer to buy near the end of the auction.

2. **History** (considers $H(p_\mathcal{M}(t_{k-1})$ in Equation 1). We further subdivide those strategies that use a history of market information as being predictive or not (i.e. whether they predict $\{p_\mathcal{M}(t_{k+1}), p_\mathcal{M}(t_{k+2}), \ldots\}$ or not). The non-predictive strategies typically use $H(p_\mathcal{M}(t_{k-1}))$ to estimate $p_\mathcal{M}(t_k)$.

   (a) *Non-predictive*: The non-predictive strategy is typically belief-based and forms a decision based on some belief of *the current market conditions*. The agent's belief is computed from the history of market information in the KL, and usually represents the belief that a particular action will benefit the agent in the market (e.g. an offer to buy that is accepted). Given its belief over a set of actions, the agent then determines the best action over the short or long term.

   (b) *Predictive*: A strategy makes a prediction about the market state in order to adapt to it. Now, because future market conditions (that the trading agent adapts to) cannot be known *a priori*, the adaptive strategy typically makes some prediction using the history of market information. The KL is required to keep track of how the market (knowledge) is changing to predict the future market, while the BL uses this knowledge about the market dynamics to improve its response in the market. Being adaptive is particularly important in situations where the environment is subject to significant changes. By tracking such changes and adapting its behaviour accordingly, the agent aims to remain competitive in changing market conditions.

3. **No External Information** (ignores $ext_1, \ldots, ext_n$ in Equation 1). In this case, the strategy does not consider any signals external to the market (e.g. the falling market price of a good affecting the client's preferences for another type of good in an auction). However, the agent can choose whether or not to use the (internal) information (e.g. the e-Snipe strategy uses the internal market information, while the ZI Strategy [10] in the CDA does not make use of any market information).

---

[5] www.esnipe.com

4. **External Information** (considers $ext_1, \ldots, ext_n$ in ESquation 1). It is possible that signals external to the market can influence the preferences of the participants, such as an event independent of the market causing the clients' preferences in the market to change (e.g. unforeseen weather conditions affecting the production of wheat and thus the market for wheat indirectly). Thus, external information can be a valuable source of information that the agent can use to strategise in the market.

Having presented our IKB model for designing trading strategies, we now consider a specific example of a market mechanism that has spawned a gamut of strategies, and discuss how our model can be applied to it.

4 Applying IKB to the CDA

The CDA is a symmetric auction with multiple buyers and sellers and presently is one of the most popular auction formats in marketplaces populated by autonomous software agents. In CDAs, traders are allowed to submit offers to buy (bids) or to sell (asks) at any time during the trading day. There is an outstanding bid (ask) which is the highest bid (lowest ask) submitted in the market at any time during the auction. Furthermore, the market clears continuously whenever a bid can be matched to an ask. Such CDAs are widely used, indeed they are the principal financial institution for trading securities and financial instruments (e.g. the NYSE and the NASDAQ both run variants of the CDA). Because there is no known dominant strategy in the CDA, several researchers have worked on competing alternatives [4,9,21], developing trading agents that have been shown to be capable of outperforming humans in experimental settings [5]. We now give a formalised definition of the single-unit, single-item CDA institution, whose market state at time t_k is $p_{\mathcal{M}}(t_k) = <g, \mathcal{B}, \mathcal{S}, price(t_k), bid(t_k), ask(t_k) >$ where:

1. g is the good being auctioned off.
2. $\mathcal{B} = b_1, \ldots, b_{nb}$ is the finite set of identifiers of bidders in the market, where nb is the number of current bidders.
3. $\mathcal{S} = s_1, \ldots, s_{ns}$ is the finite set of identifiers of sellers in the market, where ns is the number of current sellers.
4. $price(t_k)$ denotes the current market price of good g in the market. This corresponds to the most recent transaction price.
5. $bid(t_k)$ denotes the outstanding bid at time t_k.
6. $ask(t_k)$ denotes the outstanding ask at time t_k.

The agent state at time t_k, is $p_i(t_k) = < id_i, n_i(t_k), \boldsymbol{v}_i = (v_{1,i}, \ldots, v_{n_i(t_k),i}), budget_i(t_k), comp_i(t_k) >$ where:

1. id_i defines the identity of the agent as either a buyer or a seller agent.
2. $n_i(t_k)$ defines the number of items an agent wishes to buy or sell.
3. $\boldsymbol{v}_i = \{v_{1,i}, \ldots, v_{n_i(t_k),i}\}$ is the vector of limit prices [6] ordered from highest to lowest in the case of a bidder and vice versa in the case of a seller.
4. $budget_i(t_k)$ is the budget available to agent i.

---

[6] This is the highest value at which a buyer would buy or the lowest value a seller will accept.

5. $comp_i(t_k)$ is the computational resources (memory and processing power) available currently to agent i.

The action set of the agent depends on its identity (id_i). If it is a buyer, it has $\mathcal{A}_i = <bid_i, silent>$ where $bid_i \in Re^+$ and $silent$ is no bid and an action that does not impact on the market. Correspondingly, if it is a seller, its action set is $\mathcal{A}_i = < ask_i, silent >$ where $ask_i \in Re^+$. It should be noted that in the CDA, SA_i will only be singletons (i.e. an agent can only take a single action at a time). The state transfer function T_{CDA} is the rules for acceptance and rejection of bids and asks as well as the clearing rules (see below). The standard CDA is not influenced by external signals (i.e. the transfer function T_{CDA} has no $ext_1, \ldots, ext_n$ arguments[7]) and the market changes each time an agent submits a bid or an ask and thus simultaneous bidding does not occur. Thus $p_{\mathcal{M}}(t_{k+1}) = T_{CDA}(p_{\mathcal{M}}(t_k), H(p_{\mathcal{M}}(t_{k-1})), SA_i)$ whereby $T(.)$ is defined by the following rules:

- if $SA_i = bid_i$, then
  - if $bid_i < bid(t_k)$ then bid_i is rejected and $p_{\mathcal{M}}(t_{k+1}) = p_{\mathcal{M}}(t_k)$.
  - if $bid(t) < bid_i < ask(t_k)$ then $bid(t_{k+1}) = bid_i$ and all other market variables remain unchanged.
  - if $ask(t) < bid_i$, then $price(t_{k+1}) = cr(ask(t_k) + bid_i)$ (where $cr(.)$ is a clearing rule stating the transaction price at which the clearing should occur)[8], $bid(t_{k+1}) = 0$ and $ask(t_{k+1}) = max_{ask}$ (where max_{ask} is the maximum ask an agent can submit in the CDA)
- if $SA_i = ask_i$, it follows the same intuition as above.
- if $SA_i = silent \ \forall i \in \mathcal{I}$ and $t_{k+1} - t_k > inactivity_{limit}$ or $t_{k+1} = deadline$, then the auction ends. $inactivity_{limit}$ is a pre-defined period of inactivity whereby no bid or ask is submitted, and $deadline$, the preset time when the market closes.

Furthermore, an agent's state will also change, conditional on whether its bid or ask is accepted in the market. If an agent's bid bid_i results in a transaction, $n_i(t_{k+1}) = n_i(t_k) - 1$, $budget_i(t_{k+1}) = budget_i t_k - price(t_{k+1})$ and $v_i = \{v_{2,i}, \ldots, v_{n_i(t_k),i}\}$. If an agent's bid is unsuccessful, then the MS relays this private information to the agent. The agent's visibility is restricted to only bids and asks being submitted in the market (with the agent that submitted a bid or an ask, not disclosed) and successful transactions. This information is publicly available in the MS. Based on the information that describes the market conditions, the agent strategises to submit a competitive offer to buy or sell. Given this background, we now analyse a selection of the most popular strategies for the CDA, from the perspective of the IKB model. We provide a summary of the analysis in table 1.

- **The Zero-Intelligence (ZI) Strategy [10]:** The ZI has a random behaviour: it is non-predictive and does not use the history of market information. It effectively ignores the market state (MS) and considers only its limit price, $v_{n_i(t_k),i}$ (its private information state in the IL) when submitting a bid or an ask. The KL does not compute any knowledge and simply forwards $v_{n_i(t_k),i}$ from the IL to the BL.

---

[7] Thus, a CDA strategy does not consider external information.

[8] This varies according to the CDA; examples include the midway value or $ask(t_k)$.

Table 1. Analysis of five CDA strategies under the IKB model

	ZI	ZIP	Kaplan	GD	RB
Information Layer	Limit price	Limit price and transaction price and Current bid/ask and current profit margin	Limit price and Outstanding bid/ask	Limit price and history of bid/ask and transaction price	Limit price and transaction price and limit price
Knowledge Layer	None	Competitive profit margin, success of trade	Measures for heuristics	Belief that bid/ask will be accepted	Target price based on estimate of CE price, risk factor
Behavioural Layer	Random	History, predictive	No history, non-predictive	History, non-predictive	History, predictive

- **The Zero-Intelligence Plus (ZIP) Strategy [4]:** This is a predictive strategy that uses the history of market information to predict the future market condition and adapt to it. It learns the profit margin of agent i to remain competitive given the changing market conditions. The IL collects $bid(t_k)$, $ask(t_k)$ and $price(t_k)$ (as instructed by the KL). The IL forwards this data, as well as the agent's profit margin (private information in its IL), to the KL. That knowledge is then used in the BL to predict the future market and adapt its profit margin, μ_i, to it. The BL then submits $\mathcal{A}_i = <bid_i|ask_i, silent>$, where bid_i or $ask_i = (1+\mu)v_{n_i(t_k),i}$.

- **The Kaplan Strategy [7]:** This is a non-predictive strategy that makes a decision based only on simple heuristics, and ignores the history of market information. The IL collects the outstanding bid and ask ($bid(t_k)$ and $ask(t_k)$ respectively) from the MS. Thereafter, using this information from the IL, the KL calculates the measures that are used in the heuristic rules of Kaplan's BL [7]. These rules determine what action, $\mathcal{A}_i = <bid_i|ask_i, silent>$, the agent i submits in the market.

- **The GD Strategy [9]:** This is a non-predictive strategy that uses a history of market information. The BL decides on an action, $<bid_i|ask_i, silent>$, by solving a risk-neutral utility maximisation problem involving a belief that a bid or an ask at a particular value will be successful in the market, and its limit price, $v_{n_i(t_k),i}$. Thus, the BL instructs the KL that it requires such knowledge. The KL then defines the Information Filter (see figure 1), so that relevant information, namely the history of bids, asks and transaction prices ($H(bid(t_{k-1}))$, $H(ask(t_{k-1}))$ and $H(price(t_{k-1}))$ respectively) are filtered to the IL. That information, along with the agent's limit price is passed to the KL. The KL can then compute the belief and passes it, along with the limit price, to the BL.

- **The Risk-based (RB) Strategy [21]:** This strategy is predictive and uses a history of market information. Furthermore, the RB has a more complex behaviour than the ZIP. The intrinsic parameter of the strategy, which is updated in response to changing market conditions, is the risk factor associated with the current good to buy or sell. The IL is instructed (by the KL) to record $bid(t_k)$ and $ask(t_k)$ and a history of transaction prices, $H(price(t_{k-1}))$. The KL then uses $H(price(t_{k-1}))$ to estimate the competitive equilibrium price[9] and then a target price (which the agent con-

---

[9] The competitive equilibrium is a price at which transaction prices are expected to converge to as given by the classical micro-economic theory [15].

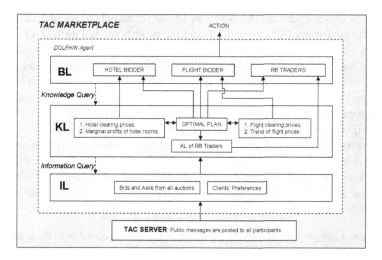

Fig. 2. Structure of the Dolphin strategy for the TAC Travel Game

siders as currently the most profitable offer price in the market). The target price (which is the market knowledge from the KL) is then used along with the agent's limit price, $v_{n_i(t_k),i}$, obtained from the IL and relayed through the KL, in a set of bidding rules in the BL. The latter then decides what offer, $< bid_i|ask_i, silent >$, the agent i submits.

Having discussed how the IKB model can be applied to existing strategies for the CDA, we consider in the next section how we can use our framework to engineer a new trading strategy given a market mechanism.

5   Design a Trading Strategy for the TAC Using the IKB

Here, we describe[10] how we employ our IKB framework to design a novel strategy for the TAC[11]. This competition involves a number of software agents competing against each other in a number of interdependent auctions (based on different protocols) to purchase travel packages over a period of 5 days (for the TACtown destination) for different customers. In more detail, in a TAC Travel Game (each lasting 9 minutes), there are 8 agents required to purchase packages for up to 8 customers (given their preferences) and that compete in 3 types of auctions which we describe next.

1. *Flight auctions.* There is a single supplier for in-flight and out-flight tickets over different days, with unlimited supply, and ticket prices updating every 10 seconds. Transactions occur whenever the bid is equal to or greater than the current asking price of the flight supplier.

---

[10] We only provide a brief description of the formalisation due to lack of space.

[11] Our IKB framework is employed in designing our agent, *Dolphin* which was ranked 4th in the final of the TAC Travel Game 2005.

2. *Hotel auctions.* There are two hotels at TACtown, namely Shoreline Shanties (SS) and Tampa Towers (TT), with TT being the nicer hotel and each hotel having 16 rooms available over 4 different days. Thus, there are 8 different hotel auctions (given the 2 hotels and rooms being available for 4 different days). Hotel rooms are traded in 16th-price multi-unit English auctions, whereby the 16 highest bidders are allocated a room for a particular day in a particular hotel, and at the end of every minute except the last minute, a hotel auction randomly closes, and the 16th and 17th highest price of each hotel auction that is still open is published.
3. *Entertainment auctions.* There are three types of entertainment in TACtown, namely a museum, an amusement park and a crocodile park, and 12 different entertainment auctions. At the beginning of the game, each agent is randomly allocated 12 entertainment tickets tradeable in the different multi-unit CDAs which clear continuously and close at the end of the game.

Given this background on the TAC environment, our objective is to design a trading strategy for an autonomous software agent participating in such a game. We develop the strategy by using the IKB framework, adopting the multi-layered approach. We now describe the strategy within the different layer prescribed by the IKB.

5.1   The Behavioural Layer

The issues associated with the bidding behaviour can be summarised as follows: (1) What item to bid for? (2) How much to bid for? (3) When to bid?

Definition 6. *Optimal Plan.* *The optimal plan is the set of travel packages, for 8 different clients, that would yield the maximum profit, given the clients' preferences (that determine the utility of the package) and the cost of the packages.*

Definition 7. *Marginal Profit*[12]. *The marginal profit of a hotel room (in a particular hotel on a particular day) is the decrease in the agent's total profit if it fails to acquire that room. Thus, the marginal profit of a hotel room that is not required in the optimal plan is 0. The marginal profit is defined only for the more competitive hotel auctions.*

Our strategy uses the history of market information, $H(p_{\mathcal{M}}(t_{k-1}))$ without any external information. The publicly viewable market state $p_{\mathcal{M}}(t_k)$ is a subset of bids and asks in all open auctions as well as the clearing price of all the closed auctions. Only the 16th and the 17th highest bid are visible for hotel auctions, and the outstanding bid and ask for the entertainment auctions.

We address the first issue by considering the *optimal plan* (see Definition 6). Thus, the agent always bids for the set of items (flight tickets, hotel rooms and entertainment tickets) required for the optimal plan, querying the optimal plan from the KL every 10 seconds. As a hotel auction closes every 60 seconds, the set of items available to the agent is further constrained and the optimal plan has to be recalculated. We address the other issues by considering the different auction formats.

First, we consider the 8 flight auctions. Given the manner in which the flight prices update, it is possible to predict the trend of the price update. Such a trend is queried

---

[12] The marginal profit described here is similar in essence to the marginal value used in [3].

from the KL. If the trend suggests a decrease in price, the BL then queries the predicted lowest ask price of the flight auction, and a bid is placed in that auction when that minimum is reached, if such flight tickets are required in the optimal plan. Conversely, if an increasing trend is predicted in a flight auction, we face a trade-off between acquiring all the tickets in such an auction immediately at the current lowest price, and waiting in case the agent does not manage to acquire the *scarce* hotel rooms required in the optimal plan, which could make the flight tickets redundant (since they are no longer required in the optimal plan and represent a loss). We implement the trade-off by spreading our bids in a flight auction over the remaining length of the TAC game. For example, if 4 tickets are required from a particular flight auction with an increasing trend, we could buy a single ticket every minute over the next 4 minutes, rather that buying all 4 immediately.

Next, we have the 8 hotel auctions, with a random one clearing (and closing) every minute. Thus, every minute, as the optimal plan changes, we update our bid in those auctions that are yet to close. Now, there is uncertainty in being able to acquire all the items required in the optimal plan, particularly at the beginning of the game. Furthermore the optimal plan typically changes during the game resulting in an item no longer being required in the optimal plan as the game progresses. Thus, bidding too high initially does not pay off since such a bid could result in that item still being acquired. Thus, our agent does not bid for a hotel room at its marginal profit (see Definition 7), but rather bid low at the beginning of the game and gradually increases its bid for a room towards its marginal profit as the game progresses, bidding its marginal cost after the 7th minute before the last hotel auction closes.

Finally, we have the 12 entertainment auctions. Here, we use the RB strategy (see Section 4) to bid in those CDAs. In particular, we have 12 RB traders that bid for the items required in the optimal plan. The agent further instructs the RB trader to buy *cheap* in auctions that do not influence the optimal plan, and sell *high* all the items that it holds, if the agent can thus be more profitable rather than using such items in its optimal plan. We now consider the knowledge required for the bidding behaviour.

5.2   The Knowledge Layer

Here, we principally require the optimal plan which is given as the solution to an optimisation problem. The agent searches for the plan that maximises its profit, which is the total utility of the packages less their estimated cost. The utility of a package is determined by a client's preferences, which is queried from the IL. Furthermore, the optimisation problem is constrained by different requirements of a feasible package, for example a client needs to stay in the same hotel for the duration of his/her stay or the client is required to stay in a hotel during the length of his/her stay [22], with additional constraints imposed as hotel auctions close. We also consider the additional knowledge of the predicted clearing price of the hotel auctions and of the flight auctions (based on the trend of flight prices in those auctions) to estimate the cost of a plan.

Now, for the hotel auctions, we calculate the marginal profit of hotel rooms required in the plan, to form the bidding price in the active hotel auctions. This is carried out by considering the next best package if a particular hotel room in the optimal plan cannot be acquired. The drop in profit then represents the marginal profit of that hotel room. Next, for the flight auctions, the KL estimates the trend of the flight prices, by considering its history. Such knowledge is used in the BL to decide when to bid for flight tickets, and in this layer, to calculate the minimum asking prices when a decreasing trend is identified. Finally, for the entertainment auctions, the agent has the same KL as the RB traders, described in Section 4.

5.3   The Information Layer

Having obtained the private information about its client preferences, the agent i then extracts all market information it requires in order to build the knowledge used in its strategy. Indeed, it tracks information relevant to the TAC Travel Game, such as the running time of the game and which auctions have closed (which are described by $H(p_{\mathcal{M}}(t_{k-1}))$), as well as the clients' preferences that do not change during the game (which are described by $H(p_i(t_{k-1}))$). When it considers the individual auctions, the agent has to record the history of published information (bids and asks where available). In the flight auctions, the history of flight prices is required to estimate the trend, which represents vital knowledge. In the hotel auctions, the history of the publicly announced 16th highest price can be recorded up to when the auction closes. Such information can be used to estimate the clearing price of the hotel auctions in future TAC games. Finally, for the entertainment auctions, the agent has the same IL as the RB traders.

6   Conclusions and Future Work

As electronic marketplaces are being used on a broader scale, we believe software agents will increasingly dominate the trading landscape. Their ability to make informed decisions, based on the plenitude of market information, to a degree that human traders can never achieve, make them ideal candidates for traders. However, as this new breed of agents are populating the markets, it is becoming a fundamental challenge to design strategies that can efficiently harness the avalanche of information that is available into efficient trading behaviour. Given this, the objective of this paper is to provide a systematic framework for designing such strategies. To this end, we proposed a framework that can be broken down into three principal components; namely the behavioural layer, the knowledge layer and the information layer. In so doing, we believe this work is an important preliminary step towards guiding the strategy designer by identifying the key models and concepts that are relevant to this task. We applied this model to analyse a selection of strategies in the CDA mechanism and showed its use when designing a novel strategy for the TAC Travel Game. Our approach allowed us to first decide upon the general outline of the strategic behaviour of the TAC strategy, and then delve into the complex task of implementing it. For the future, we obviously need to verify our framework further by applying it to different types of market institutions.

Acknowledgements

The authors would like to thank anonymous reviewers for helpful comments. Perukrishnen Vytelingum is funded by the DIF-DTC 8.6 project (www.difdtc.com) and Rajdeep K. Dash is funded by a BAE Systems studentship.

References

1. B. Bauer, J. P. Muller, and J. Odell. Agent uml: A formalism for specifying multiagent software systems. *International Journal of Software Engineering and Knowledge Engineering*, 11(3):207–230, 2001.
2. A. Chavez and P. Maes. Kasbah: An agent marketplace for buying and selling goods. In *First International Conference on the Practical Application of Intelligent Agents and Multi-Agent Technology (PAAM'96)*, pages 75–90, London, UK, 1996.
3. S. Cheng, E. Leung, K. M. Lochner, K. O'Malley, D. M. Reeves, L. J. Schvartzman, and M. P. Wellman. Walverine: A walrasian trading agent. *Second International Joint Conference on Autonomous Agents and Multi-Agent Systems (AAMAS-03)*, pages 465–472, 2003.
4. D. Cliff and J. Bruten. Minimal-intelligence agents for bargaining behaviors in market-based environments. Technical Report HPL-97-91, 1997.
5. R. Das, J. E. Hanson, J. O. Kephart, and G. Tesauro. Agent-human interactions in the continuous double auction. *Proceedings of the 17th Joint Conference on Artificial Intelligence*, pages 1169–1176, 2001.
6. T. H. Davenport and L. Prusak. *Working Knowledge: How Organizations Manage What They Know*. Harvard Business School Press, 1997.
7. D. Friedman and J. Rust. *The Double Auction Market: Institutions, Theories and Evidence*. Addison-Wesley, New York, 1992.
8. E. Gimnez-Funes, L. Godo, J. A. Rodrguez-Aguilar, and P. Garcia-Calvs. Designing bidding strategies for trading agents in electronic auctions. *Proceedings of the Third International Conference on Multi-Agent Systems*, pages 136–143, 1998.
9. S. Gjerstad and J. Dickhaut. Price formation in double auctions. *Games and Economic Behavior*, 22:1–29, 1998.
10. D. K. Gode and S. Sunder. Allocative efficiency of markets with zero-intelligence traders: Market as a partial substitute for individual rationality. *Journal of Political Economy*, 101(1):119–137, 1993.
11. M. He, N. R. Jennings, and H. Leung. On agent-mediated electronic commerce. *IEEE Trans on Knowledge and Data Engineering*, 15(4):985–1003, 2003.
12. N. R. Jennings. An agent-based approach for building complex software systems. *Comms. of the ACM*, 44(4):35–41, 2001.
13. M. Klein, C. Dellarocas, and J. Rodriguez-Aguilar. A knowledge-based methodology for designing robust multi-agent systems. *Proceedings of the Conference on Autonomous Agents and MultiAgent Systems*, pages 661–661, 2002.
14. V. Krishna. *Auction Theory*. Academic Press, 2002.
15. A. Mas-Collel, W. Whinston, and J. Green. *Microeconomic Theory*. Oxford University Press, 1995.
16. J. A. Rodriguez-Aguilar, F. J. Martin, P. Noriega, P. Garcia, and C. Sierra. Towards a test-bed for trading agents in electronic auction markets. *AI Communications*, 11(1):5–19, 1998.
17. W. F. Sharpe. Mutual fund performance. *Journal of Business*, pages 119–138, January 1966.
18. G. Tesauro and R. Das. High-performance bidding agents for the continuous double auction. *Proceedings of the Third ACM Conference on Electronic Commerce*, pages 206–209, 2001.
19. M. Tsvetovatyy and M. Gini. Towards a virtual marketplace: Architecture and strategies. In *Proceedings of the First International Conference on the Practical Application of Intelligent Agents and Multi-Agent Technology (PAAM'96)*, pages 597–613, Blackpool, UK, 1996.
20. I. A. Vetsikas and B. Selman. A principled study of the design tradeoffs for autonomous trading agents. *Proceedings of the Second International Joint Conference on Autonomous Agents and Multiagent Systems*, pages 473–480, 2003.

21. P. Vytelingum, R. K. Dash, E. David, and N. R. Jennings. A risk-based bidding strategy for continuous double auctions. *Proc. 16th European Conference on Artificial Intelligence*, pages 79–83, 2004.

22. M. P. Wellman, A. Greenwald, P. Stone, and P. R. Wurman. The 2001 trading agent competition. *Proceedings of the Fourteenth Conference on Innovative Applications of Artificial Intelligence*, pages 935–941, July 2002.

23. F. Zambonelli, N. R. Jennings, and M. Wooldridge. Developing multiagent systems: the gaia methodology. *ACM Transactions on Software Engineering and Methodology*, 12(3):285–312, September 2003.

Scaling Up the Sample Average Approximation Method for Stochastic Optimization with Applications to Trading Agents

Amy Greenwald, Bryan Guillemette, Victor Naroditskiy, and Michael Tschantz

Department of Computer Science
Brown University, Box 1910
Providence, RI 02912
{amy, gilmet, vnarodit, mtschant}@cs.brown.edu

Abstract. The Sample Average Approximation (SAA) method is a technique for approximating solutions to stochastic programs. Here, we attempt to scale up the SAA method to harder problems than those previously studied. We argue that to apply the SAA method effectively, there are three parameters to optimize: the number of evaluations, the number of scenarios, and the number of candidate solutions. We propose an experimental methodology for finding the optimal settings of these parameters given fixed time and space constraints. We apply our methodology to two large-scale stochastic optimization problems that arise in the context of the annual Trading Agent Competition. Both problems are expressed as integer linear programs and solved using CPLEX. Runtime increases linearly with the number of scenarios in one of the problems, and exponentially in the other. We find that, in the former problem, maximizing the number of scenarios yields the best solution, while in the latter problem, it is necessary to evaluate multiple candidate solutions to find the best solution, since increasing the number of scenarios becomes expensive very quickly.

1 Introduction

Stochastic programming is a natural method for solving optimization problems under uncertainty. This approach considers a problem in two stages. Decisions are made in the first stage before pertinent information about the second stage is revealed, but the objectives in the second stage are dependent on the first stage decisions. Given stochastic information available about the second stage outcomes, the goal is to find the first stage decisions that maximize the profits of the first stage plus the expected profits of the second stage. A solution is sought that is optimal in this expected sense.

One computational bottleneck in solving problems formulated as stochastic programs is the calculation of the expected profits of the second stage. This calculation typically involves enumerating all possible second stage outcomes In many problems, there are combinatorially many of these so-called *scenarios*, making it prohibitively expensive to calculate expected profits. One common means of approximating the calculation is the *expected value method* (e.g., [5]) in which the available stochastic information is collapsed into a deterministic statistic (e.g., the mean), and a deterministic variant of the

H. La Poutré, N. Sadeh, and S. Janson (Eds.): AMEC and TADA 2005, LNAI 3937, pp. 187–199, 2006.

optimization problem is solved. But ignoring large portions of the available stochastic information has been shown to be detrimental to solution quality (e.g., [6]).

Shapiro, *et al.* [1,9] proposed an alternative approximation technique called *sample average approximation* (SAA) to reduce the number of scenarios. They suggest using only a subset of the scenarios, randomly sampled according to the distribution over scenarios, to represent the full scenario space. An important theoretical justification for this method is that as the number of scenarios sampled increases, the solution to the approximate problem converges to an optimal solution in the expected sense. Indeed, the convergence rate is exponentially fast.

In this paper, we attempt to scale up the SAA method to harder problems than those previously studied (e.g., [1,9]). We tackle two stochastic optimization problems that arise naturally in the context of the annual Trading Agent Competition (TAC) (see http://www.sics.se/tac). The first problem is a bidding problem inspired by the TAC Travel game; the second problem is a scheduling problem inspired by the TAC Supply Chain Management game. Nested inside each of these problems is an NP-hard optimization problem.

We find that runtime increases linearly with the number of scenarios in the bidding problem, whereas it increases exponentially in the scheduling problem. Indeed, given reasonable time constraints we cannot reliably solve the scheduling problem with a sample size of more than 8 out of 2^{40} scenarios. We conclude that the theory which justifies the SAA method is inapplicable to some stochastic optimization problems. Consequently, we experiment with optimizing the tradeoff between the number of scenarios and the number of *policies* (i.e., candidate solutions). We generate multiple policies by sampling from the set of scenarios multiple times, and solving the ensuing approximation problems. We evaluate these policies with respect to a large, yet fixed, sample of scenarios. In the bidding problem, as the theory suggests, we find that maximizing the number of scenarios yields the best solution; in the scheduling problem, however, it is necessary to evaluate multiple policies to find the best solution, since increasing the number of scenarios becomes expensive very quickly.

2   Sample Average Approximation

Following [9], we are interested in solving optimization problems of the form:

$$v^* = \max_{x \in \mathcal{X}} g(x) \tag{1}$$

where

$$g(x) = \mathbb{E}_Q\left[G(x, Y)\right] \tag{2}$$

Here, $x \in \mathcal{X}$ is a vector of decision variables that takes values in the finite set $\mathcal{X}$; Y is a vector of discrete random variables with joint probability distribution Q over universe Ω; $G(x, \omega)$ is a real-valued function of $x \in \mathcal{X}$ and $\omega \in \Omega$; and $\mathbb{E}_Q\left[G(x, Y)\right]$ is the expected value of G at x: i.e.,

$$\mathbb{E}_Q\left[G(x, Y)\right] = \sum_{\omega \in \Omega} Q(\omega) G(x, \omega) \tag{3}$$

Each realization ω of Y, drawn according the distribution Q, is a *scenario*. Note that the number of scenarios is exponential in the number of random variables. (For example, if there are n random variables, all of which can take on binary values, there are 2^n scenarios.) Consequently, it is prohibitively expensive to compute $\mathbb{E}_Q\left[G(x, Y)\right]$. On the other hand, it is relatively less expensive to compute $G(x, \omega)$.[1]

The *sample average approximation* (SAA) method is a numerical means of approximating a solution to Equation 1 via Monte Carlo simulation. The main idea is simple: (i) generate a set of scenarios $\mathcal{S}$ of size S by sampling values of Y according to the distribution Q, and (ii) approximate the expected value in Equation 3, based on only the scenarios in $\mathcal{S}$. More specifically, generate a set of scenarios $\mathcal{S} = \{y_1, \ldots, y_S\}$, and solve the optimization problem:

$$\hat{v}_\mathcal{S} = \max_{x \in \mathcal{X}} \hat{g}_\mathcal{S}(x) \tag{4}$$

where for a set of scenarios $\mathcal{N} = \{a_1, \ldots, a_N\}$ of size N,

$$\hat{g}_\mathcal{N}(x) = \frac{1}{N} \sum_{i=1}^{N} G(x, a_i) \tag{5}$$

The SAA method, as it is applied in this paper, is shown in Algorithm 1. First, P candidate solutions, or policies, $\tilde{x}_1, \ldots, \tilde{x}_P$, are generated, by solving Equation 4 for P distinct scenario sets $\mathcal{S}_1, \ldots, \mathcal{S}_P$, each of size S. Second, these candidate policies are evaluated by computing $\hat{g}_\mathcal{E}(\tilde{x}_1), \ldots, \hat{g}_\mathcal{E}(\tilde{x}_P)$ for a fixed set of scenarios $\mathcal{E} = \{z_1, \ldots, z_E\}$ of size E. Third, the best candidate policy according to the evaluation phase is output.

Note the following:

- for all $\mathcal{X}' \subseteq \mathcal{X}$, $\hat{v}_\mathcal{S} = \max_{x \in \mathcal{X}} \hat{g}_\mathcal{S}(x) \geq \max_{x \in \mathcal{X}'} \hat{g}_\mathcal{S}(x)$
- for all $x \in \mathcal{X}$, $\hat{g}_\mathcal{N}(x)$ is an unbiased estimator of $g(x)$: i.e., $\mathbb{E}\left[\hat{g}_\mathcal{N}(x)\right] = g(x)$

It follows that the estimator $\hat{v}_\mathcal{S}$ is a statistical upper bound on v^*:

$$\mathbb{E}\left[\hat{v}_\mathcal{S}\right] \geq \mathbb{E}\left[\max_{x \in \mathcal{X}^*} \hat{g}_\mathcal{S}(x)\right] \geq \max_{x \in \mathcal{X}^*} \mathbb{E}\left[\hat{g}_\mathcal{S}(x)\right] = \max_{x \in \mathcal{X}^*} g(x) = v^* \tag{6}$$

where $\mathcal{X}^* \subseteq \mathcal{X}$ denotes the set of optimal solutions to Equation 1. On the other hand, for any feasible solution $\tilde{x} \in \mathcal{X}$, $\hat{g}_\mathcal{E}(\tilde{x})$ is a statistical lower bound on v^*:

$$v^* = \max_{x \in \mathcal{X}} g(x) \geq g(\tilde{x}) = \mathbb{E}\left[\hat{g}_\mathcal{E}(\tilde{x})\right] \tag{7}$$

The difference $\mathbb{E}\left[\hat{v}_\mathcal{S}\right] - \mathbb{E}\left[\hat{g}_\mathcal{E}(\tilde{x})\right]$ is an estimator of the optimality gap.

Using the theory of large deviations, Kleywegt, *et al.* [9] establish the following result: as $S \to \infty$, the probability that a solution to Equation 4 is an optimal solution to Equation 1 converges to 1 exponentially fast. In their implementation of SAA, the basic procedure is repeated P times, for increasing values of S (and E), until the estimate of the optimality gap is sufficiently small. However, as $S \to \infty$, the time and

---

[1] In fact, in our application domains, the exact computation of $G(x, \omega)$ is NP-hard.

Algorithm 1. Sample Average Approximation (E, S, P)

1: bestval $\Leftarrow -\infty$
2: sample a set $\mathcal{E}$ of E scenarios according to Q
3: **for all** $j = 1$ to P **do**
4:     sample a set $\mathcal{S}$ of S scenarios according to Q
5:     $\hat{x} \Leftarrow \arg\max_{x \in \mathcal{X}} \hat{g}_{\mathcal{S}}(x)$
6:     calculate $\hat{g}_{\mathcal{E}}(\hat{x})$
7:     **if** $\hat{g}_{\mathcal{E}}(\hat{x}) >$ bestval **then**
8:         bestval $\Leftarrow \hat{g}_{\mathcal{E}}(\hat{x})$
9:         bestsol $\Leftarrow \hat{x}$
10:     **end if**
11: **end for**
12: return bestsol

---

space complexity required to solve Equation 4 may increase superlinearly, making it impossible—for all practical purposes—to allow S to suitably increase, unless the desired optimality gap is sufficiently *large*. Rather than fix the number of policies P, and vary only S and E, we apply the SAA method by searching for optimal settings of E, S, and P, given the time and space constraints of the problem.

2.1 Overview

In solving stochastic optimization problems, not only can increasing the number of scenarios S increase the quality of the solution, but increasing the number of policies P can also increase the quality of the solution (the probability that the $(P + 1)$st policy outperforms the first P policies is $1/(P+1)$). Moreover, in Algorithm 1, the time complexity is linear in P and the space complexity is constant in P, but increasing S could increase time and space complexity in unpredictable ways because of the intricacies of Equation 4. In this paper, we study two stochastic optimization problems in the TAC domain, analyzing the tradeoff between solution quality and complexity, with respect to E, S, and P.

3 Sample Problem Domains

In this paper, we study two sample problem domains—stochastic bidding and stochastic scheduling—both inspired by the annual Trading Agent Competition (see http://www.sics.se/tac, [11], [2]).

3.1 Stochastic Bidding Problem

We solve a stochastic bidding problem inspired by the classic Trading Agent Competition game. In this game, each agent's objective is to maximize the profits earned by delivering combinations of 28 types of goods, on offer in 28 auctions, to eight clients. The stochastic formulation of the bidding problem can be described informally as follows: given a stochastic model of auction clearing prices, and given an agent's clients' preferences, find an optimal set of bids (and asks). It is natural to formulate this problem as a two-stage stochastic program: in the first stage an agent makes its bidding decisions; in the second stage, when the agent is informed of its winnings, it allocates those winnings to its clients. This second stage problem, TAC Travel allocation—find the utility-maximizing set of packages that an agent can assemble from its winnings, given its clients preferences—is equivalent to the (NP-hard) winner determination problem in combinatorial auctions (see Appendix B.)

A TAC Travel Stochastic Pricing Model. The bidding problem takes as input a stochastic model of clearing prices. Our stochastic pricing model is inspired by the *expected* competitive equilibrium pricing model developed for Michigan's TAC Travel Agent, Walverine [7]. To compute the *expected* competitive equilibrium price of a good, the tatonnement process is run once making use of the expected market wide demand, which is calculated based on the expected values of the opposing agents' clients' preferences. In a *stochastic* modeler, rather than run the tatonnement process only once using expected market wide demand, the process is run multiple times, each time drawing a random selection of the opposing agents' clients' preferences from the probability distributions given in the game's specification. We ran this procedure 2000 times to generate 2000 scenarios, which comprise our model of stochasticity in our experiments.

3.2 Stochastic Scheduling Problem

We solve a stochastic scheduling problem inspired by the Trading Agent Competition in Supply Chain Management. The problem is to schedule production of computers at a factory with limited capacity when demand for different types of computers is stochastic. There are 16 computer types that can be produced. The computers are produced to meet customer demand, which comes in the form of possible orders. A possible order is specified by a probability, price, computer type, and quantity. The probability indicates how likely it is that a possible order will become a real order. Real orders can be satisfied by delivering the quantity of the computer type requested. Revenue is earned by satisfying real orders. The objective is to distribute the available production capacity among computer types in a way that maximizes expected revenue.

We express the problem as a two-stage stochastic program. In the first stage, the agent makes its production decisions. In the second stage, the agent is told which of the possible orders become real orders, and chooses the profit maximizing subset of real orders to deliver using the computers produced in the first stage. The second stage problem, which we call delivery scheduling, is a 0-1 knapsack problem (see Appendix C).

A problem instance is a set of 40 possible orders. The possible orders are generated based on uniform distributions of probabilities, computer types, and quantities. A possible order's price is inversely related to the probability of it becoming a real order. To make the problem interesting, we generate a range of quantities such that the expected demand is twice the production capacity.

4   Experiments

The goal of our experiments was to optimize the parameters E, S, and P in Algorithm 1 in our two sample problems, given time (and space) constraints. At a high level, we ran multiple trials (that is, we solved multiple instances of each problem), with multiple settings of the parameters, and we averaged our results across trials to find the best parameter settings within reasonable time and space constraints. More specifically, our tests were conducted as follows: for each setting of the parameters (E, S, P), and for each trial $t = 1, \ldots, T$, we (i) generated a problem instance; (ii) ran Algorithm 1 to find the best policy; (iii) evaluated that policy using $E' > E$ scenarios.[2] For the bidding problem we set $T = 50$ and $E' = 250$, and we let $E \in \{1, 2, 4, 8, 16, 32, 64, 128\}$ and $S, P \in \{1, 2, 4, 8, 16, 32, 64\}$. For the scheduling problem, we set $T = 100$ and $E' = 5000$, and we let $E \in \{10, 100, 500, 1000\}$, $S \in \{1, \ldots, 8\}$, and $P \in \{1, \ldots, 375\}$. All experiments were run on an AMD Athlon 64 3000+ with 1GB of RAM. We used CPLEX 9.0 to solve the integer programs, solving to within .01% of optimality with the default settings.

4.1   Hypotheses

Our first set of experiments was intended to approximate the time complexity of the bidding problem and the scheduling problem. The graphs in Figure 1 depict time (in seconds) as a function of S, for fixed values of E and P. Perhaps surprisingly, in the bidding problem, this relationship is approximately linear. In the scheduling problem, however, time increases rapidly as the number of scenarios increases. The error bars in these graphs plot one standard deviation from the mean. The variance in these experiments is large, because we average results across multiple trials: i.e., problem instances of varying degrees of difficulty.

Figure 2 depicts the agent's reward in the bidding problem and its revenue in the scheduling problem, as a function of S and P. Here, we observe that increasing the number of scenarios from 1 to 64 in the bidding problem leads to an increase in reward from roughly 3300 to roughly 4200, on average. In the scheduling problem, increasing the number of policies, say from 1 to 20, leads to a substantial increase in revenue, but at 32 policies, revenue seems to stabilize. Of course, increasing the number of scenarios also leads to an increase in revenue, but in practice this may not be feasible. Indeed, revenue is still increasing between 7 and 8 scenarios, but we cannot solve this problem reliably with as few as 9 scenarios.

Based on these observations, we postulate the following: In problems, like the bidding problem, where time complexity is an approximately linear function of S, a near optimal setting of the parameters can be obtained by setting S to the maximum value possible within the time and space constraints of the application, and then perhaps increasing P if time and space permit. On the other hand, in problems like the scheduling problem, where time complexity is a superlinear function of S, it is necessary to search the space of parameter settings, within the time and space constraints of the applica-

---

[2] Anecdotally, we report that more evaluations were necessary to accurately estimate the value of a policy, but fewer evaluations were sufficient to rank policies.

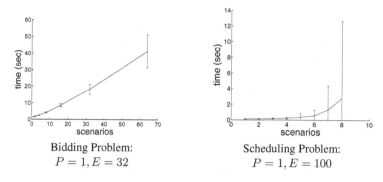

Fig. 1. Time as a function of the number of scenarios

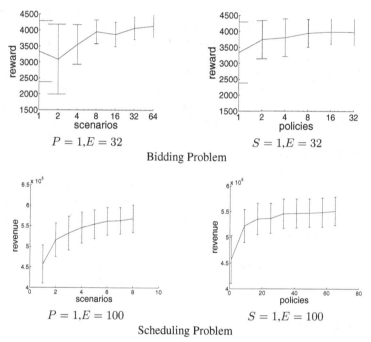

Fig. 2. Reward and revenue as a function of the number of scenarios and policies

tion, to find the best quality solution. Indeed, the next experiments provides evidence to support these hypotheses.

4.2 Optimizing E, S, and P

We tested only 243 of the 392 possible settings of the bidding parameters, and 282 of the 12000 possible settings of the scheduling parameters because of artificially-imposed time constraints. In the bidding problem, we ran all combinations of the parameter settings for which we predicted the running time would be less than 3 minutes (in TAC Travel games, hotel bidding proceeds in 1 minute rounds); in the scheduling problem, we ran all combinations of the parameter settings for which we predicted the running time would be less than 25 seconds (in TAC SCM games, each day lasts 15 seconds) We made these predictions as follows. For all values of S, we recorded the average time to solve Equation 4; call this $\alpha(S)$. For all values of E, we recorded the average time to solve Equation 5; call this $\beta(E)$. For each combination of E, S, and P, we predicted the running time would be $P(\alpha(S) + \beta(E))$. Note that because of these time constraints, we never exhausted the space limitations of our machines.

The results of our search for optimal parameter settings are depicted in Table 1. Each table was generated as follows. First, we sorted our data according to time. Then, we traversed this sorted list. Whenever the value of the solution improved, we output new parameter settings and the corresponding values. The first column in each table lists time in seconds. For the bidding problem, the second column lists rewards; for scheduling, the second and third columns list the statistical upper and lower bounds on revenue (Equations 6 and 7). The revenue earned in the scheduling problem is precisely the estimated lower bound. The last three columns list the settings of E, S, and P that generated these values.

In the bidding problem, the best performing parameter settings are those with 64 scenarios and only 2 policies, increasing the number of evaluations as time permits. It appears that the increase in solution quality obtained by increasing the number of scenarios exceeded any increase that could have been obtained by increasing the number of policies. Given that time increases only linearly with the number of scenarios in the bidding problem, but that solution quality converges to the optimal exponentially fast, this outcome is not surprising.

In the scheduling problem, the best performing parameter settings are those with 4–6 scenarios and multiple policies. When the number of scenarios was 7 or 8, the policy generation process was much slower than it was when there were fewer scenarios. Indeed, only one "algorithm" with 7 scenarios appears in the table, and no "algorithms" with 8 scenarios appear at all. We conclude that in the scheduling problem, choosing the best among multiple policies yields better solutions than increasing the number of scenarios to a point at which only a few policies can be evaluated.

5   Related Work

The sample average approximation method has been applied to a variety of stochastic optimization problems of varying degrees of difficulty. It appears to us, however, that none were quite so hard as the problems attacked here. For example, [9] experiment with the stochastic knapsack problem, with only 20 first stage binary decision variables, and [1] experiment with a stochastic optimization problem with 2 continuous first stage variables and 4 integer second stage variables. In our formulation of the bidding problem, there are 70400 first stage variables and 201216 second stage variables; in our formulation of the scheduling problem, there are 16 first stage integer variables and 320 second stage binary variables. Moreover, nested inside each of our problems are NP-hard second stage decision problems.

To our knowledge, Algorithm 1 is the best-known method for solving stochastic optimization problems. Thus, rather than compare sample average approximation with other

Table 1. Optimal settings of the parameters as a function of time

Time	Reward	E	S	P
1.47	3318	64	1	1
1.48	3456	128	1	1
1.48	3502	2	1	1
1.49	3548	16	1	1
2.45	3550	32	4	1
2.45	3577	2	4	1
3.38	3695	2	1	2
3.89	3705	4	1	2
4.12	3912	128	8	1
4.16	3947	32	8	1
8.43	3967	2	16	1
10.55	4014	8	8	2
16.75	4043	32	8	2
17.95	4045	64	32	1
18.09	4064	1	32	1
18.12	4065	32	32	1
33.50	4077	32	8	4
38.52	4099	16	32	2
41.26	4132	32	64	1
82.20	4134	1	64	2
84.81	4136	32	32	4
85.99	4141	16	64	2
88.81	4142	32	64	2
115.27	4146	128	64	2

Bidding Problem

Time	Lower	Upper	E	S	P
0.03	468310	754507	10	1	1
0.04	517559	688963	10	2	1
0.07	535059	657833	10	3	1
0.11	548218	647722	10	4	1
0.29	550930	639010	10	5	1
0.38	554046	637546	100	5	1
0.40	559796	630666	10	6	1
0.56	561418	628053	100	6	1
1.31	562798	624235	100	7	1
1.36	567807	661136	100	3	8
1.58	575676	647877	100	4	7
2.84	577965	646174	100	4	13
3.06	579369	638006	100	5	9
4.13	581433	636296	100	5	13
5.47	582306	629457	100	6	9
5.65	582504	635982	100	5	17
7.30	583621	637376	100	5	21
8.50	583998	630956	100	6	13
9.44	584043	646170	100	4	43
10.00	584287	636188	100	5	29
10.92	585094	645841	100	4	49
12.63	585543	636626	100	5	37

Scheduling Problem

techniques, we conducted an in-depth study of the SAA method itself, with one exception. We did measure the performance of the expected value method in the scheduling problem, where all random variables are replaced with their means. Much like the results reported in [4], this method performs far worse than the SAA method, even with only one scenario and one policy. The revenue earned was only 311,064 (as compared to 468,310). [3]

6   Conclusion

In this paper, we conducted an empirical study of the sample average approximation method for solving stochastic optimization problems. We discovered that runtime can increase exponentially with the number of scenarios, so that even if solution quality increases exponentially with the number of scenarios, it may be advantageous to conduct a policy search, because runtime increases only linearly with the number of policies. In particular, we applied what we call the ESP methodology, which is a means of searching

---

[3] The poor performance of the expected value method is partly due to the structure of the particular problem instances we solved. The expected value method should perform better on problem instances with higher ratios of the number of orders to the number of computer types.

for optimal settings of the parameters of the SAA algorithm, given the time and space constraints of an application. Based on our observations, we formulated a quick test to determine whether maximizing S and then P, given the constraints of an application is sufficient—namely, do time and space usage grow only linearly with S? Often, however, we expect time and space usage to grow exponentially with S, in which case it is necessary to search the space of parameter settings to optimize the tradeoffs between increasing S or P. The stochastic bidding and scheduling problems studied in this paper were inspired by the Trading Agent Competition. In both TAC Travel and TAC SCM, our agent's architecture [3, 8] is comprised of two main modules: a "modeler" and a "decider." Our modelers build stochastic models of their environments, which necessitates that our deciders solve stochastic optimization problems. In other words, decision-making under uncertainty, particularly the two problems defined and analyzed in this paper, is fundamental to our agents' designs. Generalizing from our experience in TAC Travel and TAC SCM, we expect that related stochastic optimization problems are fundamental to the design of trading agents for domains outside the scope of the Trading Agent Competition.

A   Stochastic Programming Formulations

A.1   TAC Travel Bidding Problem

Index Sets $a \in A$ indexes the set of auctions. $c \in C$ indexes the set of clients. $p \in P$ indexes the set of bid prices. $q \in Q_a$ indexes the set of goods in auction a. $s \in S$ indexes the set of scenarios. $t \in T$ indexes the set of packages.

Constants $\mathcal{G}_{at}$ is an integer constant indicating how many goods from auction a are contained in a package t. $\mathcal{B}_{aqs}$ is an integer constant indicating the closing buy price of the qth good of auction a in scenario s. $\mathcal{Z}_{aqs}$ is an integer constant indicating the closing sell price of the qth good of auction a in scenario s. $\mathcal{U}_{ct}$ is an integer constant indicating the utility gained for client c having package t.

Decision Variables $B = \{\beta_{apq}\}$ is a set of boolean variables indicating whether to bid price p for the qth good in auction a. $Z = \{\zeta_{apq}\}$ is a set of boolean variables indicating whether to ask price p for the qth good in auction a. $\Gamma = \{\gamma_{cst}\}$ is a set of boolean variables indicating whether client c gets package t in scenario s.

Objective Function

$$\max_{B,Z,\Gamma} \sum_{S} \Pr(s) \left(\overbrace{\left(\sum_{C,T} \mathcal{U}_{ct}\gamma_{cst} \right)}^{utility} - \overbrace{\left(\sum_{A,Q_a,p>\mathcal{B}_{aqs}} \mathcal{B}_{aqs}\beta_{aqp} \right)}^{cost} + \right.$$

$$\left(\overbrace{\sum_{A,Q_a,p<Z_{aqs}} Z_{aqs}\zeta_{aqp}}^{revenue} \right) \right) \tag{8}$$

The objective function (Equation 8) maximizes utility minus cost plus revenue.

Constraints

$$\sum_T \gamma_{cst} \leq 1 \quad \forall c \in C, s \in S \tag{9}$$

$$\sum_P B_{apq} \leq 1 \quad \forall a \in A, q \in Q_a \tag{10}$$

$$\sum_P Z_{apq} \leq 1 \quad \forall a \in A, q \in Q_a \tag{11}$$

$$\sum_{C,T} \gamma_{cst} \mathcal{G}_{at} \leq \left(\sum_{Q_a,p>\mathcal{B}_{aqs}} \beta_{apq} \right) - \left(\sum_{Q_a,p<Z_{aqs}} \zeta_{aqs} \right)$$
$$\forall a \in A, s \in S \tag{12}$$

Equation 9 limits each client to one package in each scenario. Equation 10 prevents the agent from placing more than one bid for the same (auction, quantity) pair. Equation 11 prevents the agent from placing more than one ask for the same (auction, quantity) pair. Equation 12 prevents the agent from allocating goods that it does not own (number allocated $\leq$ number bought $-$ number sold).

A.2   TAC SCM Production Scheduling Problem

Index Sets $i \in I$ indexes the set of RFQs. $j \in J$ indexes the set of SKUs. $n \in N$ indexes the set of scenarios.

Constants C is the production capacity. SKU s_i, quantity q_i, price p_i, and penalty ρ_i. c_j is the number of cycles required to produce SKU j. ω_{in} is set to 1 if RFQ i becomes an order in scenario n.

Decision Variables v_j is an integer variable indicating the amount of SKU j to produce. z_{in} is a boolean variable with value 1 if we fill order i in scenario n.

Objective Function

$$\max_z \sum_n \sum_i (p_i + \rho_i) z_{in} \tag{13}$$

The objective function (Equation 13) maximizes the revenue of allocating assembled computers to orders across scenarios. Note that the true value is obtained by subtracting the quantity $\sum_i \rho_i$ from the given value; but changing the objective function by a constant does not affect the solution.

Constraints Stage 1:

$$\sum_j c_j v_j \leq C \tag{14}$$

$$v_j \in \mathbb{Z}_+, \quad \forall j$$

Stage 2:

$$z_{in} \leq \omega_{in} \ \forall i, n \tag{15}$$

$$\sum_{\{i \ | \ s_i = j\}} q_i z_{in} \leq v_j, \ \forall j, n \tag{16}$$

$$z_{in} \in \{0, 1\}, \ \forall i, n$$

Constraint 14 makes sure that we do not produce beyond our production capacity. Constraint 15 does not let us satisfy an RFQ for which we did not place a winning bid. Constraint 16 makes sure that we do not allocate to orders more computers than we assembled in the first stage.

B   TAC Travel Allocation is NP-Hard

Generally speaking, *allocation* is equivalent to the winner determination (WD) problem in combinatorial auctions, an NP-hard problem [10]. The role of the agent is analogous to that of an auctioneer. In WD, an auctioneer is given a set of combinatorial bids in the form of package–price pairs, and seeks an allocation of goods to bids so as to maximize his profits, subject to the constraint that he cannot allocate more goods than he owns. Analogously, in *allocation*, the agent is given a set of "bids" in the form of package–utility pairs, and seeks an allocation of goods to packages so as to maximize the sum of the corresponding utilities, subject to the constraint that it cannot allocate more goods than it owns.

In TAC Travel, agents are subject to the further constraint that only one package can be allocated to each client. TAC Travel allocation and (general) allocation are polynomial-time reducible to one another. An arbitrary instance of TAC Travel allocation reduces to an instance of allocation by adding to every bid from client c a dummy good c of which the agent owns exactly one, so that every feasible allocation assigns at most one package per client. An arbitrary instance of allocation reduces to TAC Travel allocation by associating a unique client with each bid.

C   Delivery Scheduling is NP-Hard

The NP-hardness of the Delivery Scheduling Problem (DSP) [3] follows from the fact that DSP is equivalent to 16 parallel 0-1 knapsack problems, one per SKU. In the knapsack problem, a set of items of varying weights and values is given, along with a knapsack of a fixed capacity (i.e., a weight limit). An optimal solution is a subset of the items that maximizes the total value, with a total weight that does not exceed the knapsack's capacity. Equivalently, in DSP with only one SKU, a set of orders of varying quantities and prices is given, along with a fixed inventory. An optimal solution to DSP is a subset of the orders that maximizes the total profit for which the total quantity does not exceed inventory.

References

1. S. Ahmed and A. Shapiro. The sample average approximation method for stochastic programs with integer recourse. *Submitted for publication*, 2002.
2. R. Arunachalam and N. Sadeh. The 2003 supply chain management trading agent competition. In *Third International Conference on Autonomous Agents and Multi-Agent Systems Workshop on Trading Agent Design and Analysis*, July 2004.
3. M. Benisch, A. Greenwald, I. Grypari, R. Lederman, V. Naroditskiy, and M. Tschantz. Botticelli: A supply chain management agent. In *Third International Conference on Autonomous Agents and Multiagent Systems*, volume 3, pages 1174–1181, July 2004.
4. M. Benisch, A. Greenwald, V. Naroditskiy, and M. Tschantz. A stochastic programming approach to TAC SCM. In *Fifth ACM Conference on Electronic Commerce*, pages 152–160, May 2004.
5. John Birge and Francois Louveaux. *Introduction to Stochastic Programming*. Springer, New York, 1997.
6. H. Chang, R. Givan, and E. Chong. On-line Scheduling Via Sampling. In *Artificial Intelligence Planning and Scheduling (AIPS)*, pages 62–71, Breckenridge, Colorado, 2000.
7. S.F. Cheng, E. Leung, K.M. Lochner, K.O'Malley, D.M. Reeves, L.J. Schvartzman, and M.P. Wellman. Walverine: A Walrasian trading agent. *Decision Support Systems*, page To Appear, 2004.
8. A. Greenwald and J. Boyan. Bidding algorithms for simultaneous auctions: A case study. In *Proceedings of Third ACM Conference on Electronic Commerce*, 115-124 2001.
9. A.J. Kleywegt, A. Shapiro, and T. Homem de Mello. The sample average approximation method for stochastic discrete optimization. *SIAM Journal of Optimization*, 12:479–502, 2001.
10. M.H. Rothkopf, A. Pekeč, and R.M. Harstad. Computationally manageable combinatorial auctions. *Management Science*, 44(8), 1998.
11. M.P. Wellman, P.R. Wurman, K. O'Malley, R. Bangera, S. Lin, D. Reeves, and W.E. Walsh. A Trading Agent Competition. *IEEE Internet Computing*, April 2001.

Who to Listen to: Exploiting Information Quality in a ZIP-Agent Market

Dan Ladley[1] and Seth Bullock[2]

[1] Leeds University Business School,
University of Leeds, UK
danl@comp.leeds.ac.uk
[2] School of Computing,
University of Leeds, UK
seth@comp.leeds.ac.uk

Abstract. Market theory is often concerned only with centralised markets. In this paper, we consider a market that is distributed over a network, allowing us to characterise spatially (or temporally) segregated markets. The effect of this modification on the behaviour of a market populated by simple trading agents was examined. It was demonstrated that an agent's ability to identify the optimum market price is positively correlated with its network connectivity. A better connected agent receives more information and, as a result, is better able to judge the market state. The ZIP trading agent algorithm is modified in light of this result. Simulations reveal that trading agents which take account of the quality of the information that they receive are better able to identify the optimum price within a market.

1 Introduction

The study of the centralised market has been one of the key areas of economic research for many years. There have been many attempts to understand the behaviour of markets and that of the traders within them. These attempts range from analytical studies (e.g., [1]), to experiments on real subjects (e.g., the studies of Smith [2]).

In addition to analytical and experimental results, the use of simulation has become increasingly important [3,4,5,6,7]. In particular simulation has allowed the modelling of trader micro-behaviour, which would be analytically intractable and experimentally time consuming. In virtually all of these micro studies, the market is assumed to occupy a single location. All bids and offers are submitted in the same place, where all others may see and respond to them. Not all markets, however, are like this. Retail markets, for instance, are spatially embedded and consequently impose costs in terms of the time and effort that it takes to visit other traders and acquire information. As a consequence of this, it is usually impossible for a trader to visit *all* possible partners. Instead, the trader will probably restrict information gathering to nearest neighbours, or key operators in the market. In this case the market no longer has a central location to which information is submitted and, as a result, different traders within the market may have access to different histories of bids and offers.

H. La Poutré, N. Sadeh, and S. Janson (Eds.): AMEC and TADA 2005, LNAI 3937, pp. 200–211, 2006.
© Springer-Verlag Berlin Heidelberg 2006

It is not only spatially embedded markets which may limit the ubiquity of market information. Traders in a financial market have ready access to all trading information. However, in this case the shear quantity of information may segregate the market. The traders incur very little cost in gathering information, instead the main cost is that of analysis. Analysing information takes time, meaning that it may be impossible for a single trader to study and accurately respond to all of the information within the market. Traders are therefore likely to ignore some of the information available and fail to take it into account when making decisions. In effect the trader will not be hearing some of the information even though it is available in principle. One possible consequence of this is to focus the attention of traders on a small subset of market products, leading to specialisation. There is, however, an important difference between these cases. Although a market may be segregated in terms of information flow, trade is not as restricted as it is in the spatially extended case.

In either of these cases, however, assumptions about centralisation of market processes no longer hold. Different traders within the market have access to different histories of bids and shouts and, potentially, a propensity to deal with particular partners rather than others. These problems aren't necessarily limited to human traders. It is possible to conceive of markets that are sufficiently large and complex that even computer programs would find it inefficient to analyse all information present, or consider trading with every agent in the market. Recently models have started to appear that examine these types of problems. For instance [8] and [9] have both examined trading scenarios that take place across networks.

This paper aims to investigate the valuation of information within distributed markets. As has previously been described, traders in these markets will have access to different information sources and therefore different pictures of the market state. This will be particularly apparent if some traders are more connected than others, i.e., they have more information sources and trading partners. These better connected traders are, on average, likely to have a better understanding of the market than those traders who are less well connected. This paper will first examine the advantage this inequality provides to the better connected traders along with the effect this has on trading within the market.

The effect of this imbalance is important because to some extent the degree to which a trader is connected can be altered by the trader itself. It is well known that resources must be expended to gather information and that properly analysing information takes time. In many situations it is possible for a trader to change the proportion of its resources dedicated to gathering and analysing information, however, it is important to know under which circumstances to do this. This paper will begin to investigate this question. It will consider a market where both trade and information flow are restricted in a manner represented by an explicit, fixed network of possible agent-agent interactions. The network will govern which agents are able to communicate with each other and, therefore, which agents are able to trade with each other. Importantly, this network will not be complete (fully connected), i.e., some traders within the market will not be able to communicate directly with others. In this initial work we wish to gain an understanding of the value of information in a simple segmented market so the market network is fixed. Trader are not permitted to change their connections during the simulation. In future we hope to develop this system so as to better understand the circumstances in which it is favourable to change connectivity. The market used for these simulations is very simple, it is not designed to reflex the intricacies of any particular distributed market in particular. Instead it is designed to provide general insight into the valuation of information in segmented markets. The results found within this paper could be applied to any markets where information cannot flow freely. This includes retail markets, OTC markets, and many others.

This model will differ from previous work in that it will model the micro-behaviour of the traders. In both of the previous studies mentioned above [8,9], trade between agents was abstract. When two agents were chosen to trade, their utility functions were examined and an allocation of resources was calculated such that the utilities of both agents were increased. In this study, we will use a well-established trading agent algorithm to investigate the effect of the market constraints on the ability of agents to identify the optimum price. In addition, an attempt will be made to modify the trading agent algorithm to better cope with, or exploit, this situation.

2   Method

This section will first describe the structure and function of the markets that will be investigated, before detailing the trading agents that will populate them.

2.1   Network Generation

Trading networks were constructed in which nodes represented traders and edges represented bi-directional communication channels. There are many possible network configurations which could be investigated for their effect on market performance, including lattices, Erdős-Rényi random graphs, small worlds, and graphs resulting from preferential attachment. This paper will focus on the latter class of networks since they exhibit some interesting properties, including the presence of well-connected "hubs", which have an intuitive appeal in terms of real world markets, where it would be expected that certain major investment banks would be much better connected than individual investors.

An existing preferential attachment scheme is employed here [10]. A network of N unconnected nodes is gradually populated with Nm edges. In random order, each node is consulted, and allocated an edge linking it to a second node chosen according to probabilities calculated as $p_i = (n_i + \delta)^P$. Here, P is the exponent of preferential attachment and remains constant, n is node's current degree (number of edges), and δ is a small constant (0.1 for all results reported here) that ensures unconnected nodes have a non-zero probability of gaining a neighbour. Self-connections and multiple connections between the same pair of nodes were not allowed. All probabilities, p_i, were updated after every edge was added. After m cycles through the population, the network was complete. Note that every node will have a minimum of m edges, and a maximum of $N - 1$.

Markets explored here have a relatively high preferential exponent of $P = 1.5$ in order to generate networks that display a wide range of degrees. For all results reported here, $m = 10$. Initial tests showed that if m was significantly less than this value, the market failed to converge as few agents were able to trade with their limited number of neighbours.

2.2   Auction Dynamics

The market functioned according to an adapted continuous double auction mechanism. The standard continuous double auction allows buyers and sellers to submit bids to the rest of the market for consideration at any time. First, in order to simplify the implementation of a continuous double auction on a network, we adopted the system presented by Cliff and Bruten [4]. In their simulations, the auction mechanism acts in discrete time and has no order book. Each time period, one active agent (one who is still able to trade) is selected at random to make an offer or a bid. The other agents in the market are then polled in random order for responses to the shout. If the response and the shout cross then a trade is executed at the first shouted price, if not the next agent is polled. If no trader accepts the shout then the shout is removed. Second, we limit an agent's ability to trade such that they are only able to make offers to, or accept bids from, their network neighbours. Each market was simulated for a fixed number of time steps.

2.3   Trading Agents

Here, the ZIP trading algorithm is used to govern agent behaviour. ZIP, or Zero Intelligence Plus, agents were created by Cliff and Bruten [4] in response to work by Gode and Sunder [3], who created the "Zero Intelligence" trading algorithm in some of the first agent-based market simulations. The Zero Intelligence algorithm was designed to be the simplest possible algorithm that would allow trade to occur in a market. Two types of Zero Intelligence trader were introduced. The first, unconstrained traders (ZI-U), choose shout prices at random from a uniform distribution across the whole range of possible prices permitted, disregarding any limit prices. It was found that markets populated by these traders exhibited none of the normal properties associated with markets, such as convergence to the equilibrium price. The second type of zero intelligence traders (ZI-C) were *constrained* in the range of prices that could be shouted. Shout prices were again drawn at random from a uniform distribution. However, this distribution was now constrained by an agent's limit price. In the case of sellers, shouts were constrained to be greater than the limit price, while in the case of buyers, shouts had to be less than the specified limit price. Importantly, markets populated by traders using this algorithm were shown to behave analogously to real markets in that they converged to the theoretical equilibrium price [3]. This was interpreted as indicating that the market mechanism itself was the most significant factor in market behaviour, and that the design of the trading algorithm was not as important. Cliff and Bruten [4], however, showed this to be incorrect, demonstrating that the convergence observed during each trading period was an artifact of the supply and demand schedules used by Gode and Sunder. They demonstrated that, for a certain type of supply and demand schedule that was close to symmetric, the probability distribution of likely ZI-C bids and offers would result in convergence to the mean price. They then performed simulations to verify these results with a broader range of supply and demand schedules. For non-symmetric schedules, markets populated by ZI-C traders failed to converge, or converged to a non-market-equilibrium value.

The ZIP agent differs from the ZI-C agent in that it learns from the market. Each ZIP trader has a profit margin associated with its limit price. In the case of buyers, the profit margin is the amount by which they wish to undercut their limit price to make a trade, and in the case of sellers, it is the amount by which they wish to exceed there limit price. When a ZIP trader shouts, the price is constrained by its limit price and profit margin. The agent uses the market's response to its activity (and the observable activity of others) to update its profit margin. For instance, buyers observe the bids made on the market and whether they are accepted or not and adjust their profit margin accordingly (for full details of this algorithm, see [4]). The ZIP algorithm employs the Widrow-Hoff learning rule with momentum [11] to adapt these profit margins throughout each agent's lifetime—maximising for each agent the possibility of making a profitable trade. This learning rule allows the agents to rapidly converge on the optimal price, while the momentum term allows blips in the market to be ignored. Unlike ZI-C, ZIP agents are capable of finding the market equilibrium under a wide range of supply and demand schedules.

Here, each ZIP agent was initialised with a random profit margin drawn from a uniform distribution $[0.05, 0.35]$. Each agent was also initialised with a random learning rate drawn from a uniform distribution $[0.1, 0.5]$ and random momentum value drawn from a uniform distribution $[0.2, 0.8]$.

3   Initial Results

Experiments were performed using markets populated by 100 ZIP traders. Each agent was randomly allocated a limit price in the range $[100, 200]$, and either the ability to buy one unit or sell one unit of an unnamed indivisible commodity. Each market simulation lasted for 400 time steps. Markets were constrained by networks, constructed as described above, with $P = 1.5$ and $m = 10$, and all markets operated through the continuous double auction mechanism.

Figure 1(left) shows the price deviation from the theoretical optimum averaged over forty thousand repetitions. Each agent's valuation was obtained at each time step of each repetition, and the average calculated. Notice that timeseries are shown for agents with connectivity *rank* ranging from 1st (most well-connected) to 100th (least well-connected). Over time, the average price shouted by all agents, regardless of connectivity, approaches the equilibrium price. This is to be expected, as it is a fundamental property of markets that they tend to converge to equilibrium. The agents do not all converge at the same rate, however. Those agents who have most connections converge fastest. Agents who are more connected receive more frequent information and so have a better impression of the state of the market. They are, therefore, better able to accurately judge the equilibrium price.

Agents converge on a market price that deviates from the equilibrium price. This is due to the allocation of supply and demand. As the market converges, it will become increasingly difficult for agents who have been allocated limit prices beyond the market's theoretical equilibrium price to find partners prepared to trade with them. Since agents cannot alter their limit price, and are not prepared to trade at a value below it, some will effectively price themselves out of the market. Indeed, some agents will be unable to trade despite the presence of willing partners in the market as a whole, because they will not have a *neighbour* prepared to trade with them.

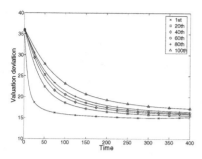 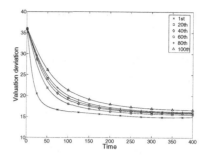

Fig. 1. Absolute deviation from optimum price averaged over 40000 runs for agents ranked in decreasing order of connectivity for (left) standard ZIP agents, and (right) ZIP agents with a learning rule adapted to exploit market topology information

3.1 Extension

As described, traders in the market assume that all of the information that they hear is of equal quality, regardless of its source, i.e., the ZIP learning rule makes no distinction between the information it receives from different individuals. It has been demonstrated, however, that there is a relationship between agent connectivity and accuracy of valuation. How, therefore, could the traders take advantage of this fact?

In reality, it is known that some sources of information are of better quality than others. This may be for a number of reasons, including market experience, quality of information sources, reputation, or size. For reasons such as these, people are more likely to trust information about financial markets obtained from a market trader than information from a pub landlord. Alternatively they are more likely to trust the manager of a large importer than a market trader for information about the fruit market.

In order to incorporate this factor into the model, the traders were modified to *weight* the quality of information received. Information judged to be of high quality was weighted strongly when adapting profit margins. There are many (possibly sophisticated) ways to evaluate the quality of information received by an agent, especially as each agent has multiple sources of information each of which may have sent messages several times in the past. It could be possible to construct an algorithm that determined a profit margin by comparing the most recent bid received to all previous bids received from that and other traders, and the relative information quality of those bids. The complexity of such an algorithm, however, would seem to be inappropriate for a model of this simplicity at this stage. Here, a very simple method for evaluating the quality of information was implemented, based on the results presented above.

ZIP agents adapt their price using the Widrow-Hoff rule every time they hear a shout from another trader in the market. This rule includes a learning rate which influences how quickly an agent is able to learn. Currently a fixed learning rate is assigned to each individual in the simulation from a uniform distribution $[0.1, 0.5]$.

In order for the agents to take account of information quality, the learning rate was modified so that instead of being fixed, the value would be calculated for each piece of information received. This alteration results in ZIP agents placing more weight on information obtained from well-connected individuals than from less well-connected individuals.

The Widrow-Hoff "delta" learning rule was modified by removing the learning rate and replacing it with the function $f(s,r)$, where s and r are the sender and recipient of a piece of information (a shout).

$$
f(s,r) = \begin{cases} 0.3 + \dfrac{0.2 \log \frac{E(s)}{E(r)}}{\log(R_{max})} & : E(s) \geq E(r) \\[3mm] 0.3 - \dfrac{0.2 \log \frac{E(r)}{E(s)}}{\log(R_{max})} & : E(s) < E(r) \end{cases}
$$

The function, E, gives the number of neighbours (degree) of an agent, and R_{max} is the largest ratio of edges between two adjacent agents within the market. This adaptive learning rate weights information according to relative connectivity within the market, i.e., the ratio of the sender's connectivity to the recipient's connectivity determines the learning rate. When the sender is more highly connected than the receiver the information received is more likely to be accurate and so more adaptation occurs. When the receiver is more connected, the receiver's current picture of the market state is likely to be more accurate than the senders and so less adaptation occurs. The value is normalised by the maximum ratio present in the market in order to ensure that the learning rate remains within the same bounds as standard ZIP traders. Connectivity ratios are log-scaled to ensure that learning rate adaptation is sensitive to the small differences in connectivity that characterise most sender-recipient pairs in a network generated by a preferential attachment process (where there will be only a few very well-connected individuals).

4   Results

Figure 1(right) shows the results obtained with the modified learning rule. All other parameters are the same as the previous scenario. As before the deviation of the valuations decreases over time. Again the most connected agents converge more quickly than the least connected agents. Figure 2(left) affords an easier comparison between the two studies. The least well-connected agents converge more quickly when using the modified learning rule than when using a fixed learning rate. At all times they have a lower deviation from the optimum price than agents using a fixed learning rate. By the end of the market they are significantly closer to the optimum price than those using fixed learning rates (t-test, $p < 0.0001$). Over longer experiments they may, however, eventually converge to the same value. The convergence of the better-connected agents is very similar, with or without the presence of the modified learning rule, although convergence is slightly retarded in the former case. By the end of the market, however, both groups have attained very similar values. It must be remembered that, as a consequence of the preferential attachment scheme that generates the market network, the distribution of agent connectivities exhibits a power law. Poorly-connected individuals vastly outnumber well-connected agents. As a result, even if the adaptive learning rate does significantly retard the convergence of well-connected agents, only a very small

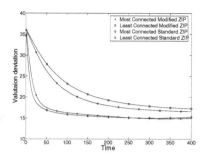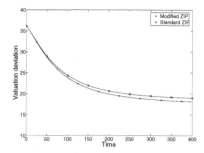

Fig. 2. Absolute deviation from optimum price averaged over 40000 runs for (left) the most and least connected agent in each experimental condition, and (right) for the single monitored agents in markets designed to control for learning rate

number of traders will suffer (although these agents may in some sense be of above average "importance").

Before discussing these results further, a slight bias introduced by the adaptive learning rate scheme must be dealt with. Although the adaptive learning rate is constrained to lie within the same bounds that constrain regular ZIP agents, the average learning rate employed by the adaptive ZIP agents is higher than that of standard ZIP traders. Recall that there are a greater number of weakly connected agents than strongly connected agents. In the case of the weakly connected agents, nearly all of their neighbours will be at least as well-connected, if not better-connected. This means that the typical learning rate employed by an agent will rarely be below the population mean. As a result, the average learning rate of these agents is increased, so faster convergence is not necessarily surprising. In order to demonstrate that the modified rule has an effect on convergence above that which would be expected to result from a simple increase in average learning rate, a further study was designed.

Two equal-sized groups of standard ZIP agents are initialised, the first group forming a completely connected clique, while the second forms a minimally connected ring. The quality of information being exchanged in the first group should, therefore, tend to be much higher than that being trafficked in the second group. A final modified ZIP trader with an equal number of connections to random agents within each group is added to the market. This agent does not make any shouts, nor respond to shouts. It simply adapts its valuation based on the information it hears. This study was run under two conditions: using a standard ZIP algorithm for the final agent, or using the adaptive learning rule instead. In the second condition, the connections from the final agent to the rest of the market are ignored by the adaptive learning rate rule, as they are never used to convey information *to* the market.

In the second condition, it is possible to set the number of connections from the final agent such that its average learning rate is equal to the average learning rate of a standard ZIP agent (0.3 in the studies reported here). The learning rates of the modified ZIP traders lie within the range $[0.1, 0.5]$. The following equation for the average adaptive learning rate, $\bar{\eta}(n)$, for a modified ZIP trader with n neighbours may be written given that all agents within each of the two groups share the same connectivity and the final agent has an equal number of connections to each group.

$$\bar{\eta}(n) = \frac{1}{2} \left(0.3 + 0.2 \frac{\log\left(\frac{E_{max}}{E(n)}\right)}{\log(R_{max})} + 0.3 - 0.2 \frac{\log\left(\frac{E(n)}{E_{min}}\right)}{\log(R_{max})} \right)$$

Where E_{max} is the connectivity of agents in the fully connected group and E_{min} is the connectivity of agents in the weakly connected ring, and n is the number of connections of the final agent. If we require this average to be the standard ZIP average of 0.3 this equation can be solved to give:

$$n = \sqrt{E_{max}E_{min}}$$

Here, we employ a fully-connected clique of fifty-one agents and a ring of fifty-one agents, giving $E_{max} = 50$ and $E_{min} = 2$, requiring $n = 10$ connections in total, or five connections to each population.

The results of 40000 repetitions are shown in figure 2(right). As can be seen, the modified ZIP agent using an adaptive learning rate converges faster and to a significantly lower asymptotic value than the standard ZIP agent (t-test, $p < 0.0001$). Hence, the adaptive learning rate rule has a positive effect on convergence beyond simply increasing the learning rate.

5 Discussion

In this paper we wished to explore the effect on convergence of market structure in terms of trader connectivity. The result obtained in the first part of this paper clearly show that the more connected an agent is, the faster it is able to converge, and the closer it is able to get to the optimum price. In the short term the more well-connected traders receive more information, and so are able to adapt faster. In the longer term, this greater volume of information means that they have a better overall picture of the market, and so may evaluate the optimum price more accurately.

As a consequence, the source of a shout has an impact on the quality of the information obtained. This was demonstrated by factoring information quality into the Widrow-Hoff adaptation rule via an adaptive learning rate. Our results show that agents who employ this strategy value the commodity more accurately in the majority of cases.

The fact that a small number of well-connected agents do worse by adopting this adaptive learning rate rule demonstrates that it is not of universal utility. The reason for this may be related to who these individuals are connected to. In the market structures studied here, for the vast majority of the time, highly connected agents will receive their information from less well-connected individuals. Since such information is judged (by the learning rule) to be of relatively low quality, less attention is paid to it. This may be a good decision in the long run. However, when the market opens this proves to be detrimental. At the beginning of a market every agent has a random valuation. Therefore, it would pay to attend to any information, even if it originates from poorly connected individuals. Whereas the most poorly-connected individuals do just this, the most well-connected agents tend to trust their initial valuation to a greater extent. This results in the slower initial convergence seen in the most well-connected agents. One might imagine that since these well-connected, but initially misguided individuals have a very significant influence on their neighbours, they might retard the market's convergence as a whole. Results suggest that this does not occur for the topologies considered here, but one could imagine market structures in which the hubs are so large and scarce that they could disturb the market for some time. As it stands, the simple adaptive learning rate rule could obviously be modified to better suit the more well-connected individuals, or, alternatively, separate rules could be used.

The adaptive learning rate rule used in this paper is very simple. It was chosen in order to demonstrate that the quality of an information source could be an important factor in making trading decisions, and that this could be used by trading agents to improve their valuations. It is not an attempt to provide an optimal rule. Their are many other possible factors which could be incorporated in order to make this rule more sophisticated.

As it currently stands this rule has several weaknesses. The most obvious is that it relies on information which may not be publicly known. First, it uses the maximum connectivity ratio present within the market in order to normalise the rate of change. This is necessary in order to ensure that learning rates were scaled to fall within the same range as that employed by standard ZIP agents. Second, whenever an agent adapts, it uses the connectivity of the shouter in order to determine how much attention should be paid to the shout. In real situations it seems unlikely that an agent would have access to either of these kinds of information. In order for an agent to know the maximum connectivity ratio, it would be necessary for the agent to know how the whole of the market was structured. For the simulations reported here, this information is easy to obtain. However, in real markets it seems highly unlikely that this information would be available. The only probable way for an agent to know the whole market structure is to be in contact with every agent in the market. If this were possible, then it is likely that other agents would also be completely connected, and an individual agent's connectivity would cease to be an issue. The connectivity of an individual trader may be even more difficult to obtain. In the studies reported here, every agent knows its own connectivity and that of its neighbours. In reality it is unlikely that the agent would possess this second piece of information, or perhaps even the first. The only realistic way to determine how well-connected another agent is, is to obtain the information from the agent directly. As has been suggested, however, it seems unlikely that agents would want to give this information away, as our results suggest that it is valuable.

This begs the question, if it is impossible to obtain the necessary connectivity information in reality, what practical significance do the results presented here have? Although it may be impossible to obtain exact connectivity information, it is not impossible to generate an evaluation of the information quality of ones trading partners in a real market. Moreover, information quality can be measured via indicators other than connectivity. In the case of human markets, traders may implicitly evaluate many aspects of their trading partners when deciding the significance of a piece of information. These aspects may include estimates of the partner's size (is it an investment bank with many traders or is it an sole trader), reputation, market position, market experience, etc. As yet, it may be difficult for an artificial trader operating in a real market, i.e., the stock market, to do this, due to the complexity of the information processing involved. It could be possible, however, for such automatic trading algorithms to be provided with human-generated estimates of known trading partners. The problem becomes even more complex in the case of markets solely populated by artificial trading agents. However, as mentioned above, if sufficient information is available it may be possibly to analyse the time series of shouts by a particular agent in order to estimate the quality of its information. There is obviously a great deal of further work to be done in this area, particularly in examining the effect of different evaluation rules and the effect of different market structures on market (and agent) behaviour.

This paper has been more concerned with the performance of the market as a whole rather than the situation of any one group of traders. There are, however, many interesting question which can be asked about the ways in which information may be used. In particular it would be interesting to consider how the better connected traders could exploit their advantageous positions to make a larger profit and also how they could exploit the knowledge that other agents gain an advantage by considering information quality. In order to properly understand these issues, however, it may be necessary to make the market more sophisticated. Currently, traders may only trade once. This effectively limits the ways in which traders can exploit information because as soon as a trader makes a trade they are effectively removed from the market. As a consequence some areas of the market may become stagnant as all available trades are made. This could be remedied by the introduction of a continuous flow of buy and sell orders entering the market. Allowing traders to interact multiple times and to develop more sophisticated strategies, whilst preventing the market from stagnating.

In this paper only a small (but significant) difference between traders using the new strategy and those not using it is demonstrated. Two points should be noted, firstly this rule was not chosen as an optimal rule for increasing valuation accuracy, instead it was chosen for its simplicity in demonstrating a point. Secondly the market employed in these experiments is by its nature "one-shot" in that all traders only trade once for one unit of the commodity. This naturally limits the opportunities for making profits, in particular in eliminates reselling. In real markets, however, this is not the case. Traders in real markets often trade many times for large volumes of products. A small increase in accuracy when dealing with large volumes may make a significant difference to the profit obtained. In the extreme case, foreign exchange markets have a turn over in the region of one trillion dollars a day. Even very small increases in valuation accuracy in contexts such as these can results in huge increases in profits.

6   Conclusion

This paper has demonstrated that simple markets populated by simple trading agents may function despite trading constraints represented by an explicit, fixed network of possible agent-agent interactions. We have not attempted to classify or analyse the effect of topology in general. However, for one particular type of market, some interesting and encouraging results have been shown. We have demonstrated that more well-connected agents have an informational advantage within a market. Having more neighbours ensures that a trading agent has a better picture of the market and, as a result, a better valuation of the commodity being traded. By making a simple modification to the ZIP trading algorithm to take account of this observation, improved performance was demonstrated for all but the most well-connected individuals.

In a more general sense, these results show that if it is possible to estimate the quality of a trader's knowledge, it may be beneficial to factor this information into the way in which the trading agent learns. This result isn't necessarily restricted to trading agents. In general, in any market with incomplete information flow, it may be beneficial to pay more attention to the most significant players within the market. However, care is necessary. Currently the ZIP trading strategy does not allow the more well-connected agents to exploit their informational advantage. However, this could be changed fairly easily. It is not difficult to imagine methods that allow simple trading agents to exploit informational advantages in order to make profit. It is, however, difficult to imagine ways in which to modify trading strategies in order to prevent this occurring in network based markets. The only solution to this problem may be to design market systems which minimise informational asymmetries. This may require research into more sophisticated market mechanisms to replace the continuous double auction. Alternatively, it may require the addition of completely new processes to the market. For instance, a process analogous to the financial press may allow agents to regularly gain an overview of the behaviour of the entire market.

References

1. DeLong, J.B., Shleifer, A., Summers, L.H., Waldmann, R.J.: Noise trader risk in financial markets. Journal of Political Economy **98** (1990) 703–738
2. Smith, V.L.: An experimental study of competitive market behaviour. Journal of Political Economy **70** (1962) 111–137
3. Gode, D.K., Sunder, S.: Allocative efficiency of markets with zero-intelligence traders: Market as a partial substitute for individual rationality. Journal of Political Economy **101** (1993) 119–37
4. Cliff, D., Bruten, J.: Minimal-intelligence agents for bargaining behaviors in market-based environments. Technical Report HPL-97-91, Hewlett-Packard Labs, UK (1997)
5. Gjerstad, S., Dickhaut, J.: Price formation in double auctions. Games and Economic Behavior **22** (1998) 1–29
6. Das, R., Hanson, J.E., Kephart, J.O., Tesauro, G.: Agent human interactions in the continuous double auction. In Nebel, B., ed.: Proceedings of the International Joint Conference on Artificial Intelligence, Morgan Kauffman, San Francisco, CA (2001) 1169–1187
7. Farmer, J.D., Patelli, P., Zovko, I.I.: The predictive power of zero intelligence in financial markets. Proceedings of the National Academy of Science **102** (2005) 2254–2259
8. Wilhite, A.: Bilateral trade and 'small-world' networks. Computational Economics **18** (2001) 49–64
9. Bell, A.M.: Bilateral trading on a network: a simulation study. In: Working Notes: Artificial Societies and Computational Markets. (1998)
10. Noble, J., Davy, S., Franks, D.W.: Effects of the topology of social networks on information transmission. In Schaal, S., Ijspeert, A.J., Billard, A., Vijayakumar, S., Hallam, J., Meyer, J.A., eds.: Eighth International Conference on Simulation of Adaptive Behavior, MIT Press, Cambridge, MA (2004) 395–404
11. Widrow, B., Hoff, M.E.: Adaptive switching circuits. IRE WESCON Convention record **4** (1960) 96–104

On Correctness and Privacy in Distributed Mechanisms*

Felix Brandt and Tuomas Sandholm

Carnegie Mellon University, Pittsburgh PA 15213, USA
{brandtf, sandholm}@cs.cmu.edu

Abstract. Mechanisms that aggregate the possibly conflicting preferences of individual agents are studied extensively in economics, operations research, and lately computer science. Perhaps surprisingly, the classic literature assumes *participating agents* to act selfishly, possibly untruthfully, if it is to their advantage, whereas the *mechanism center* is usually assumed to be honest and trustworthy. We argue that cryptography offers various concepts and building blocks to ensure the secure, *i.e.*, correct and private, execution of mechanisms. We propose models with and without a center that guarantee correctness and preserve the privacy of preferences relying on diverse assumptions such as the trustworthiness of the center or the hardness of computation. The decentralized model in which agents jointly "emulate" a virtual mechanism center is particularly interesting for two reasons. For one, it provides privacy without relying on a trusted third-party. Second, it enables the provably correct execution of *randomized* mechanisms (which is not the case in the centralized model). We furthermore point out how untruthful and multi-step mechanisms can improve privacy. In particular, we show that the fully private emulation of a preference elicitor can result in unconditional privacy of a (non-empty) subset of preferences.

1 Introduction

Mechanisms that aggregate the possibly conflicting preferences of individual agents are studied extensively in economics, operations research, and lately computer science. Distributed mechanisms are used in such diverse application areas as auctions, voting, resource sharing, routing, or task assignment.

In the heart of a mechanism lies the so-called "mechanism center" or "mechanism infrastructure" to which agents privately send reports about their preferences and that computes the mechanism outcome (*e.g.*, allocation of goods, election winner, network route, *etc.*). The main focus of existing work has been on creating mechanisms whose outcome has various desirable properties (efficient computability has been added recently) and in which agents have an incentive to submit their preferences truthfully. Perhaps surprisingly, the classic literature assumes *participating agents* to act selfishly, possibly untruthfully, if it is to their advantage, whereas the *mechanism center* is usually assumed to be honest and trustworthy, even when it has an incentive to be untruthful, *e.g.*, by overstating the second-highest bid in Vickrey auctions if it gains a fraction of the selling price (see for example [PS03]).

---

* This paper was originally presented at AMEC-04.

H. La Poutré, N. Sadeh, and S. Janson (Eds.): AMEC and TADA 2005, LNAI 3937, pp. 212–225, 2006.
© Springer-Verlag Berlin Heidelberg 2006

In this paper, we investigate how to ensure the *correctness of the mechanism outcome* and the *privacy of individual preferences* by using various building blocks that have been developed in the field of cryptography over the years. As a matter of fact, cryptography and mechanism design have major objectives in common. To a large extent, both fields are concerned about agents who deviate from a given distributed mechanism (respectively protocol) in an undesirable manner (violating global objectives such as social welfare maximization or privacy). One could say that mechanisms allocate utility optimally with respect to certain constraints such as individual rationality, social welfare maximization, or budget-balance. For example, utility is allocated by redistributing goods or imposing payments on participants. Cryptographic protocols, on the other hand, allocate information optimally with respect to constraints like privacy, correctness, or fairness. However, while mechanism design assumes adversaries to be *rational* (according to some definition of utility), cryptography traditionally deals with "*worst-case*" adversaries, *i.e.*, any strategy, regardless of rationality is considered. In fact, in cryptography, it is considered a bad concept to assume rationality of the adversary (*e.g.*, [Gol01]). Yet, the mechanism design approach has its merits. For example, cryptographic protocols are incapable of eliciting truthful behavior since they cannot provide incentives. Generally speaking, proper behavior of agents in a mechanism is enforced by making deviations "uneconomic", *i.e.*, no utility can be gained by manipulating the mechanism. In cryptography, on the other hand, the correctness of a protocol is ensured by forcing agents to prove the correctness of each of their actions without revealing any information but the correctness itself. This is achieved by relying on computational intractability, *i.e.*, the existence of computationally hard problems, the polynomially bounded computational power of agents, *etc.*. Interestingly, using computational intractability as a barrier against undesirable behavior, which has a long tradition in cryptography since Diffie and Hellman's seminal paper [DH76], was recently also applied in mechanism design [BTT89, CS03c].

This paper establishes a link between cryptography and mechanism by using cryptographic primitives to provide correctness and privacy in distributed mechanisms. Correctness and privacy are defined as follows. Correctness means that in the end of a mechanism each agent is convinced that the outcome was computed correctly whereas privacy states that an agent does not learn anything about others' preferences that he cannot infer from the (correct) outcome and his own preferences. Correctness and privacy are not only complementary but also deeply intertwined (see Section 3). In mechanisms, privacy of preferences is crucial not only because sensible information might be of importance for future mechanisms or negotiations but also because a lack of privacy heavily affects the equilibria of mechanisms in execution. We will use the following notations. Agent i's preferences are denoted by $\theta_i \in \Theta_i$. The outcome function of a mechanism is $f : \Theta_1 \times \Theta_2 \times \cdots \times \Theta_n \to O$. θ is a short notation for $(\theta_1, \theta_2, \ldots, \theta_n)$. n is the number of agents participating in a mechanism.

The remainder of this paper is structured as follows. Section 2 summarizes existing work at the boundary between cryptography and mechanism design. Section 3 introduces basic security models that ensure correct mechanism execution, with or without a center. In Section 4, we consider randomized, multi-step, and untruthful mechanisms in the context of correctness and privacy. The paper concludes with a summary of the obtained results and a brief outlook on future research in Section 5.

2   Related Work

In [MPS03], a connection between mechanism design and multiparty computation has been established for a purpose that is slightly different from the one we pursue in this paper. The authors integrate "cryptographic objectives" such as the wish to keep other agents from learning one's preferences, the wish to learn other agents' preferences, the wish to know the correct mechanism outcome, and the wish to prevent others from knowing it into the utility functions of agents and then investigate the possibility of incentive-compatible mechanism design in this novel framework. A similar approach without a mechanism center was recently analyzed in [HT04]. [MT99] consider a model where agents are not directly connected to the center, but are rather nodes in a more general communication network.

To our knowledge, the first paper to explicitly present a security model and generic protocol for arbitrary mechanisms was [NPS99]. This model basically consists of two centers that are assumed not to collude. The decentralized model presented in Section 3.2 is based on preliminary results lately proposed in [Bra03b]. The importance of considering the privacy of agents in distributed mechanisms has been stated in [FNR+02, FS02].

In recent years, there has been a large body of research on cryptographic auction protocols, *i.e.*, protocols that privately compute the outcome of sealed-bid auction mechanisms (*e.g.*, [Bra03a, Kik01, NPS99]). These special-purpose protocols implicitly contain security models (of which almost all are based on using more than one center).

3   Security Models

In this section, we investigate which sets of assumptions (general model, communication channels, existence of one-way functions, *etc.*) allow the provably correct execution of deterministic single-step mechanisms. In particular, we examine whether *unconditional* privacy, *i.e.*, privacy that can never be breached, even when unbounded computational power becomes available, can be achieved in a given model.

In order to enable the notion of unconditional privacy in the first place, we have to make the following distinction. While we (in some models) allow unbounded computational power to breach privacy *after* the protocol/mechanism terminated, super-polynomial computational power is *not* available *during* the protocol. The deep relation between correctness and privacy makes this assumption necessary.[1] Nevertheless, this assumption seems reasonable since the time needed to perform super-polynomial computation is presumably longer than the typically short execution time of a mechanism. Furthermore, we generally assume the availability of a public key infrastructure. In some cases, we will assume "private channels" between certain parties. These are

---

[1] Otherwise, privacy could be breached by violating correctness (*e.g.*, by forging perfect zero-knowledge arguments).

authenticated means of communication between two parties that are unconditionally secure without relying on any computational assumption. Quantum channels, for example, would meet this definition.

It has turned out that the existence of almost all cryptographic primitives can be reduced to the existence of certain notions of one-way functions. A *one-way function* is a function that can be evaluated efficiently (in polynomial time), but there is no polynomial-time algorithm that can invert the function more accurately than guessing at random. A *one-way permutation* is a one-way function that is a bijective mapping of a domain onto itself. A *trapdoor permutation* is a one-way permutation that, given some extra information (the trapdoor), can be inverted in polynomial time. To give two examples, it has been shown that secure digital signatures exist if (and only if) there are one-way functions. Secure public-key encryption, on the other hand, is known to be feasible if trapdoor permutations exist.

The actual existence of one-way functions would imply $\mathcal{P} \neq \mathcal{NP}$. However, the reverse is not true: Although it might be hard to invert a function in the *worst-case*, it can be easy in many practical instances or even in the *average-case*. This uncertainty plus the technological assumptions one has to rely on—even when one-way functions exist—motivate the exploration of security that is based on alternative models such as in unconditionally secure multiparty computation [BGW88, CCD88].

The approach of the subsequent sections is as follows. We believe correctness to be fundamentally important and thus only consider models that guarantee correctness. On top of that, we investigate which sets of assumptions are necessary to provide differing degrees of privacy, *e.g.*, privacy that relies on a trusted center or privacy that relies on computational intractability. The proofs in the following sections will make use of cryptographic primitives such as *commitment schemes*, (computational) *zero-knowledge proofs*, and *perfect zero-knowledge arguments*[2]. We refer to cryptographic textbooks (*e.g.*, [Gol01]) for definitions of these building blocks.

3.1   Centralized Mechanism Execution

Let us first start by trying to obtain a provably correct single center without caring for privacy. It might seem to be sufficient to provide private channels, *e.g.*, based on public-key cryptography, from each agent to the center in order to transmit the preferences and a signature scheme that allows agents to sign their submissions. The center would then be able to prove the correctness of the outcome by just broadcasting all signed preferences. However, the center could collude with an agent and make him sign and send preferences that the center chooses *after* having seen preferences that were submitted earlier.[3] For this reason, publishing a so-called commitment to one's preferences *prior* to submitting the preferences becomes inevitable. By applying zero-knowledge proofs

---

[2] Perfect zero-knowledge arguments are a variant of zero-knowledge proofs in which there is no information revelation even to computationally unbounded adversaries, but computationally unbounded agents can produce "forged" proofs.

[3] Even if communication from the center to any agent could be prohibited, a manipulated agent would be able to send various signed messages. The center could then choose the appropriate one after it has seen all other preferences.

to the commitment values, we essentially get computational privacy for free, *i.e.*, without having to make further assumptions.

Theorem 1. *Correct deterministic mechanism execution can be guaranteed given that trapdoor permutations exist. Privacy can be breached by the center or exhaustive computation.*

Proof. Agents broadcast unconditionally binding commitments to preferences. Both the commitment scheme and the broadcasting can be based on the existence of one-way functions (and the availability of a signature scheme infrastructure) [LSP82, Nao89]. In order to prevent an agent from copying somebody else's commitment (and thus his preferences), each agent proves in computational zero-knowledge (which can be based on one-way functions as well [BOGG+88]) that he knows how to open the commitment, *i.e.*, he proves that he knows what he committed to. These proofs are executed sequentially to avoid the copying of proofs.[4] After all agents have submitted their commitments (this can be publicly verified due to the broadcasting), agents send information on how to open their commitments to the center using public-key encryption (based on trapdoor permutations). The center privately opens all preferences and rejects malformed by publicly opening the commitment value (on the broadcast channel). The center cannot reject preferences illegitimately as the commitment value is uniquely defined. Finally, it privately computes and declares the outcome with an accompanying proof of correctness in computational zero-knowledge.   □

In order to obtain privacy that does not rely on intractability, we also consider a model that is based on somewhat stronger assumptions.

Theorem 2. *Correct deterministic mechanism execution can be guaranteed given that there are private channels from each agent to the center and one-way permutations exist. Privacy can only be breached by the center.*

Proof. Agents broadcast unconditionally hiding commitments to their preferences and sequentially prove their correctness using perfect zero-knowledge arguments. After that, agents send information on how to open their commitments to the center on private channels. The center then privately opens the preferences and rejects malformed by publicly opening the corresponding commitment. In the following, it privately computes the outcome and then declares the outcome with an accompanying argument of correctness in perfect zero-knowledge. All these operations can be based on one-way permutations.   □

Zero-knowledge proofs and arguments allow the center to privately send parts of the outcome to each agent (and prove its correctness), so that a single agent learns only the part of the outcome that it is required to know. This can be of advantage in auctions so that *only* winning bidders learn about the goods they are awarded and the prices they have to pay while still guaranteeing correctness [Bra03a].

---

[4] There are more efficient, yet less intuitive, ways of achieving the same functionality.

3.2 Decentralized Mechanism Execution

In order to decentralize the trust that agents need to have in a single center, the computation of the outcome can be distributed across several distinct centers. This is just a straight-forward application of secure multiparty computation [GMW87, BGW88, CCD88]. It is possible to generate shares of a secret piece of information so that a single share is "worthless", *i.e.*, it reveals no information at all, but all shares put together uniquely determine the original piece of information.[5] Assume that agents distribute shares of their preferences so that each center receives one share from each agent. Multiparty computation protocols allow the centers to jointly compute the mechanism outcome using these shares. Depending on the protocol and the underlying security model, privacy may rely on computational intractability. In any case, privacy also relies on the assumption that a coalition of *all* centers is ruled out. When all centers collude and share their information, they can reconstruct each agent's private preferences. Nevertheless, this model is used in almost all existing cryptographic auction protocols. Especially the special case for two centers, as introduced by [Yao82], has been widely used.

In this section, we aim to obtain a more satisfying level of privacy by omitting the center(s) completely and letting agents resolve the mechanism by themselves. In other words, the mechanism's *participants* engage in a multiparty computation protocol. The key observation underlying this model is that if there is a coalition of *all* agents, there are no preferences left to be private. Thus, if the protocol is designed so that a coalition of up to $n - 1$ agents does not gain any information, collusion becomes pointless (in order to breach privacy). This will be called "full privacy" in the following.

Definition 1 (Full privacy). *A protocol is* fully private[6] *if no information about any agent's preferences can be uncovered, other than what can be inferred from the outcome and all remaining preferences.*

By introducing full privacy, we shift the focus from mechanisms to *protocols*. These protocols enable agents to jointly determine the outcome of the mechanism by exchanging messages according to some predefined rules without revealing any information besides the outcome. We say that a protocol fully privately *emulates* a mechanism. When relying on computational intractability, *any* mechanism can be emulated by fully private protocols.

Proposition 1. *Correct mechanism execution can be guaranteed without a center given that trapdoor permutations exist. Privacy can only be breached by exhaustive computation.*[7]

---

[5] As an easy example, consider a single secret bit that is shared by choosing n bits at random so that the exclusive-or of these n bits yields the original bit. A single share, and even up to $n - 1$ shares, reveal no information at all about the secret bit.

[6] In cryptographic terms, a fully private protocol is $(n-1)$-private, which means that a coalition of up to $n - 1$ agents is incapable of breaching privacy.

[7] Propositions 1 and 2 are based on modifying the classic results of multiparty computation [GMW87, BGW88, CCD88] for a setting of full privacy by introducing "weak robustness". Due to a very strict security model, the original results rely on a fraction, *e.g.*, a majority, of the agents being trusted (see [Bra03b] for more details).

It turns out that replacing intractability assumptions with the existence of unconditionally private channels (like in Section 3.1), only enables the fully private emulation of a *restricted* set of mechanisms. These mechanisms will be called "simple mechanisms" in the following.

Definition 2 (Simple Mechanism). *A mechanism is* simple *if its outcome function is privately computable in the sense of [Kus89, CK89]. E.g., the only Boolean outcome functions that are privately computable are of the form $f(\theta) = B_1(\theta_1) \oplus B_2(\theta_2) \oplus \cdots \oplus B_n(\theta_n)$ where $B_i(\theta_i)$ are Boolean predicates and $\oplus$ is the Boolean exclusive-or operator.*

There is yet no complete characterization of privately computable functions (except for special cases like Boolean [CK89] and 2-ary functions [Kus89]). However, by using known necessary conditions for private computability, it has been shown that first-price sealed-bid auctions are simple mechanisms whereas second-price sealed-bid auctions are not [BS04].

Proposition 2. *Correct mechanism execution can be guaranteed for simple mechanisms without a center given that there are private channels between all agents and one-way permutations exist. Privacy cannot be breached.*[7]

As in the previous section, both models also allow the (correct) computation of *different* outcomes (or parts of an outcome) for each agent, *e.g.*, so that losing bidders in an auction do not learn the selling price.

4 Intertwining Cryptography and Mechanism Design

In this section, we will relax three restrictions that we made so far, namely that mechanisms are deterministic, single-step, and incentive-compatible. The revelation principle, a central theorem of mechanism design, suggests that one restrict attention to direct-revelation mechanisms, *i.e.*, truthful, single-step mechanisms, as all remaining mechanisms can be simulated by (possibly randomized) direct-revelation mechanisms. Although this a striking result in mechanism design, its consequences are debatable as it does not consider the following important aspects: communication complexity, computational abilities of the agents and the center (see also [CS03b]), and, which is our main concern here, privacy of agents' preferences. But first of all, let us consider the effects of randomization on the correctness of a mechanism.

4.1 Randomized Mechanisms

Randomized mechanisms, *i.e.*, mechanisms in which the outcome function is probabilistic, are of increasing interest. It has been shown in [CS02a] that the automated design of an optimal deterministic mechanism for a constant number of agents is $\mathcal{NP}$-complete in most settings whereas the design of randomized mechanisms for the same purpose is always tractable (by linear programming). Furthermore, randomized mechanisms are always as good or better than deterministic ones in terms of the expected value of the designer's objective (*e.g.*, a 2-item revenue maximizing auction has to be randomized [AH00, CS03a]). Finally, as mentioned above, the revelation principle only holds if we allow for the possibility that the resulting direct-revelation mechanism may be randomized.

Randomization has severe consequences on the notion of correctness. Whereas a single mechanism center can prove the correctness of the outcome of a deterministic mechanism (see Section 3.1), this is not possible for randomized mechanisms. There is no way a mechanism center can actually *prove* that it is using real random numbers in order to compute the outcome (without introducing a third-party that is assumed to reliably supply random data). The advantages of randomized mechanisms (*e.g.*, that manipulating the mechanism can be $\mathcal{NP}$-hard [CS03c]) in fact rely on the trustworthiness of the mechanism center. These advantages become void if the center is corrupt. Forcing the center to commit to its random choice before the agents submit their preferences only reduces the problem as the center might still choose a random value that is beneficial to itself (and possibly colluding agents).[8]

In the decentralized model proposed in Section 3.2, on the other hand, the "competition" between agents allows the unbiased joint generation of random numbers (unless *all* agents collude).

Theorem 3. *Randomized mechanisms can be emulated correctly by computationally fully private protocols. Randomized simple mechanisms can be emulated correctly by unconditionally fully private protocols.*

Proof. The following construction builds on a cryptographic primitive that is called "coin tossing into the well" [Blu82]. Before computing the mechanism outcome, each agent broadcasts an unconditionally hiding commitment to a freely chosen bit-string r_i and proves the correctness of the commitment (*i.e.*, that he knows what is inside) with a perfect zero-knowledge argument. These proofs are arranged sequentially to avoid proof duplication as in Theorem 1. After that, agents commit to their preferences and start emulating the mechanism. In the following computation of the outcome, agents can use $r = r_1 \oplus r_2 \oplus \cdots \oplus r_n$ (which can be privately computed, even in the unconditionally private model according to Definition 2) as a source of pure random data. We stress the fact, that this procedure works for the computationally private emulation of arbitrary mechanisms as well as the unconditionally private emulation of simple mechanisms. As the agents generate the random bit-string *before* committing to their preferences, the correctness of the (randomized) outcome can still be guaranteed if *all* agents collude after knowing the submitted preferences of each other for sure (in the form of commitments). This is desirable as there are mechanisms in which it might be beneficial for all agents to manipulate the randomization of the outcome after they know their submissions.[9]   □

---

[8] Even though *truthfulness* is preserved when the random choice is known beforehand in *strongly truthful* mechanisms [MV04], other properties such as revenue maximization might be lost when agents are able to manipulate the random choice by colluding with the mechanism center.

[9] There might also be randomized mechanisms where the opposite is true, *i.e.*, *all* agents benefit from a manipulation of their preferences after they know the common random string, but we doubt that they are of any significance.

4.2 Multi-Step Mechanisms

Multi-step mechanisms are mechanisms in which the center gradually asks questions to the agents in multiple rounds until enough preferences have been elicited to compute the outcome (see *e.g.*, [CS01]). Ascending (*e.g.*, English) or descending (*e.g.*, Dutch) auctions are special cases of this definition. Besides the limited preference revelation, multi-step mechanisms have an important advantage that is not considered in cryptography: Agents do not need to completely determine their own preferences. This is important because determining one's own preferences may be tedious task and can even be intractable [San93].

While executing multi-step mechanisms in the single center models presented in Section 3.1 is straightforward, it is interesting to examine whether the fully private emulation of multi-step mechanisms is possible. By fully privately emulating a multi-step mechanism, we can improve the level of privacy guaranteed in Proposition 1 because some preferences might never be elicited and thus remain unconditionally private. However, the main problem is that queries may implicitly contain information on agents' preferences revealed so far. We define a certain class of mechanisms which always benefit from private elicitation.

Definition 3 (Privately Elicitable Mechanism). *A mechanism is called* privately elicitable *if it satisfies the following two conditions:*

- *There are cases in which a subset of the preferences is sufficient to compute the mechanism outcome.*[10]
- *There is a function that maps the mechanism outcome and the preferences of one agent to the complete sequence of queries that this agent received.*

The second condition ensures that agents do not learn information about others' preferences from the queries they are asked (see the proof of Theorem 4 for details). English auctions, for example, are privately elicitable mechanisms: The first condition holds because it is irrelevant (for the mechanism outcome) how much the highest bidder would have bid, as long as it is made sure that everybody else bid less than him. The second condition is satisfied because the only prices not "offered" to a bidder are prices above the selling price.

Theorem 4. *Privately elicitable mechanisms can be emulated by fully private protocols so that it is impossible to reveal* all *preferences, even by exhaustive computation.*

Proof. Without loss of generality, the preference elicitor can be emulated by the following protocol. We jointly and iteratively compute a query function and a stop-function for several rounds, and once, at the end of the protocol, evaluate the outcome function. Let $\gamma_i \in \Gamma_i$ be the (iteratively updated) set of agent i's statements on his preferences, $\gamma = (\gamma_1, \gamma_2, \ldots, \gamma_n)$, and $\Gamma = \Gamma_1 \times \Gamma_2 \times \cdots \times \Gamma_n$. All γ_i are initialized as empty sets. The following procedure is repeated round by round. The query function $q : \{1, 2, \ldots, n\} \times \Gamma \to Q$, which is fully privately computed by all agents (using

---

[10] Otherwise, preference elicitation would be pointless, regardless of privacy. Almost all practical mechanisms satisfy this condition.

Proposition 1), outputs a private query for each agent (Q is some set of available queries including an empty query $\perp$). Agents reply to these queries by publicly committing to their answer on a broadcast channel (without revealing their answer). Thus, γ_i is defined as the set of commitments agent i made so far. Whenever no more information is needed from a particular agent i, $q(i, \gamma_i) = \perp$. Agents reply to that by committing to an "empty answer". Agents then jointly compute the Boolean stop function $s : \Gamma \to \{0, 1\}$ and proceed to the next round (by asking more queries) if it is 0, or compute the outcome function $f' : \Gamma \to O$ if $s(\gamma) = 1$.

So far, all agents get to know the number of rounds, *i.e.*, the maximal number of queries asked to a single agent, and could infer information from that. Sometimes this information can be inferred from the outcome (*e.g.*, in an English or Dutch auction). However, as this is not the general case, the number of rounds needs to be hidden. For this reason, we execute the protocol for the maximal number of rounds that *could* be needed to compute the outcome and use the modified query function

$$q'(i, \gamma) = \begin{cases} q(i, \gamma) & \text{if } s(i, \gamma) = 0 \\ \perp & \text{otherwise} \end{cases} .$$

The only information an agent learns is the sequence of queries he is asked. According to Definition 3, the agent can infer this information from the mechanism outcome anyway, thus giving him no information advantage than to just being informed of the outcome. What remains to be shown is that there *always* is a protocol that hides some part of the preferences unconditionally. If we define the query function to ask completely at *random* for information that has not been revealed by that agent so far (satisfying the second condition of Definition 3), some preferences always remain unelicited (in expectation).

There certainly exist particular mechanisms that allow for more efficient elicitation protocols than this general proof construction. Also, in some specific mechanisms, queries may depend on others' preferences if the information revealed through the queries can be inferred from the outcome.   □

Together with Proposition 1 and Proposition 2 this result gives a nice classification of private mechanisms: *All mechanisms* can be emulated guaranteeing computational privacy, *privately elicitable mechanisms* can additionally provide unconditionally privacy of a (non-empty) subset of preferences, and *simple mechanisms* provide unconditional privacy of all preferences. A striking advantage of private elicitation over the approach given in Proposition 2 is that it enables unconditional privacy of some preferences *without* assuming private channels.

It is important to note that elicitation can invalidate strategy equilibria existing in the single-step version of a mechanism if the queries asked to an agent depend on other agents' preceding answers [CS02b]. When preference elicitation is used to implement a mechanism that would be a dominant-strategy direct-revelation mechanism if implemented as a single-step mechanism, then each agent's best (even in hindsight) strategy is to act truthfully *if* the other agents act truthfully [CS01]. In other words, truthful strategies form an *ex post* equilibrium. *Ex post* equilibria are not as robust as dominant-strategy equilibria, but are more robust than Bayesian Nash equilibria in that they are prior-free.

The emulation of multi-step mechanisms is a powerful tool to guarantee strong privacy (partially unconditional) *and* reduce the amount of agents' deliberation required to evaluate their preferences. For example, consider a veto voting mechanism: Preferences are single bits (veto or not) and the outcome function is defined as $f(\theta) = \bigvee_{i=1}^{n} \theta_i$. This mechanism is not simple according to Definition 2. As a consequence, there is no unconditionally fully private veto protocol. However, we can construct a protocol in which *most* preferences remain unconditionally private by emulating a preference elicitor. The protocol consists of n rounds. In each round, a randomly selected agent that has not been queried so far is privately asked for his preference (veto or not). All other agents receive empty queries and reply with empty queries. Once an agent privately submits a veto, *all* agents receive empty queries in the following rounds. Since the query function is computed fully privately, only some agents (those who are queried) learn some probabilistic information on the number of vetoers.

4.3   Untruthful Mechanisms

Untruthful mechanisms may not only lead to greater social welfare in some settings (relying on computational assumptions) [CS03b], but they can also support the protection of preferences. As a matter of fact, the probably most prominent truthful mechanism, the Vickrey auction, is said to be rare because bidders are reluctant to reveal their preferences truthfully as required by the dominant strategy [RTK90]. This problem and the possibility of an untruthful mechanism center (which is stated as the other major reason for the Vickrey auction's rareness) can be tackled by the techniques presented in Section 3.2. Yet, even in the centralized model, preferences can be protected (at least partially) by inducing strategic behavior in a mechanism. We sketch two different ways how to achieve this, of which the second one relies on computational intractability.

When the mapping from preferences to a strategy is a *non-injective* function, *i.e.*, different preferences can yield the same strategy, it is obviously impossible to uniquely invert a strategy. This naturally is the case when the set of strategies S_i is smaller than the set of preferences ($|\Theta_i| > |S_i|$). For instance, in most voting protocols with more than two candidates, a complete ranking of candidates (the preferences) is mapped to a single strategic vote (the strategy). For example, when considering the US presidential election in 2000 (plurality voting with three candidates), it is impossible to tell if someone who voted for Gore, truthfully preferred Gore over Nader or not (even given the prior beliefs of that voter, *e.g.*, that Nader would be far behind). The same argument applies to most other voting protocols.

Based on these considerations, it might be interesting to construct mechanisms that induce equilibria consisting of *"one-way strategies"*. Here, the mapping from preferences to a strategy is computationally easy while the inversion is intractable (preferably even given the beliefs that the agent had). This requires that $|\Theta_i|$ is exponentially large or somehow enriched, possibly by random data padding. We do not know whether such mechanisms can be constructed (for relevant problems), but note that this might be another interesting application of computational intractability in mechanism design.

5   Conclusion and Future Work

In this paper, we suggested that the fields of cryptography and mechanism design have several similarities and can both greatly benefit from each other. We proposed two security models for centralized mechanism execution in which the center proves its correctness (in zero-knowledge) and that provide differing degrees of privacy. However, in these models, privacy always has to rely on the trustworthiness of the mechanism center. For this reason, we showed how participating agents can emulate a (correct) "virtual" mechanism center by jointly computing the mechanism outcome without a trusted third-party. The emulation of a restricted class of mechanisms, so-called simple mechanisms, can provide unconditional privacy of preferences whereas all mechanisms can be emulated so that privacy can only be breached by unbounded computation. In these models, privacy builds upon the fact that it can be ruled out that *all* agents are forming a coalition in order to breach privacy. Furthermore, the decentralization allows for the provable correctness of *randomized* mechanisms. Table 1 summarizes the proposed models for secure mechanism execution. Even though the centralized models provide questionable privacy, there are certainly applications in which they would be favored over the decentralized models due to practical considerations (efficiency, lack of communication between agents, robustness, *etc.*).

Table 1. Comparison of security models with provable correctness

	Center	Privacy can be breached by	Requirements
Th. 1	yes	**center** or computation	trapdoor perm., **det. mech.**
Th. 2	yes	**center**	$A \to C$-channels, one-way perm., **det. mech.**
Pr. 1	no	computation	trapdoor perm.
Pr. 2	no	—	$A \to A$-channels, one-way perm., **simple mech.**

$A \to C$-channels: private channels from each agent to the center
$A \to A$-channels: complete network of private channels between all agents

In addition to the revelation principle criticisms stated in [CS03b], we pointed out that multi-step and untruthful mechanisms can drastically improve *privacy* in a variety of social choice settings. In particular, we identified a class of mechanisms, so-called privately elicitable mechanisms, for which there are fully private protocols that emulate a preference elicitor so that a part of the preferences is never elicited and thus remains unconditionally private and does not have to be determined by the agents.

Besides further investigation of preference protection by multi-step and untruthful mechanisms, future directions include

- the construction of *efficient* zero-knowledge proofs/arguments for the outcome of relevant mechanisms,
- the investigation of which mechanisms can be emulated by unconditionally fully private protocols (a first step has been made in [BS04]), and
- the construction of *efficient* protocols that (computationally) fully privately emulate relevant mechanisms.[11]

---

[11] We already constructed a protocol that (computationally) fully privately emulates the Vickrey auction in just three rounds of broadcasting without any direct interaction between bidders [Bra03a].

Acknowledgements

This material is based upon work supported by the Deutsche Forschungsgemeinschaft under grant BR 2312/1-1, by the National Science Foundation under grants IIS-9800994, ITR IIS-0081246, and ITR IIS-0121678, and a Sloan Fellowship.

References

[AH00]   C. Avery and T. Hendershott. Bundling and optimal auctions of multiple products. *Review of Economic Studies*, 67:483–497, 2000.

[BGW88]   M. Ben-Or, S. Goldwasser, and A. Wigderson. Completeness theorems for non-cryptographic fault-tolerant distributed computation. In *Proc. of 20th STOC*, pages 1–10. ACM Press, 1988.

[Blu82]   M. Blum. Coin flipping by telephone. In *Proc. of 24th IEEE Spring Computer Conference*, pages 133–137. IEEE Press, 1982.

[BOGG⁺88]   M. Ben-Or, O. Goldreich, S. Goldwasser, J. Håstad, J. Kilian, S. Micali, and P. Rogaway. Everything provable is provable in zero-knowledge. In *Proc. of 14th CRYPTO Conference*, volume 403 of *LNCS*, pages 37–56. Springer, 1988.

[Bra03a]   F. Brandt. Fully private auctions in a constant number of rounds. In R. N. Wright, editor, *Proc. of 7th Conference on Financial Cryptography*, volume 2742 of *LNCS*, pages 223–238. Springer, 2003.

[Bra03b]   F. Brandt. Social choice and preference protection - Towards fully private mechanism design. In N. Nisan, editor, *Proc. of 4th ACM Conference on Electronic Commerce*, pages 220–221. ACM Press, 2003.

[BS04]   F. Brandt and T. Sandholm. (Im)possibility of unconditionally privacy-preserving auctions. In C. Sierra and L. Sonenberg, editors, *Proc. of 3rd AAMAS Conference*, pages 810–817. ACM Press, 2004.

[BTT89]   J. Bartholdi, III, C. A. Tovey, and M. A. Trick. The computational difficulty of manipulating an election. *Social Choice and Welfare*, 6(3):227–241, 1989.

[CCD88]   D. Chaum, C. Crépeau, and I. Damgård. Multi-party unconditionally secure protocols. In *Proc. of 20th STOC*, pages 11–19. ACM Press, 1988.

[CK89]   B. Chor and E. Kushilevitz. A zero-one law for Boolean privacy. In *Proc. of 21st STOC*, pages 36–47. ACM Press, 1989.

[CS01]   W. Conen and T. Sandholm. Preference elicitation in combinatorial auctions. In *Proc. of 3rd ACM Conference on E-Commerce*, pages 256–259. ACM Press, 2001.

[CS02a]   V. Conitzer and T. Sandholm. Complexity of mechanism design. In *Proc. of 18th Conference on Uncertainty in Artificial Intelligence (UAI)*, pages 103–110, 2002.

[CS02b]   V. Conitzer and T. Sandholm. Vote elicitation: Complexity and strategy-proofness. In *Proc. of 18th AAAI Conference*, pages 392–397. AAAI Press, 2002.

[CS03a]   V. Conitzer and T. Sandholm. Applications of automated mechanism design. In *Proc. of UAI workshop on Bayesian Modeling Applications*, 2003.

[CS03b]   V. Conitzer and T. Sandholm. Computational criticisms of the revelation principle. In *Proc. of 5th Workshop on Agent Mediated Electronic Commerce (AMEC)*, LNCS. Springer, 2003.

[CS03c]   V. Conitzer and T. Sandholm. Universal voting protocol tweaks to make manipulation hard. In *Proc. of 18th IJCAI*, pages 781–788, 2003.

[DH76]   W. Diffie and M. E. Hellman. New directions in cryptography. *IEEE Transactions on Information Theory*, IT-22(6):644–654, 1976.

[FNR⁺02]   J. Feigenbaum, N. Nisan, V. Ramachandran, R. Sami, and S. Shenker. Agents' privacy in distributed algorithmic mechanisms. Position Paper, 2002.

[FS02]   J. Feigenbaum and S. Shenker. Distributed algorithmic mechanism design: Recent results and future directions. In *Proc. of 6th International Workshop on Discrete Algorithms and Methods for Mobile Computing and Communications*, pages 1–13. ACM Press, 2002.

[GMW87]   O. Goldreich, S. Micali, and A. Wigderson. How to play any mental game or a completeness theorem for protocols with honest majority. In *Proc. of 19th STOC*, pages 218–229. ACM Press, 1987.

[Gol01]   O. Goldreich. *Foundations of Cryptography: Volume 1, Basic Tools.* Cambridge University Press, 2001.

[HT04]   J. Halpern and V. Teague. Rational secret sharing and multiparty computation. In *Proc. of 36th STOC*. ACM Press, 2004.

[Kik01]   H. Kikuchi. (M+1)st-price auction protocol. In *Proc. of 5th Conference on Financial Cryptography*, volume 2339 of *LNCS*, pages 351–363. Springer, 2001.

[Kus89]   E. Kushilevitz. Privacy and communication complexity. In *Proc. of 30th FOCS Symposium*, pages 416–421. IEEE Computer Society Press, 1989.

[LSP82]   L. Lamport, R. Shostak, and M. Pease. The Byzantine generals problem. *ACM Transactions on Programming Languages and Systems*, 4(3):382–401, 1982.

[MPS03]   R. McGrew, R. Porter, and Y. Shoham. Towards a general theory of non-cooperative computation. In *Proc. of 9th International Conference on Theoretical Aspects of Rationality and Knowledge (TARK)*, 2003.

[MT99]   D. Monderer and M. Tennenholtz. Distributed games: From mechanisms to protocols. In *Proc. of 15th AAAI Conference*, pages 32–37. AAAI Press, 1999.

[MV04]   A. Mehta and V. Vazirani. Randomized truthful auctions of digital goods are randomizations over truthful auctions. In *Proc. of 5th ACM Conference on E-Commerce*, pages 120–124. ACM Press, 2004.

[Nao89]   M. Naor. Bit commitment using pseudorandomness. In *Proc. of 9th CRYPTO Conference*, volume 435 of *LNCS*, pages 128–137. Springer, 1989.

[NPS99]   M. Naor, B. Pinkas, and R. Sumner. Privacy preserving auctions and mechanism design. In *Proc. of 1st ACM Conference on E-Commerce*, pages 129–139. ACM Press, 1999.

[PS03]   R. Porter and Y. Shoham. On cheating in sealed-bid auctions. In *Proc. of 4th ACM Conference on E-Commerce*, pages 76–84. ACM Press, 2003.

[RTK90]   M. H. Rothkopf, T. J. Teisberg, and E. P. Kahn. Why are Vickrey auctions rare? *Journal of Political Economy*, 98(1):94–109, 1990.

[San93]   T. Sandholm. An implementation of the contract net protocol based on marginal cost calculations. In *Proc. of 10th AAAI Conference*, pages 256–262. AAAI Press, 1993.

[Yao82]   A. C. Yao. Protocols for secure computation. In *Proc. of 23th FOCS Symposium*, pages 160–164. IEEE Computer Society Press, 1982.

Author Index

Lecture Notes in Artificial Intelligence (LNAI)

Vol. 4087: F. Schwenker, S. Marinai (Eds.), Artificial Neural Networks in Pattern Recognition. IX, 299 pages. 2006.

Vol. 4068: H. Schärfe, P. Hitzler, P. Øhrstrøm (Eds.), Conceptual Structures: Inspiration and Application. XI, 455 pages. 2006.

Vol. 4065: P. Perner (Ed.), Advances in Data Mining. XI, 592 pages. 2006.

Vol. 4062: G. Wang, J.F. Peters, A. Skowron, Y. Yao (Eds.), Rough Sets and Knowledge Technology. XX, 810 pages. 2006.

Vol. 4049: S. Parsons, N. Maudet, P. Moraitis, I. Rahwan (Eds.), Argumentation in Multi-Agent Systems. XIV, 313 pages. 2006.

Vol. 4048: L. Goble, J.-J.C.. Meyer (Eds.), Deontic Logic and Artificial Normative Systems. X, 273 pages. 2006.

Vol. 4045: D. Barker-Plummer, R. Cox, N. Swoboda (Eds.), Diagrammatic Representation and Inference. XII, 301 pages. 2006.

Vol. 4031: M. Ali, R. Dapoigny (Eds.), Advances in Applied Artificial Intelligence. XXIII, 1353 pages. 2006.

Vol. 4029: L. Rutkowski, R. Tadeusiewicz, L.A. Zadeh, J.M. Zurada (Eds.), Artificial Intelligence and Soft Computing – ICAISC 2006. XXI, 1235 pages. 2006.

Vol. 4027: H.L. Larsen, G. Pasi, D. Ortiz-Arroyo, T. Andreasen, H. Christiansen (Eds.), Flexible Query Answering Systems. XVIII, 714 pages. 2006.

Vol. 4021: E. André, L. Dybkjær, W. Minker, H. Neumann, M. Weber (Eds.), Perception and Interactive Technologies. XI, 217 pages. 2006.

Vol. 4020: A. Bredenfeld, A. Jacoff, I. Noda, Y. Takahashi (Eds.), RoboCup 2005: Robot Soccer World Cup IX. XVII, 727 pages. 2006.

Vol. 4013: L. Lamontagne, M. Marchand (Eds.), Advances in Artificial Intelligence. XIII, 564 pages. 2006.

Vol. 4012: T. Washio, A. Sakurai, K. Nakajima, H. Takeda, S. Tojo, M. Yokoo (Eds.), New Frontiers in Artificial Intelligence. XIII, 484 pages. 2006.

Vol. 4008: J.C. Augusto, C.D. Nugent (Eds.), Designing Smart Homes. XI, 183 pages. 2006.

Vol. 4005: G. Lugosi, H.U. Simon (Eds.), Learning Theory. XI, 656 pages. 2006.

Vol. 3978: B. Hnich, M. Carlsson, F. Fages, F. Rossi (Eds.), Recent Advances in Constraints. VIII, 179 pages. 2006.

Vol. 3963: O. Dikenelli, M.-P. Gleizes, A. Ricci (Eds.), Engineering Societies in the Agents World VI. XII, 303 pages. 2006.

Vol. 3960: R. Vieira, P. Quaresma, M.d.G.V. Nunes, N.J. Mamede, C. Oliveira, M.C. Dias (Eds.), Computational Processing of the Portuguese Language. XII, 274 pages. 2006.

Vol. 3955: G. Antoniou, G. Potamias, C. Spyropoulos, D. Plexousakis (Eds.), Advances in Artificial Intelligence. XVII, 611 pages. 2006.

Vol. 3949: F.A. Savacı (Ed.), Artificial Intelligence and Neural Networks. IX, 227 pages. 2006.

Vol. 3946: T.R. Roth-Berghofer, S. Schulz, D.B. Leake (Eds.), Modeling and Retrieval of Context. XI, 149 pages. 2006.

Vol. 3944: J. Quiñonero-Candela, I. Dagan, B. Magnini, F. d'Alché-Buc (Eds.), Machine Learning Challenges. XIII, 462 pages. 2006.

Vol. 3937: H. La Poutré, N.M. Sadeh, S. Janson (Eds.), Agent-Mediated Electronic Commerce. X, 227 pages. 2006.

Vol. 3930: D.S. Yeung, Z.-Q. Liu, X.-Z. Wang, H. Yan (Eds.), Advances in Machine Learning and Cybernetics. XXI, 1110 pages. 2006.

Vol. 3918: W.K. Ng, M. Kitsuregawa, J. Li, K. Chang (Eds.), Advances in Knowledge Discovery and Data Mining. XXIV, 879 pages. 2006.

Vol. 3913: O. Boissier, J. Padget, V. Dignum, G. Lindemann, E. Matson, S. Ossowski, J.S. Sichman, J. Vázquez-Salceda (Eds.), Coordination, Organizations, Institutions, and Norms in Multi-Agent Systems. XII, 259 pages. 2006.

Vol. 3910: S.A. Brueckner, G.D.M. Serugendo, D. Hales, F. Zambonelli (Eds.), Engineering Self-Organising Systems. XII, 245 pages. 2006.

Vol. 3904: M. Baldoni, U. Endriss, A. Omicini, P. Torroni (Eds.), Declarative Agent Languages and Technologies III. XII, 245 pages. 2006.

Vol. 3900: F. Toni, P. Torroni (Eds.), Computational Logic in Multi-Agent Systems. XVII, 427 pages. 2006.

Vol. 3899: S. Frintrop, VOCUS: A Visual Attention System for Object Detection and Goal-Directed Search. XIV, 216 pages. 2006.

Vol. 3898: K. Tuyls, P.J. 't Hoen, K. Verbeeck, S. Sen (Eds.), Learning and Adaption in Multi-Agent Systems. X, 217 pages. 2006.

Vol. 3891: J.S. Sichman, L. Antunes (Eds.), Multi-Agent-Based Simulation VI. X, 191 pages. 2006.

Vol. 3890: S.G. Thompson, R. Ghanea-Hercock (Eds.), Defence Applications of Multi-Agent Systems. XII, 141 pages. 2006.

Vol. 3885: V. Torra, Y. Narukawa, A. Valls, J. Domingo-Ferrer (Eds.), Modeling Decisions for Artificial Intelligence. XII, 374 pages. 2006.

Vol. 3881: S. Gibet, N. Courty, J.-F. Kamp (Eds.), Gesture in Human-Computer Interaction and Simulation. XIII, 344 pages. 2006.

Vol. 3874: R. Missaoui, J. Schmidt (Eds.), Formal Concept Analysis. X, 309 pages. 2006.

Vol. 3873: L. Maicher, J. Park (Eds.), Charting the Topic Maps Research and Applications Landscape. VIII, 281 pages. 2006.

Vol. 3864: Y. Cai, J. Abascal (Eds.), Ambient Intelligence in Everyday Life. XII, 323 pages. 2006.

Vol. 3863: M. Kohlhase (Ed.), Mathematical Knowledge Management. XI, 405 pages. 2006.

Vol. 3862: R.H. Bordini, M. Dastani, J. Dix, A.E.F. Seghrouchni (Eds.), Programming Multi-Agent Systems. XIV, 267 pages. 2006.